Britain's 'brown babies'

MANCHESTER
1824

Manchester University Press

Some of the children at Holnicote House, Somerset

Britain's 'brown babies'

The stories of children born to black GIs and white women in the Second World War

Lucy Bland

Manchester University Press

Published by Manchester University Press
Altrincham Street, Manchester M1 7JA
www.manchesteruniversitypress.co.uk

British Library Cataloguing-in-Publication Data
A catalogue record for this book is available from the British Library

ISBN 978 1 5261 3326 7 hardback

First published 2019

The publisher has no responsibility for the persistence or accuracy of URLs for any external or third-party internet websites referred to in this book, and does not guarantee that any content on such websites is, or will remain, accurate or appropriate.

Typeset by
Servis Filmsetting Ltd, Stockport, Cheshire
Printed in Great Britain by
Bell & Bain Ltd, Glasgow

To the British 'brown babies' who made this book possible:
this is for you.
And in memory of my beloved sister Annabel

Contents

Acknowledgements

My thanks to the British Academy for their Small Research Grant (Reference: SG151118) which funded interview travel costs and interview transcription. Thank you to my four excellent transcribers: James Burton, Steve Carey, Nicola Clay and my friend Anne Partlett. Thanks also to archivists and librarians of the following libraries: Barnardo's Library, Barkingside; The British Library; Liverpool Record Office; The National Archives; Rhodes House Library, Oxford; Schomburg Center for Research in Black Culture, New York; Somerset Heritage Centre, Taunton. My history colleagues at Anglia Ruskin University have always been encouraging: Richard Carr, Jonathan Davis, Susan Flavin, Sean Lang and Rohan McWilliam, as has my head of department, Alison Ainley, who supported my semester sabbatical, essential for the book's completion.

Many people have given helpful advice and information: Disa Allsopp, Charlotte Brunsdon, Erica Carter, Laura Doan, Bob Farrer, Leslie James, Mary Joannou, Angela Joyce, David Killingray, Sabine Lee, Elina Moriya, Lynn Nead, Pauline Nevins, Michael Rainsberry, Denise Riley, Sonya Rose, Norris Saakwa-Mante, Sue Sharpe, Pat Thane, Sally Vincent, Sophie Watson. David Killingray generously shared some archives, Clive Webb kindly forwarded some US newspapers, Hazel Carby generously sent me the draft of part of her forthcoming book, David Stanley and Graham Smith both lent me various papers that greatly helped, Philipp Rohrbach, unsolicited, sent me the records of NAACP from the Library of Congress. Others have given useful references: Peter Aspinall, Chamion Caballero, Lucy Delap, Annie Hudson, Claire Langhamer, Sarah Waters. Many thanks to you all.

A number of friends have read chapters and given thoughtful and encouraging feedback. Caroline Lawrence read the entire manuscript, for which I cannot thank her enough. Annie Hudson, Angela McRobbie, Elina Moriya, Cynthia Pine and Dave Phillips gave constructive feedback on certain chapters as did my two terrific writing groups, 'The History Girls' (Carmen Mangion, Clare Midgley, Alison Oram, Krisztina Robert, Katharina Rowold, and Cornelie Usborne) and 'The Emmets' (Lucy Delap, Julia Laite and Deborah Thom). A number of people put me in touch with potential interviewees: Brian with Jim H, Adrian and Roger, Pauline Nat with Sandra S and Joyce, Laura Doan with Sandi H, Louisa Parker with John S, Valerie Bergson with Leon L, Paul Mackney with Dave B, David Skinner with Billy, Billy with David M, Deborah with Janet B, Yvonne Buckle with Jennifer K; Sue Mitchell put me in touch with Vanessa, Liam McCarthy with Terry and Jennifer B, as well as forwarding me his excellent MRes dissertation; Suzann Savidge put me in touch with Dave G and journalist Tammy McAllister. Thanks to Tammy for doing a radio programme about my project for BBC Somerset, and to Jon Green, my university's press officer, for organising the *Woman's Hour* programme on Radio 4. Huge thanks to Dave Phillips for all his practical, intellectual and emotional support and to our daughter Rosana Phillips for helping me enter the twenty-first century and keeping me young at heart!

My greatest thanks go to all the people I have interviewed for this book: Adam (who talked about his father, John F), Adrian, Ann, Arlene, Babs, Bec (who talked about her mother, Jean), Billy, Brian, Bryn, Carol E, Carole B, Carole M, Carole T, Catherine, Edward and Colette (who talked about their father/husband, Peter), Celia (who talked about her ex-husband, Colin), Cynthia, Dave B, Dave G, David M, Deborah, Elaine, Eugene, Gillian, Heather P, Heather T, James A, Janet B, Janet J (and her daughter, Karen), Janine (who talked about her father, Michael), Jennifer B, Jennifer K, Jim H, John S, Joyce, Karla, Leon L, Lesley and Amy (who talked about their husband/father, Leon Y), Lesley (who talked about her husband, Stephen), Lloyd, Mary and Jo (daughter and granddaughter of Lillian), Monica, Pauline Nat, Richard, Roger, Sandi H, Sandra S, Tabitha (who talked about her uncle, Tony B), Terry, Tony H, Tony M, Trevor, Vanessa. This book could not have happened without you. It is dedicated to you all.

Illustrations

Introduction

Frances, a bus conductress in her early twenties, was living at home in Portsmouth during the war with her parents and had concealed her pregnancy. In January 1945 her younger sister, Molly, aged ten, found her in her bedroom giving birth and rushed downstairs. Joyce (Frances's daughter) recalls: 'She said "Frances has had a baby!" and my nan said "Don't talk silly." ... She [Molly] said, "Well you go up and have a look." ... My nan never knew right up until I was born.' Frances wanted to give Joyce up for adoption, but Joyce's grandparents wanted to keep her – they loved children:

> So my grandmother sent a telegram straight to my granddad, he was in China [as a merchant sailor] and said, 'Frances had a baby, a little girl' and he sent a telegram back and said ... 'If we can name her Joyce we'll keep her, we'll bring her up as our own' ['Joyce' because they had lost a little girl called Joyce] and they had seven at the time ... The youngest one was ten [Molly] ... When I became adopted, they became my brothers and sisters. My nan always said to me, 'Don't forget you've got an American dad.'[1]

Joyce's father was an African-American GI.

In contrast, when Carole B was born in December 1944 to a white mother and a black American serviceman, her mother was disowned by her family. Her mother was 21, single, living in Birkenhead, near Liverpool, and was in the army. Carole B remembers:

> My mum's family, they just shunned her ... it was horrible. I can remember walking down the street with her ... and she said 'Hello' to them and they just ignored her ... My mum's sister Gladys, if she saw me walking down the road, she would cross over the road in case she had to tell people who I was.[2]

0.1 Joyce

Joyce and Carole B are two examples of children born during the war to black GIs and white British women. I first heard about such children when in October 2011 I watched the second episode of the three-part BBC series *Mixed Britannia* – a history of mixed-race people in Britain in the twentieth century.[3] It opens with the presenter, George Alagiah, going off to meet his brother-in-law, Tony Martin, a mixed-race GI baby. Later in the programme another war baby, Brian Lawrenson, also talks about his childhood. Both had been fathered by black American servicemen and given up by their mothers, but while Tony had been happily fostered, Brian had remained in Liverpool children's homes until he was fourteen. I had never heard of these GI war babies. At the time I was working on a book on the 1920s, but I resolved that I would return to the topic of these children at a later date. So in 2013, with my 1920s book about to be published,[4] I went back to the subject and discovered that not much had been written beyond several case studies. Graham Smith, in his ground-breaking book *When Jim Crow Met John Bull* about black GIs in Britain during the war, briefly discusses three mixed-race babies.[5] A few more children are mentioned, also briefly, in two 1992 books about GI babies generally: Shirley McGlade's *Daddy, Where Are You?* and Pamela Winfield's *Bye Bye Baby*.[6] Janet Baker has written a Masters thesis (2000) on eleven of these children, and is herself the child of a black GI. Her insightful analysis largely focuses on the psychological issues of identity, grief and loss as well as the resilience that many of the eleven have developed. Her numbers though are small.[7] Sabine Lee compares British policies towards GI children with the German response but does not address individual cases.[8]

Given that relatively few accounts of the children were presented in these publications, there was clearly room for further work. Finding some of these mixed-race war babies (now in their early seventies) and hearing their stories seemed the best way to learn more about their upbringing. To elicit their stories I had a series of questions that I wanted to cover, such as where and when they was born, who their parents were (if they knew), where they grew up, whether they had suffered stigma or racism, whether they had looked for their father, whether they had found him, how they had identified racially and so on. But I did not want to impose a tight structure on the interviews and many were indeed fairly free-ranging.

What drew me to this research? This appeared to be a history that was very largely unknown. Histories of the British experience of the Second World War are extensive but they rarely feature these war babies. Further, everyone knows about the arrival of the ship *Empire Windrush* in 1948, and this is generally assumed to be the starting point for the growth of a post-war black British population. But about 2,000 mixed-race GI babies were born in Britain a few years prior to the *Windrush*'s arrival. That might not sound a large number, but if we take into account that the pre-war black British population was an estimated 7,000–10,000, these children represented a not insignificant 20–28 per cent increase in the numbers of people of colour over a couple of years.

Another reason why I was drawn to the study of these wartime babies is more personal. I would suggest that many historians (and probably researchers in other fields) work on subjects that resonate in some way with their own lives. My father was a law lecturer at Sussex University, and when I was eighteen he went on a year's exchange to teach at the University of West Indies. He fell in love with a Guyanese woman of mixed heritage (African, Scottish and Amerindian); my parents divorced, and my father got a permanent job in Barbados, where the university's law faculty was based. Thus by the age of twenty I had acquired a Guyanese stepmother and a Barbadian stepsister ('Barbadian' is her self-definition as someone who had largely grown up in Barbados). One of my nephews has mixed-race children and my partner and I have an adopted daughter from Guatemala. I write all this to illustrate why I, a white woman, am interested in interracial relationships and mixed-raceness: it is largely because they exist in my own family, an enriching diversity that may possibly be typical of many twenty-first-century families.

Finding and interviewing 'brown babies'

I wanted to hear the stories of as many of the 'brown babies' as I could find. 'Brown babies' was the name given in the 1940s and 1950s by the African-American press to mixed-race children born to black GIs and British and continental European women (the vast majority of whom were white) during or soon after the war. The term stood in contrast to the widely used label 'half-caste'. The word 'caste' comes from the Latin 'castus', meaning pure or guiltless, and the derivative Spanish 'casta', meaning race.[9] To be 'half-caste' thus implied impurity.[10] I later discovered that 'brown babies' is today a self-definition for a number of these children, including some of the people I interviewed and those in Germany;[11] as it is also a quicker reference than 'mixed-race GI babies', I have adopted it in this book.

How was I to contact these 'brown babies'? I managed to find and then interview Tony and Brian from the BBC programme. Brian in turn put me in touch with three other men who had been with him in the same Liverpool children's homes. Through the online organisation GI trace, which helps people find their GI fathers and relatives, I interviewed more people, and contacts snowballed.[12] But the biggest breakthrough came when I appeared on BBC Radio 4's *Woman's Hour* in October 2016 alongside Deborah, a 'brown baby' who I had recently interviewed. Although I also talked on a lot of local radio programmes, it was the *Woman's Hour* programme that led to the greatest response, with more than twenty-five people contacting me. In the end I talked to thirty-five 'brown babies' born in the 1940s, eight relatives of 'brown babies' where the person was ill or deceased, and I also drew on two memoirs, giving accounts of forty-five British, wartime, mixed-race GI babies in all. I also talked to two mixed-race war babies with Jamaican fathers, because their situation was very similar to that of the GI babies, and to six 'brown babies' born in the 1950s.

I travelled the country interviewing people and hearing their fascinating stories. I learned that all the children were born illegitimate, as the US army would not allow black GIs to marry their white girlfriends. I also learned that many of the children and their mothers had faced stigma and racism and that those put in children's homes were rarely adopted. The sense of lacking a father was hugely troubling for many of them and compounded their existing sense of being marginal as mixed-race children. That many have searched for their fathers and some have found them, or at least found American relatives, is a central part of their quest for a sense of belonging. It was a privilege to be trusted with these illuminating and moving stories from which I have learned so much.

Oral history

At the heart of this book are oral histories: interviews, mostly recorded, about personal memories of growing up in the late 1940s and 1950s as a mixed-race child in what was then a very white Britain. The interviews are combined with analysis of official records of central and local government and various organisations, reports from children's homes, newspapers (British and American), letters and memoirs. Oral history is 'the study and investigation of the past by means of personal recollections, memories, evocations, or life-stories, where the individuals talk about their experiences, life-styles, attitudes and values to a researcher'.[13] The importance of oral history is that it can access information and memories of events and emotions that are not documented elsewhere. Forgotten or hidden pasts can be recovered and recognised, a voice given to people who have often not been heard before and can now tell their stories in their own words.[14] People make sense of their past – and their present – through constructing a narrative; as historian Lynn Abrams succinctly puts it: 'our past is "storied", with each memory packaged within a story or narrative'.[15] The memories recalled through interviews for this book illuminate aspects of the British histories of race and of childhood that have very largely remained undocumented.

Some historians are suspicious of oral history, pointing out that memories can be unreliable and contradictory, dates misremembered, and accounts subjective, selective or affected by public representations of certain historical events. But all sources drawn on by historians have their drawbacks. Written sources, even minutes of a meeting, say, are written after the event, and what is remembered by the minute-writer will inevitably be selective. Memoirs are often written long after the events they record, and newspaper accounts take a particular 'angle'.[16]

There is also the issue of the relationship between the interviewer and the interviewee, which obviously affects what is said in the interview. How did my being white affect my interviewing of people who are not white? Whiteness is seen as the norm in Britain; as cultural critic Richard Dyer expresses it: 'As long as race is something only applied to non-white people ... they/we function as a human norm. Other people are raced, we are just people.'[17] When I visited my father and stepmother in Barbados I found it difficult because it meant 'encountering my whiteness'.[18] My father's wife, his stepdaughter, his students and nearly all his friends were black. At my father's home in Barbados I now realised something of how it felt to be an outsider because of racial difference. But of course my being aware of my whiteness did not take away the reality that whiteness carries privilege. There is also class privilege, a huge dividing factor in Britain. I am a white, middle-class academic. Over a third of my interviewees are today middle class, although most of them had parents who were working class, with various exceptions, such as Deborah's mother who was a respected schoolteacher, Janet J's adoptive parents who were managers or Cynthia's father who had been to university. Whatever the differences or similarities of race, class, accent and other factors between myself and my narrators, I, as interviewer, set the agenda, asked the questions, recorded the interview, interpreted what I heard, selected which parts of the interview to reproduce in this book and will be given the credit. I have tried to counter some of this inequality in the interviewer/interviewee relationship by showing all the participants everything I have written about them to make sure they are happy with it. I have changed, deleted or added anything they have requested. Although it is my name on the book, it is their words that fill it, bring it to life and of course made it possible in the first place.

The book uses the interviewees' first names, and where more than one person has the same first name (for example, there are a lot of

Caroles, Davids and Tonys – an indication of what names were popular at the time) the initial of their surname is added. Nearly all my interviewees were happy for me to use their surname, but one or two were not, so for consistency surnames are generally not used, except where a name is already in the public domain, through publications, television or radio. Not all the interviews were taped: a few were done over the telephone and notes were taken and emails exchanged. Thirty taped interviews have been edited, with the interviewees' cooperation, and are housed in the Black Cultural Archives in London.

Terms and labels

People often disagree as to which terms are acceptable to describe racial issues and identities. The terms are all culturally and historically specific; it was polite in the 1940s and 1950s to refer to black people as 'Negro' or 'coloured' ('black' was impolite) and the term 'half-caste' was widely used. As Pauline Black, lead singer of the ska band The Selecter and herself mixed-race, says of the 1950s: 'the growth of politically-correct phrases liked mixed-race, dual-heritage, people of colour, Afro-Caribbean, Anglo-African were as yet unknown'.[19] In this book I use the terms 'coloured' and 'half-caste' only when I am quoting directly. Although few people today still use the term 'half-caste', many refer to mixed-race people as 'half' a nationality or 'colour', which still has the negative connotation of not being 'pure' bred.[20] In the 1970s and 1980s, the term 'Black' (capital B) started to be used to refer not just to people of African descent but also those of Asian heritage – all peoples who suffered racism.[21] This in turn was criticised for obscuring differences, so the all-inclusive term has now generally been dropped.[22] 'Black' today is usually used to refer to those with African heritage, but it can include those who are mixed-race of white/black mix. Another inclusive term is 'people of colour', which journalist Reni Eddo-Lodge uses 'to define anyone of any race that isn't white'.[23]

I largely use the terms 'black' and 'mixed-race'. Some people argue that you should not use the term 'race' as it has no basis in reality: biologically we are all the same race – the human race. But people act in the world as if there are real racial differences, and racism and discrimination are unfortunately very much in evidence. As the cultural critic Stuart Hall argues: 'race is *both* a socio-economic "fact" *and* a social construct'.[24] The psychologists Barbara Tizard and Ann Phoenix explain why they use 'race' rather than 'ethnicity' when discussing people of mixed heritage:

> An ethnic group refers to people who share a common history, language, religion and culture ... people with the same skin colour do not always share a common culture ... What sets them apart from white people, and is the basis for their stigmatisation by racists, is their appearance, not their culture. It is because racial categories continue to have both political and psychological importance that we prefer the term 'race'.[25]

Given that race is socially constructed, it can be argued that inverted commas should be used, as in 'race'. However, I follow historian Catherine Hall in not using inverted commas, because otherwise, as she suggests, 'the text would ... be littered with them'.[26] The 'mixed' part of the term mixed-race is not always liked; as one of my interviewees said to me, 'it implies that we are mixed up!' The alternatives of biracial or dual heritage are fine if there are only two heritages involved; many people have more than two though. Multiracial is another alternative, but I generally use mixed-race because that is the term that the vast majority of my interviewees use today to describe themselves.[27] But of course these terms do not define anyone in their entirety. They categorise people by their race/biology, which might not reflect anything about their personal history, their cultural heritage or their own self-definition. In other words, we continue to label people by their biological heritage, and neglect other factors that make up each unique individual. The psychologist Stephen Murphy-Shigematsu poses a pertinent question: 'Is biology the determining factor in the creation of a cultural self? While we deny the scientific validity of race, do we persist in believing that something genetic remains the overriding factor in forming an authentic self?'[28]

Structure of the book

The first chapter sets the scene, explaining why there were black American servicemen in Britain during the war, where they were based, how they were segregated, how they met local women and how they were prevented from marrying them. The second chapter focuses on the children born to the black GIs who were kept by their mothers or grandmothers – just over half of the forty-five born in the war whose stories I am drawing on. Their experiences of illegitimacy and racism and their sense of difference are charted, including having hair that was seen as 'unmanageable' and an inexplicably different skin tone, as well as lacking a father. Chapter 3 examines the various children's homes set up for the 'brown babies' and looks at the experiences of those who were put in such homes. Chapter 4 explores fostering and adoption stories. Very few of the 'brown babies' were in fact adopted; I consider the reasons for this, including why attempts to have the children adopted in the US were blocked by the British government. Chapter 5 presents accounts of searching for and sometimes finding mothers and fathers. Most of the 'brown babies' knew very little about their fathers. This gaping hole in their history of origin and the extraordinary relief and completeness on finding fathers or even simply US relatives demonstrates movingly the huge importance of having a sense of one's heritage. The final chapter moves to the post-war period and considers 'brown babies' born in Europe during the years of occupation of Germany and Austria – 1945–55. Some of the parallels with the British situation but also the differences are noted; for example, German children were adopted into the US in their hundreds. Six case studies of 1950s' British 'brown babies' are also presented, their upbringing contextualised in terms of the changing racial landscape of Britain, as West Indians and many from the Indian subcontinent arrived in their thousands. Finally identity, belonging and Britishness are examined and the way in which after all these years of living in Britain, the 'brown babies' still face the indignity of being asked their country of origin. The assumption that to be British is to be white is unfortunately still in wide circulation, although the ever-growing presence of black and mixed-race people as UK citizens is making such a supposition increasingly untenable.[29]

Notes

1 Interview with Joyce, 12 August 2014.
2 Interview with Carole B, 1 September 2014.
3 *Mixed Britannia*, episode 2, 1940–65 (dir. Kate Misrahi, BBC2, 2011).

4   Lucy Bland, *Modern Women on Trial: Sexual Transgression in the Age of the Flapper* (Manchester, 2013).

5   Graham Smith, *When Jim Crow Met John Bull* (London, 1987).

6   Shirley McGlade, *Daddy, Where Are You?* (London, 1992); Pamela Winfield, *Bye Bye Baby: The Story of the Children the GIs Left Behind* (London, 1992).

7   Janet Baker, '"Lest We Forget": The Children We Left Behind: The Life Experience of Adults Born to Black GIs and British Women during the Second World War', unpublished Masters thesis, University of Melbourne, 2000.

8   Sabine Lee, 'A forgotten legacy of the Second World War: GI children in post-war Britain and Germany', *Contemporary European History*, 20.2 (2011), pp. 157–81. As I finish writing this book, Chamion Caballero and Peter Aspinall's wonderful *Mixed Race Britain in the Twentieth Century* (London, 2018) has been published, which also discusses these mixed-race children.

9   See Francisco Bethencourt, *Racisms: From the Crusades to the Twentieth Century* (Princeton, NJ, 2013), pp. 163–72.

10 In Germany the equivalent term was *Mischling* – meaning mixed or hybrid – which had previously been applied to those who were part-Jewish, but in the post-war years was used to refer to children born to German woman and African-American GIs. Heide Fehrenbach, *Race after Hitler: Black Occupation Children in Post-War Germany and America* (Princeton, NJ, 2005), pp. 74–106. The racist history of the term precludes its use as a self-definition for mixed-race German and Austrian people today. Personal communication from Austrian historian Vanessa Spanbauer.

11 I met a number of German mixed-race GI babies at a GI trace gathering in Berlin in autumn 2017.

12 www.gitrace.org.

13 A useful definition quoted in Penny Summerfield, *Reconstructing Women's Wartime Lives: Discourse and Subjectivity in Oral Histories of the Second World War* (Manchester, 1998), p. 32, n. 1; see also Lynn Abrams, *Oral History Theory* (London, 2010), p. 2; Lynn Abrams, 'Memory as both source and subject of study: the transformations of oral history', in Stefan Berger and Bill Niven (eds), *Writing the History of Memory* (London, 2014), pp. 89–109.

14 See Robert Perks and Alistair Thomson (eds), *The Oral History Reader* (London, 3rd edn, 2016).

15 Abrams, *Oral History Theory*, p. 106. See also Allessandro Portelli, 'The peculiarities of oral history', *History Workshop*, 12 (1981), pp. 96–107.

16 See Penny Summerfield, *Histories of the Self* (London, 2018).

17   Richard Dyer, *White* (London, 1997), p. 1.

18   Catherine Hall, *Civilising Subjects: Metropole and Colony in the English Imagination, 1830–1867* (Cambridge, 2002), p. 5, on her experience when visiting Jamaica. This book's introduction is exemplary.

19   Pauline Black, *Black by Design: A 2-tone Memoir* (London, 2011), p. 6.

20   See Stephen Murphy-Shigematsu, *When Half is Whole* (Stanford, CA, 2012). Thanks to Elina Moriya for drawing this theorist to my attention.

21   See Stuart Hall, 'New ethnicities', in James Donald and Ali Rattansi (eds), *'Race', Culture and Difference* (London, 1992), pp. 252–9.

22   See Elizabeth Buettner, '"Would you let your daughter marry a Negro?": race and sex in 1950s Britain', in Philippa Levine and Susan R. Grayzel (eds), *Gender, Labour, War and Empire* (London, 2009), p. 234, n. 10.

23   Reni Eddo-Lodge, *Why I Am No Longer Talking to White People about Race* (London, 2018), p. xvi. Dyer, interestingly, objects to this term because 'we need to recognise white as a colour too'; Dyer, *White*, p. 11.

24   Stuart Hall, with Bill Schwarz, *Familiar Stranger* (London, 2017), p. 105.

25   Barbara Tizard and Ann Phoenix, *Black, White or Mixed Race? Race and Racism in the Lives of Young People of Mixed Parentage* (London, 1993), pp. 4–5.

26   Hall, *Civilising Subjects*, p. 22.

27   See Jayne O. Ifekuwunigwe, *'Mixed Race' Studies: A Reader* (London, 2004), pp. xvix–xxi, on why she uses the term mixed-race.

28   Stephen Murphy-Shigematsu, *Multicultural Encounters* (New York, 2002), p. 74.

29   In the 2011 census, 2.2 per cent of the population ticked one of the 'mixed' boxes; Caballero and Aspinall, *Mixed Race Britain*, p. 478. Nearly 13 per cent of the British population is black, Asian or mixed: https://www.ons.gov.uk/peoplepopulationandcommunity/cultural identity/ethnicity/articles/2011censusanalysisethnicityandreligionof thenonukbornpopulationinenglandandwales/2015-06-18 (accessed 13 August 2018).

1

British women meet black GIs

On 26 August 1945 the front page of the *Sunday Pictorial*, a popular British paper, carried the following headline: 'All This Happened in England Yesterday'. The heading implied a very un-English happening. The article opens:

> The scene was Bristol, most English of all English cities. The time was 2 am. The actors were a mob of screaming girls aged between 17 and 25. Their hysteria was caused by news that four companies of American negro soldiers in the city were leaving for home. The girls besieged the barracks where the soldiers were and began singing 'Don't Fence Me In'. This was too much for the coloured men, who began to break down the barbed wire surrounding their quarters. In a few minutes hundreds of girls and US soldiers were kissing and embracing.

'Don't Fence Me In', written by Cole Porter, had been sung the previous year by Bing Crosby; it was a quintessentially American song but was widely known in Britain. The *Sunday Pictorial* article ends: 'Most of them [the young women] had been waiting since 7 pm the night before, and although it was pouring with rain, they decided to wait. "I don't mind getting wet," said one eighteen-year-old girl. "I intend to give my sweetie a good send-off."'[1] What were black Americans doing in Britain at this time? How had these young women met the black GIs and with what consequences?

Black GIs and the US military

The black Americans were in Britain as wartime allies, coming to the country as servicemen. Their presence in the US military had not been inevitable. President Roosevelt's re-election in early November

1940 had relied heavily on the black vote, and seizing an opportunity to make demands, in September that year black leaders had met with Roosevelt to press for racial integration of the military and an end to discrimination in the defence industries.[2] The black leaders presented him with a seven-point programme of demands, including desegregation, training of black officers and the opening of all branches of the army air corps to black Americans.[3] A few days later the War Department announced that African Americans would be admitted to the military in the same proportion as that of the US's black population as a whole, namely 10 per cent.[4] (In the event, black troops in the European Theatre of Operations probably only ever constituted 7.5–8 per cent.)[5] Officer training expanded: there were only five black officers before the US entered the war in December 1941 (of whom three were chaplains), rising to 7,000 by the end, although they were never allowed to command white troops. A black flying programme at Tuskegee, Alabama, was established (the Tuskegee pilots were widely respected for their prowess during the war).[6] Many black Americans believed that if they could fight and die for their country, they could no longer be denied equality. When Japan attacked Pearl Harbor, Hawaii, in December 1941, the US finally joined the war. Already in place was the 1940 Selective Training and Service Act, which required able-bodied men aged 21–35 to serve in the military for at least one year.[7] The US War Secretary did not want blacks in the military and he certainly did not want them to bear arms; he thought they could not be trusted to fight, a viewpoint labelled by the black press as the 'Negro-is-too-dumb-to-fight' policy.[8] By the end of the war, of the approximately 500,000 African Americans who had served overseas, the vast majority had been in support, not combat, units.[9]

The hypocrisy of the US fighting against fascism yet remaining racist and segregated led in February 1942 to the African-American newspaper the *Pittsburgh Courier* launching the 'Double V' campaign for 'victory at home and abroad': victory against Hitler and against Jim Crow.[10] The following year the leading African-American poet Langston Hughes wrote the powerful poem, 'Beaumont to Detroit: 1943', about this two-pronged battle. (The towns were sites of 1943 race riots.) The last three verses read:

You jim crowed me
Before hitler came to power

And your're STILL jim crowing me
Right now, this very hour.

Yet you say we're fighting
For democracy.
Then why don't democracy
Include me?

I ask the question
Cause I want to know
How long I got to fight
BOTH HITLER – AND JIM CROW.[11]

As the war progressed, African Americans' resolve to force an end to segregation and discrimination increased. At the war's end, when the black journalist Roi Ottley toured Europe and asked black GIs what message they wanted to send to their fellow Americans, he was told: 'Tell them we want to see the end of ole Jim Crow in America and equal treatment for everyone.'[12]

It was not just African Americans who were determined to shift racist attitudes and behaviour. In 1943 Nancy Cunard, the daughter of a wealthy English baronet but a socialist and anti-racist, published a pamphlet with the Trinidadian socialist George Padmore called *White Man's Duty*. Written largely as a conversation between the two of them, it suggested that the war should lead to greater awareness of racial prejudice and the enactment of legislation to tackle the colour bar as well as colonial self-government.[13] Although India obtained independence in 1947, it was a long time before any real shifts in attitudes and law took place in Britain.

GIs in wartime Britain

Approximately three million American troops passed through Britain in the period 1942–45, many arriving for the subsequent invasion of France. The first tranche arrived in January 1942 and were based in Northern Ireland. The exact number of black GIs is not known; if we assume that approximately 8 per cent of all the US troops who came to Britain were black, the figure would be in the region of 240,000, although of course there were never that many at any one time.[14] The

American troops were based all over the country, but in greatest concentration in south and south-west England, South Wales, East Anglia
and Lancashire. What knowledge did people have of Americans before
their arrival? As a Ministry of Information report noted, 'by far the
most important source of ideas about life in America is the cinema'.[15]
Most girls and young women went to the cinema about twice a week
and it was very largely Hollywood movies that they saw – hugely popular films such as *Gone with the Wind* (with its racist romanticising
of the 'deep South'), the Western *Stagecoach*, *The Wizard of Oz* (all
three released in 1939) and *Citizen Kane* (1941).[16] A group of British
probation workers later reflected on the role of Hollywood in girls'
perception of GIs: 'To girls brought up on the cinema, who copied the
dress, hair styles and manners of Hollywood stars, the sudden influx
of Americans, speaking like the films, who actually lived in the magic
country, and who had plenty of money, at once went to the girls'
heads.'[17]

Here in Britain were now billeted men who spoke with 'exotic'
Hollywood accents and did indeed have 'plenty of money', for American
soldiers were paid on average five times as much as British soldiers.[18]
Despite rationing, the Americans regularly distributed cigarettes,
chocolate (which they called candy), chewing-gum and coca-cola,
known as 'the four Cs'. 'Got any gum, chum?' children would cheekily
demand, while the GIs would insouciantly reply: 'Got a sister, mister?'
It was estimated that GIs received about twelve ounces of meat per day
– three times the British civilian ration and twice as much as British
troops in the UK.[19] It was not for nothing that comedian Tommy
Trinder described the Americans as 'over-paid, over-fed, over-sexed,
and over here'.[20] British soldiers did not get the hand-outs of cigarettes and chocolate, let alone access to nylons (stockings), an especial
delight for British women who, faced with stringent rationing, were
resorting to staining their legs brown with gravy powder and drawing
a seam up the back with an eye pencil.[21] The American response to the
name calling was predictable: Brits were 'underpaid, underfed, under-
sexed and under Eisenhower' (US General Eisenhower was Supreme
Commander of the Allied Expeditionary Forces in Europe).

Controlling relationships between black Americans and British women

From the moment the British government knew that US troops would be coming to Britain there was concern in official circles about the consequences of the presence of *black* GIs. The Home Secretary Herbert Morrison, for example, was anxious that 'the procreation of half-caste children' would create 'a difficult social problem'.[22] He and others in the War Cabinet would have preferred no black GIs to be sent at all. The Foreign Secretary Anthony Eden argued that the British climate was 'badly suited to negroes' and suggested that they would be better off in Italy.[23] The government's misgivings were to no avail, for black GIs did indeed arrive; almost immediately there were various official attempts to prevent interracial relationships. In August 1942 Major-General Dowler, in charge of Southern Command, where a large proportion of black GIs were stationed, issued a paper headed 'Notes on Relations with Coloured Troops' and sent it to District Commanders in his area; it was subsequently distributed more widely. The paper was not official, and indeed it had been decreed by the War Cabinet that no *written* instructions should be distributed on the subject of 'coloured troops' as the issue was very 'delicate'; however, Dowler's notes were subsequently largely approved by the War Office, and informed its own written advice given out later to the British Army and RAF. Dowler's paper was overtly racist, with remarks such as 'coloured men ... work hard when they have no money and when they have money they prefer to do nothing until it is gone. In short they do not have the white man's ability to think and act to a plan.' One of Dowler's proposals was that 'white women should not associate with coloured men. It follows then, they should not walk out, dance, or drink with them.'[24] The War Cabinet paper did not go quite this far, but suggested that 'for a white woman to go about in the company of a Negro American is likely to lead to controversy and ill-feeling, it may also be misunderstood by the Negro troops themselves'.[25] Further, Home Secretary Morrison warned his colleagues in the War Cabinet that the 'morale of British troops is likely to be upset by rumours that their wives and daughters are being debauched by American coloured troops'.[26]

The War Office decreed that the British Army should lecture its troops, including the women of the Auxiliary Territorial Service

(ATS), on the need to keep contact with black GIs to a minimum.[27] The ATS had a (very probably unfair) reputation for sexual promiscuity, being known as the 'groundsheet of the army'.[28] Local police were to report women soldiers found with black GIs. There was also discussion in government circles about how to guide the civilian population. Whispering campaigns were promoted by the Women's Voluntary Services, hinting at the high rate of venereal disease among black Americans.[29] And the Defence of the Realm Act was deployed, prosecuting women for trespass or loitering if found with black GIs on military premises.[30] Further, girls under eighteen were subject to apprehension under the Children and Young Person's Act of 1933 if police thought that they were in 'grave moral danger' – a state assumed more likely if the soldiers they were with were black.[31]

In contrast, the 1943 film *Welcome to Britain* presented a more progressive view of Britons' attitudes towards black GIs. The film was commissioned by the Ministry of Information and made for newly arriving US troops, aiming to give a sense of what British culture was like. It was directed by Anthony Asquith (son of the former Prime Minister) and starred the well-known US actor Burgess Meredith. In one scene a black and a white GI emerge from a railway carriage and shake hands with an elderly white British woman. She remarks to the black GI how odd it is that they should both come from Birmingham (his would have been in Alabama, site of some of the worst racism), and that if he should ever be in *her* Birmingham, he must come to her home and have a cup of tea. The white GI, Meredith, turns to the camera confidentially and comments:

> Now look men, you heard that conversation; that's not unusual here … there are less social restrictions in this country … You heard an Englishwoman asking a coloured boy to tea … that might not happen at home but the … point is, we're not at home … if we bring a lot of prejudice here [he is clearly speaking to a white audience], what are we going to do about that?

In the next scene the two GIs come across US General Lee (who oversaw Services of Supply, where most black GIs were employed). Lee, who is filmed in person, not played by an actor, makes a slightly stilted speech about how 'Everyone's treated the same when it comes to dying.'[32] The overall message is that white GIs must look at their own racism and that the US stands for democratic values.

Despite this officially sanctioned film showing a white woman asking a black soldier to tea, there were some British women who were advocating precisely the opposite. In late summer 1942 Mrs May, wife of the vicar of Worle, a village adjoining Somerset's seaside town of Weston-Super-Mare, called the women of the village together and presented her six-point code on how women should relate to black Americans. It is worth quoting in full for its extreme racism and the subsequent reaction:

1. If a local woman keeps a shop and a coloured soldier enters, she must serve him but must do so as quickly as possible and indicate that she does not desire him to come there again.
2. If she is in a cinema and notices a coloured soldier next to her, she moves to another seat immediately.
3. If she is walking on the pavement and a coloured soldier is coming towards her, she crosses to the other pavement.
4. If she is in a shop and a coloured soldier enters, she leaves as soon as she has made her purchases or before that if she is in a queue.
5. White women, of course, must have no social relationships with coloured troops.
6. On no account must coloured troops be invited into the homes of white women.[33]

One woman told the popular newspaper *Sunday Pictorial*: 'I was disgusted, and so were most of the women there. We have no intention of agreeing to her decree.' The newspaper presented a declaration, italicised for emphasis: '*Any coloured soldier who reads this may rest assured that there is no colour bar in this country and he is as welcome as any other Allied soldier. He will find that the vast majority of people here have nothing but repugnance for the narrow-minded, uninformed prejudices expressed by the vicar's wife.*'[34] This was wishful thinking; prejudice was widespread, although not usually as blatant as Mrs May's. One example is the response to a reader's letter in the magazine *Woman's Own*. The reader enquired of agony aunt Leonora Eyles in November 1943:

There are a lot of coloured US soldiers in our town and I feel sorry for them, far from home and very few nice girls being friends with them. Only the cheap sort of girls speak to them and some of them are so polite and friendly. Is it all right to be friends – and I mean friends only – with them, they are fighting for us?

Eyles replied: 'it would not be fair either to them or you to form such a close friendship as may lead to romance. It is not a question of their being "inferior" but *different*, and … on the very rarest occasions do such marriages succeed.'[35] Claiming the barrier of 'difference' avoided the overt racism of Mrs May, but it was still clearly a prejudicial statement against interracial relationships.

Some white Americans tried to turn British civilians against interracial contact through spreading spiteful but often absurd rumours, such as that black servicemen had tails or could not speak English but could only bark. The African American Walter White heard of a black sergeant invited to eat with an English family who 'noticed that every chair to which he was directed had a cushion on it, though none of the other folk seemed to enjoy such a luxury'. Two months later, when he knew the family better, he learned that a white American had told them that 'all Negroes had tails which made it impossible for them to sit in the ordinary hard-bottomed chair without first becoming extremely uncomfortable, then excited and dangerous'. The 'tail' idea was still around after the war. Cynthia, a 'brown baby' whose parents met during the war, remembers that 'my mother told me once they went to Scotland … and he got off the train and … somebody said, "Where's your tail?" Like he was a monkey.'[36] White also heard of towns where the response of black GIs to the barking rumour had led them to act it out, barking at passing Britons. In their turn the British apparently barked back, the shared joke leading to friendship rather than ridicule.[37]

The Americans believed relations between black men and white women to be the chief cause of interracial tension among their servicemen. In July 1944 *The Crisis*, the paper of the National Association for the Advancement of Colored People (NAACP), reported on

a white Southern lieutenant in a Negro anti-aircraft company who just could not stand to see his men enjoying the courtesies extended by the white women of a certain Eastern town. He posted a notice that *any* type of association with white women is regarded as rape and reminded his men that the penalty for rape during wartime is death.[38]

There were many violent incidents in Britain involving fights between white and black GIs, some resulting in deaths and most predicated on whites' resentment of interracial relationships.[39] To address the potential conflict between their troops, the Americans introduced segregation of leisure pursuits. Although Britain was formally opposed to US military segregation (the army stayed segregated until 1948), it did not interfere with the segregation arrangements that the Americans put in place around the country. The British government clearly wished to be discreet about its tacit support, for it was caught in a dilemma: it needed to keep on the right side of the US, and thus was not going to oppose segregation openly, but it also did not want to disaffect the West Indians who had come over to join the British armed forces or to work in munitions. Parliamentary papers show ongoing disagreements between the Colonial Office and other departments.[40] The segregation set up across the country involved passes for entry to towns near to American bases; in some towns, access for blacks and whites was given on different days, while other towns were permanently designated 'whites only' or 'blacks only' for the war's duration. In many villages, pubs too were segregated along colour lines, and dances were held for black GIs one evening, whites the next. The historian Graham Smith points to the irony of the government contributing 'to a policy encouraging the British to respect segregation because that was the *American* way, making a film the following year [*Welcome to Britain*], with American actors and senior American staff officers, encouraging the Americans to respect racial integration in Britain because that was the *British* way!'[41]

Many Britons were shocked by the segregation and by the racism of the white GIs. Many felt strongly that 'discrimination is undemocratic, particularly when black and white are *both* fighting for democracy'.[42] It was not as if the British were without racism themselves, Mrs May being one example, but casting white Americans as the 'true' racists gave Britons a sense of superiority.[43] Yet British attitudes were frequently condescending and informed by negative racist stereotypes. For example, the June 1943 Home Intelligence Report on *British Public Feeling about America* drew together some of the remarks that people had made over the previous year-and-a-half and noted (without comment) 'a tendency to regard the negroes as "childish, happy and naïve fellows who mean no harm"'.[44] As the cultural critic Stuart Hall points out: 'cultural stereotypes [can] be thought of as *like colour*:

fixed and immovable because – apparently – derived not from history, but from nature'.[45] The Hollywood films that many British people watched certainly contributed to the stereotypes. As Harold Moody, a Jamaican living in London, observed, these films 'largely show the black man in some menial position or as a buffoon or as a semi-nude savage. Never as a skilled or cultured individual. Never in any position of authority. Thus the stereotype of the black man is always one of a menial or an idiot.'[46] One could add: or a happy and loyal slave, as in *Gone with the Wind*.

As for whether there was a nationwide 'colour bar', the famous Trinidadian cricketer Learie Constantine, who lived in Britain from 1929 to 1949, certainly experienced it first-hand. For example, while employed by the Ministry of Labour as a welfare officer in Lancashire, he came to London with his family in autumn 1943 on four days' leave, booked in at the Imperial Hotel, but on his arrival he was told he was unwelcome 'because other guests would object'.[47] And when in 1949 *Picture Post* published an article entitled 'Is there a British colour bar?' it concluded that it was very real, with prejudice 'almost always based on ignorance'.[48] The British were hypocritical: they disparaged the racism of the white Americans, rooted in the history of slavery, but were themselves seeped in prejudices against non-white peoples that were inextricably tied to British imperialism.[49] British obsession with social class also contributed to viewing blacks as inferior, for black people were widely assumed to be low class.[50] In his 1954 study *Colour Prejudice in Britain*, the sociologist Anthony Richmond suggested that already by the war there was a stereotype of black people, at least in Liverpool, as being 'of low social status, little skill and doubtful moral habits'.[51]

The particular appeal of the black GI

If the attraction of the GIs to British women was unsurprising, given their relative wealth and glamour, what did surprise – and worry – the Home Secretary, Herbert Morrison, as he informed the War Cabinet in October 1942, was that 'some British women appear to find a peculiar fascination in associating with men of colour'.[52] In September 1942 a black GI stationed in Northern Ireland confirmed this when he wrote home: 'all the girls are going crazy about us'.[53] What was this 'peculiar fascination' with black Americans?

Part of the 'fascination' was surely unfamiliarity: many Britons had never seen a black person before, other than on cinema screens. Writing at the time, the sociologist Kenneth Little surmised that 'it is doubtful if as many as five per cent of us have ever had any personal contact with a coloured man or woman'.[54] Outside Cardiff and Liverpool, and before the arrival of many people from the Caribbean and the Indian subcontinent in the 1950s and 1960s, Britain was very largely a white country. An estimated 7,000–10,000 non-white people lived in Britain before the war, mostly concentrated in seaports.[55] These included those born to interracial relationships.[56]

It was not just women and girls who liked the black GIs; from all accounts the British public largely felt positive about their arrival, at least initially. Reports from the Home Intelligence Unit (set up in November 1939 to monitor British morale) frequently mentioned people's appreciation of 'the extremely pleasing manners of the coloured troops'.[57] Many may have agreed with the response of a West Country farmer when asked about the GIs: 'I love the Americans, but I don't like those white ones that they have brought with them.'[58] Britons were especially impressed by their singing, such as the 200-strong African-American choir which played to great acclaim in the Albert Hall with the London Symphony Orchestra.[59]

African-American GIs were often appreciative of British friendliness; for example, one black sergeant wrote back home in September 1942: 'This is a great country here and the people are very friendly, We like them very much … I am living the happiest days of my life.'[60] According to Walter White, 'for many of the Negroes, it was their first experience in being treated as normal human beings and friends by white people'.[61] An example of Britons' especial affection for the black GIs was a story White heard of 'a pub keeper who had posted a sign over his entrance reading: "THIS PLACE FOR THE EXCLUSIVE USE OF ENGLISHMEN AND AMERICAN NEGRO SOLDIERS."'[62] Kenneth Little learned of a case of white Americans rebuking a pub landlady for serving black troops, to which she replied: 'Their money is as good as yours and we prefer their company.'[63] There were a number of pubs that refused to introduce segregation, such as the Colston Arms in Bristol. Ironically, the pub was named after Edward Colston, a Bristol slave trader.[64] There are many anecdotes of locals taking the side of the black GIs and choosing to drink with them. For example, Bob Farrer (not a GI baby), who was born in 1947 and grew up in Bovingdon, Hertfordshire, where there was an American air base during the war, relates how 'my father told me about extraordinary racial tension between the white US aircrew and the often black aircraft mechanics. The locals sided with the blacks and drank with them in the Bull pub while the Wheatsheaf, over the road, became a US "officer only" [white] enclave.'[65] The historians Juliet Gardiner and David Reynolds both show the same 1942 photograph of black troops sitting drinking outside a pub in Bovingdon; it was very probably the Bull.[66] Farrer continues:

> Dad was amazed by the racism and the arrogance of the white aircrew. There was visceral hatred between white and black ... Dad said racism got worse as the war continued – partly because the Eighth [US] Air Force suffered very heavy losses in late 1943: daytime raids and up to half of the men didn't come back. There were [unfounded] rumours that black mechanics were sabotaging the aircraft.[67]

The African-American writer Ralph Ellison (best known for his 1953 novel *The Invisible Man*) served in the merchant marines and was greatly impressed by the hospitality of the Welsh. In a third-person autobiographical short story he writes of 'Mr Parker' being attacked by white Americans soon after his arrival in Wales. Mr Parker is saved by a group of Welshmen, taken to the pub and then to hear a local choir. The music enfolds him. 'He liked the Welsh. Not even on the ship, where the common danger and a fighting union made for a degree of understanding, did he approach white men so closely.'[68]

A number of commentators contrasted the manners of black and white GIs. Walter White, leader of the NAACP, visited Britain in early 1944 to assess the morale of black servicemen.[69] White was of African-American heritage but lived up to his surname in being able to 'pass' as white, enabling him to infiltrate racist organisations (even briefly joining the Ku Klux Klan) or work as a 'white' investigative journalist. (Describing his appearance he wrote: 'I am a Negro. My skin is white, my eyes are blue, my hair is blond. The traits of my race are nowhere visible upon me.'[70] His father was a quarter black, his mother a sixteenth, but with America's 'one drop of black blood' rule, he was classified as black.)[71] He noted the contempt of some white GIs towards the British: 'the absence of telephones and radios, electric refrigerators and vacuum cleaners to most soldiers ... denoted an inferior civilization and a backward people'. But he realised that black Americans,

> like the British, were not so accustomed to highly mechanized gadgets. Therefore they were not so prone to derogatory comments upon British living as were some of their white fellow Americans. So, too, did somewhat better manners restrain them from giving offense. Learning this in time, the British developed respect and friendship for Negro soldiers which they, in turn, cherished.[72]

Back in the US, black Americans on average earned half the income of white Americans while Britons earned only about a third.[73] And unlike post-war black immigrants, black GIs were seen as temporary visitors and not a threat to employment.[74] Writing soon after the war, two other African Americans also commented on the superiority of black GIs' manners over white. The prominent black activist, journalist and sociologist W. E. B. DuBois noted how 'The Negroes were often diffident and apologetic ... [they] asked at bars for a drink; they asked if they could be served in restaurants; they did not, like so many white Americans, order, demand and swagger.'[75] To the black journalist and former GI Ormus Davenport, 'The simple fact is, as most of the British girls in the villages who dated the American Negro can testify, the Negro was on the whole more courteous, more considerate, and more sincere than the white GI, whose attitude was far more frequently superior, condescending and insincere.'[76]

It was not just unfamiliarity or good manners that attracted young British women to black GIs. The attraction may have also related to the association of black American culture with new forms of dance and cutting-edge modern music. As the African-American magazine *Ebony* observed in 1946: 'The average Negro GI had one advantage over his white army brother: he knew how to jitterbug. English girls love to dance.'[77] For British women, dancing was their main leisure pursuit throughout the 1920s, 1930s and into the 1940s – along with visits to 'the pictures'.[78] The cultural critic Mica Nava suggests that 'dancing for English girls was both narcissistic display and a form of sexual foreplay ... at a time when full intercourse was both risky and disreputable'.[79] Women's attraction to black GIs as men with whom to have a good time could be seen as buying into the stereotype of black men as 'fun-loving' and 'having the beat' but not (necessarily) the brains. 'Having a good time', however, was precisely what young women wanted; most of them were not looking for a husband (many already had husbands, temporarily absent), or indeed for a father of future children. Apart from the English dance the 'Lambeth Walk', there had been no new dance in England since the Charleston of the mid-1920s.[80] The jitterbug and the lindy hop were dances associated with swing, jazz and black American culture; they were novel and daring. The black GIs had their own swing bands. These new forms of dance and music transformed the dance hall: as one young woman remembers: 'We English girls took to it like ducks to water. No more slow, slow, quick, quick, slow, for us. This was living.'[81] The widely circulated British magazine *Picture Post* photographed some of the dance encounters of British women and black GIs in 1943 London. Known for its progressive politics, the magazine's visual depiction of interracial relationships was indeed a radical challenge to Jim Crow. Less radical was its accompanying text, the magazine resorting to racial – and racist – determinism: the claim that dancing ability was an *inherent* attribute: 'Dancing is to the coloured people what spirit is to the British or warfare to the Germans – their truest form of self-expression. It is a racial heritage, tracing back to the dark ritual of the tom-tom [an African drum].'[82] Thus even the liberal press had a notion of inherited racial difference.

White Americans were far from happy that British women were choosing black GIs over them. One wrote home resentfully: 'It seems that several outfits of colored troops preceded us over here … the girls really go for them in preference to the white boys, a fact that irks the boys no end.'[83] Another white GI expressed similar sentiments: 'I have seen nice-looking white girls going with a coon. They think they are hot stuff. The girls are so dumb it's pitiful.'[84] Not all Britons were happy about these relationships either. Although they stressed British tolerance, they did not necessarily condone intimacy, and indeed were often hostile to interracial sex and marriage. While most were committed to being friendly, polite and welcoming hosts, what the historian Wendy Webster usefully refers to as 'friendly but brief', many people, particularly the older generation, drew the line at sexual relations.[85] As a *Home Intelligence Report* in August 1942 noted: 'adverse comment is reported over girls who "walk out" with coloured troops'.[86] The girls and women tended to be seen as the instigators, as another home intelligence report made clear:

1.1 A black and white couple dancing at Frisco's International Club, Piccadilly, London. Originally published in *Picture Post*, 1486, 'Inside London's Coloured Clubs', 1943

The women and girls concerned ... in many cases are said to make most of the running. Blame of the girls is more widespread, and sometimes stronger, than of the men. Their predatoriness is particularly censured; some girls are said to be dunning as many as three or four US soldiers to provide for their coming child.[87]

British women in relationships with black GIs were frequently condemned as sluts. As Kenneth Little was informed: 'For a girl to walk out with a coloured man would mean a very definite loss in social standing; the girl would be generally considered a very loose and undesirable sort of person.'[88] A statement in *British Public Feeling about America* implicitly added to the explanation of why it was the women who were blamed: 'the coloured men are looked on as "not really responsible persons"', a view that went hand in hand with the idea that black people were 'childish, happy and naïve'.[89]

This censuring of young women meant that the 'over-sexed' GI caricature was matched by that of the British 'good-time girl': an irresponsible, selfish young woman who sought nothing but pleasure, especially sexual pleasure.[90] War work had taken many young women away from home, and they were generally earning far more money than before.[91] Often for the first time in their lives they were outside the control of family and community and they understandably wanted adventure and romance. The epithet 'good-time girl' was applied not only to single girls and women, but also to married women who pursued extramarital relationships; with their husbands usually away fighting they also had more freedom.[92] The June 1944 *Home Intelligence Report* mentioned concerns about 'the increase in moral laxity – particularly of married women, whose husbands are abroad – with Dominion and US troops'. Reflecting after the war on wartime interracial relationships in Liverpool, the African-American newspaper *Liberty* was sympathetic to the women: 'You shouldn't judge the Liverpool girls too severely ... Their own men had been away, overseas ... The bombings had made their shabby homes shabbier; the war had made it impossible to brighten their drab lives.' The article also noted that 'American Negroes treated for the first time in their lives "like white folks" ... eager to find someone to spend their incredible wealth on, could give the girls fun and luxuries their husbands had never been able to give them.'[93] DuBois, writing earlier that year (1946) in the *Chicago Defender*, took a similar position: 'I did not blame the women of England nor gloat over them. Their lives were torn apart, their men sent away and their incomes uncertain.'[94] African Americans may not have blamed the women, but to many in Britain the women's sexual behaviour, whether pre-marital or adulterous, was seen as damaging to Britain's national reputation – their actions were deemed 'unpatriotic' and transgressive of the 'sexual patriotism' expected of them.[95]

Meeting black GIs

Where did British women and black GIs meet? As explained in my introduction, I have interviewed a number of people born to British women and black GIs during or soon after the war. Although the interviews were primarily about the interviewees' own lives, I also asked them about their parents and where they met. There is little information about what the relationships between British women and black GIs were like at the time, and most of these people are no longer alive to tell their own stories. Clearly what is heard in the narratives of these women's children, years after the events described, does not give the 'voice' of the women as such, but they give a few memories of what the children had been told and what they believed their mothers had experienced. However, these accounts have their limits: they are inevitably second-hand, and many children have little knowledge of what their mothers went through during the war, not least because many of the mothers told their children very little about their fathers or any difficulties the couples may have faced.

Many of my interviewees mention dance halls or pubs as their parents' first meeting place; these were the two key social spaces where black GIs and local women were able to socialise, generally on evenings designated 'blacks only'. If a woman was known to have danced with black GIs she ran the risk of ostracism. According to a fifteen-year-old factory worker from Pollock, near Glasgow, the girls and women were identifiable because their names were noted: 'if you danced with the coloured Americans you were blacklisted by the white ones. They kept a list at the camp of these girls.'[96] Pam, an English woman whose sister married a white American GI, attended a 'black night' dance. Her nephew recounts:

A local photographer would apparently go to dances and take pictures of dancing couples. Some of them would be posted in his shop window (presumably with the aim of selling them to the couples involved). Anyway, there was a photo of Pam and a black soldier dancing, which, the story went, she was terrified would get back to her mother.[97]

Her fear was not ostracism but maternal disapproval. White American disapproval could lead to worse than ostracism, however. Gilbert Murray, professor of classics at the University of Glasgow and a well-known humanist, complained to the Colonial Office that he had heard white Americans 'talk of lynching any [black men] whom they find dancing with white girls'. The rationale for such a violent reaction, reported Murray, was as 'an American colonel said in so many words, that the great ambition of every one of these blacks was to rape a white woman!'[98] (This had also generally been the justification given for past lynchings in the American South.)[99]

James A's mother met his father at a dance in Long Eaton, Derbyshire, on a 'black night'. She went to the dance with a friend, despite having four children and a husband at home. As James expresses it: 'probably she deserved to have a little bit of life for herself, having had four children rather quickly, one after the other'.[100] Trevor's mother met his father at a dance in Honeybourne, Worcestershire, near where his father was stationed.[101] The mother of Pauline Nat met her father at a dance in Hampshire.

> My mother was in the Women's Land Army here in Hampshire, not too far from Winchester and my father was a US Army Medic based at what is now Saint Swithun's School. It was a hospital unit and apparently they met at a dance almost in between. There was a dance in Eastleigh.[102]

Unlike the mothers of James A and Trevor, the dance that Pauline's mother attended was unlikely to have been 'blacks only' as Pauline's father was Mexican-American and not subject to segregation. Pauline is included as an interviewee because although her father was not a black GI, she is nevertheless a mixed-heritage GI war baby.

If they did not meet at a dance, the alternative was likely to have been a pub. Many more women were entering pubs during the war than

1.2a Pauline Nat's mother in the land army

1.2b Pauline Nat's father

previously. In February 1943 Mass-Observation undertook a survey of attitudes towards 'women in public houses'. (Mass-Observation was a British social research organisation set up in 1937 to record everyday life through volunteers' diaries and questionnaires.)[103] Before the war few women went to pubs – they were male territory. One woman remembers: 'only the women of the street went in pubs'.[104] With the war all this changed, as women entered 'male' jobs and male preserves. Mass-Observation claimed that while the majority of pubgoers did not object to women in pubs, some of their respondents disliked young women regarding the pub as a pick-up site. One commented: 'There's a certain type who just go in to pick up men. Get what they can, sort of thing … they're the ones who go after Canadians and Americans and spread disease.'[105] Whether or not they were looked on as women 'who just go in to pick up men' (and 'spread disease'), a number of my interviewees' mothers met black GIs in pubs. Sandra S's mother attended a Bristol pub called the Spread Eagle on a so-called 'black' night, where she met Sandra's father.[106] Tony H's parents met at the Bluebell in Burtonwood, Cheshire.[107] Monica explained how her parents met:

She found out that there was a dance being held in Prescot [near where she lived in Liverpool] for the black GIs. One of her friends invited her out ... Mum said she wasn't allowed in the dance hall this time. Her and her friends went to the local pub that the GIs would go in before and after the dance ... The Wellington and ... one night one of the groups came in and my dad was among the group.[108]

Sometimes the meeting came about through the woman working in the pub, as was the case with Carole T's mother. 'My mum was an orphan by the time she was fourteen', so she went to live with an older half-brother. 'He was running a pub in Poole called the Swan, on the Quay where my dad was stationed ... She also used to help out in a pub called the Jolly Sailor and I think that is where they met.'[109] Her father romantically sang 'Goodnight Irene' to her mother when it was time to leave (her second name was Irene).[110] Joyce thinks her parents met either at the Clacton pub in Cosham, Portsmouth, or at a local dance hall. Her father would then visit her mother at her home in Portsmouth where she lived with her own mother: 'my nan used to play the piano, so the Yanks [black GIs] used to buy crates of beer and they used to come up and have a sing-song with the piano'.[111]

Not all of my interviewees' mothers met their fathers at a dance or in a pub. Billy was told by his mother that in Callington, Cornwall, 'she was walking along the street with a friend and he was walking along with a friend and they got into a conversation'.[112] John S's mother 'had a guest house [in Weymouth, Dorset] from 1941, and in 1944, I believe, there were some black soldiers billeted with her'.[113] Cynthia's mother 'had a nursing background. And I was advised she was driving an ambulance in the war. She couldn't drive – never learned to drive – so I don't know how they let her drive. And she knocked my father down, in the fog!' Despite this unpropitious beginning, they got together, married in 1950 and remained married for the rest of their lives. Cynthia's father was from British Guiana but had been studying in the US when it entered the war and was 'then caught up in the draft', coming to Britain as a GI.[114]

As already mentioned, British women in relationships with black GIs were frequently labelled 'loose'. Some of my interviewees told me that their mothers experienced hostility when seen with a black

GI. For example, Dave G recounts how his mother, who worked at Westland Industries making aircraft components,

> told me stories of what it was like being out with my father, and the stick they used to get. Particularly from white American soldiers … when my father and her went into a pub or café or anything like that … Mum used to say the white Yanks used to kick off and say: 'Yeh nigger lover'.[115]

It was not only racist abuse that women in relationships with black GIs had to confront. According to the American anthropologist Margaret Mead, who came to Britain in summer 1943 to study relations between the Americans (white and black) and the British, there were fundamental cultural misunderstandings about how to behave on a 'date'. In the US, where there were more men than women, girls and young women were much more used to 'casual', 'wise-cracking' inter-actions with boys and men. The men would push at the boundaries 'by boldly demanding innumerable favours' while the girls would refuse them. But in Britain, where there were many more women than men,

1.3a Cynthia's mother   **1.3b** Cynthia's father

Mead suggests that some of the girls took 'his words which sound like wooing for wooing, and give a kiss with real warmth, which surprises him very much. Some of them think he is proposing when he isn't.'[116] It is easy to see how this could have led to the sexes having different assessments of the seriousness of the relationship. However, even had both parties wanted to marry, it was not permitted during wartime if the GI was black.

Marriage bar

All American troops had to receive permission to marry from their commanding officers (who in the UK were nearly all white); avoidance of this permission was a court-martial offence. For black GIs wanting to marry white British women, permission was invariably refused. As the *Chicago Defender* pointed out: 'The white officers in command of Negro troops are reluctant to grant such permission ... There is documentary evidence that permission has been denied solely on the basis of race. This even in cases where the girl may be pregnant.'[117] As Ormus Davenport noted in the popular British left-leaning Sunday newspaper *Reynolds's News* in 1947: 'some [women] had acquired parental permission to wed – but could not get the permission of the US army authorities'.

> Scores of young couples to whom these children were born were genuinely and legitimately in love ... There were a few couples who were able to marry secretly, but it was not easy for a coloured man to adopt an assumed name and get a birth certificate in order to marry. In any case, all registrars were aware of the fact that anyone in uniform must be armed with official permission.[118]

According to Davenport, the US army 'unofficially had a "gentleman's agreement" which became in practice official policy. The agreement said "No negro soldier or sailor will be given permission to marry any British white girl!" ... Not one GI bride going back to the US under the US government scheme is the wife of a Negro.'[119] At least 40,000 British brides travelled to the US, the vast majority with white husbands,[120] although new research has revealed that there were over seventy marriages between black GIs and mixed-race women from

Tiger Bay, Cardiff – then the most ethnically diverse area of Britain.[121] Mixed-race women entering the US would have been seen as 'black' and thus in marrying black GIs would not have transgressed state laws forbidding interracial marriage. Thirty of the (then) forty-eight US states still had anti-miscegenation laws.

After reading Davenport's article, the Labour MP Tom Driberg raised the issue in the House of Commons. In response the Foreign Office approached the American Embassy, whose officials denied any knowledge of such a ban, although the Foreign Office did note that 'it seems very unlikely that the US army would publicly admit to having issued such orders'. It also commented, 'I doubt if the "policy" amounted to anything more than the prejudice of the Southern officers who usually ran the coloured units of the US Army.'[122] Even had interracial marriage been permitted, marriages may well have been deemed illegal in the US because of the anti-miscegenation laws. One white English woman, Margaret Goosey, a shoe factory worker, went in 1947 to Virginia to marry her black ex-GI fiancé. He was imprisoned and she was sent to an industrial farm then deported.[123] Driberg was again on the case and in Parliament he pointed out that it was 'an elementary right that men and women should be allowed to get married, irrespective of race or creed'. The Foreign Secretary Ernest Bevin, however, dismissed the objection, as the prohibition was 'in accord with Virginia State Law'.[124] The Eighth US Air Force, based in East Anglia, was explicit about banning interracial marriages: Commander General Hugh Knerr dismissed all requests as 'against public policy'. In 1944 he was challenged on the grounds of civil rights when a black GI from Dallas applied to marry a woman who was pregnant with his child. When Knerr predictably rejected the application, the woman and her father took the case to their local MP who raised it with the Foreign Office. It was decreed that the Commanding Officer had the final say, and the case was dropped.[125]

The fact that black GIs could not marry their white British girl-friends and might be suddenly transferred elsewhere appears to have been known to some women. This knowledge was apparent when Carole B asked her mother about her father:

> I said, 'Why didn't you marry him?' She said, 'It wasn't allowed …
> If they'd have found out that he had a child … he would have gone
> and I think that's what happened really' … I said, 'Did you love him,

Mum?' and she said, 'Yes I did … I really did, he was a gentleman' and I went 'He wasn't that much of a gentleman, mother!' and she started laughing and she said, 'He was a gentleman' … and I said, 'Why didn't you marry him?' She said, 'It wasn't allowed … if they found out, he would have gone.'[126]

Heather T's mother and black GI father were both 27 when she was born and both single. They had met in or near Ipswich. Heather's mother worked as a domestic servant; Heather thinks her father was stationed at Martlesham Heath, Suffolk, a US air base. Heather was born on VE Day (8 May 1945). 'He [her father] kept in touch. They wanted to be together but they thought there was no way. His mother used to send some money. They were constantly in touch initially, but both married other people and the contact stopped.' Heather's mother told her daughter that 'he was the light of her life. She absolutely really did love him … so that must have been horribly hard for her.'[127] Presumably they thought that 'there was no way' they could stay together because of legal and social barriers. There was also the financial barrier. He was from North Carolina and worked on his parents' cotton and potato fields. As Heather's husband Tim suggests:

1.4 Heather T's father

'He was a young black man, just after the war. No rights, probably no money – or very little money. Dirt farmers, maybe, scratching a living and just making a living – just to keep themselves fed. What could he have done?'[128]

James A remembers that his mother

> said that she loved my dad, and she would have liked to have gone back to America with him. He wanted to take me back to America, but she wouldn't allow him to do so because she thought I would have a worse time out there than probably here. Because at the time in America things weren't very good for black people.[129]

Whether or not Britain was good for the children born out of these relationships is the focus of the chapters that follow.

Notes

1   *Sunday Pictorial*, 26 August 1945, p. 1.
2   Linda Hervieux, *Forgotten: The Untold Story of D-Day's Black Heroes, at Home and at War* (New York, 2015), pp. 26–7.
3   Neil A. Wynn, *The African American Experience during World War II* (Plymouth, 2010), p. 27.
4   'United States Coloured Troops in the United Kingdom: Memorandum by the Secretary of State for War', September 1942, PREM 4/26/9, the National Archives (hereafter TNA), Kew, London.
5   Wynn, *The African American Experience*, p. 53, suggests 8 per cent, while David Reynolds, *Rich Relations: The American Occupation of Britain, 1942–1945* (London, 1996), p. 83, suggests it was 7.4 per cent.
6   See J. Todd Moye, *Freedom Flyers: The Tuskegee Airmen of World War II* (Oxford, 2010).
7   Hervieux, *Forgotten*, p. 19.
8   Ibid., p. 30.
9   Wynn, *The African American Experience*, p. 51.
10 *Pittsburgh Courier*, 14 February 1942. The *Pittsburgh Courier* was one of the largest black newspapers, with a circulation of over 200,000; Wynn, *The African American Experience*, p. 26.
11 Reproduced in Wynn, *The African American Experience*, p. 124.
12 Quoted in Hervieux, *Forgotten*, p. 259.

13 Nancy Cunard and George Padmore, 'The White Man's Duty: an analysis of the colonial question in light of the Atlantic', in Maureen Moynagh (ed.), *Essays on Race and Empire: Nancy Cunard* (Peterborough, Ont., 2002), pp. 127–77; Leslie James, *George Padmore and Decolonization from Below* (London, 2015), pp. 52–3.

14 According to Reynolds, *Rich Relations*, pp. 227, 323, and Smith, *When Jim Crow Met John Bull*, p. 192, there were 130,000 black GIs in the UK on D-Day, representing one in thirteen of the GIs – nearly 8 per cent. Smith's book remains the leading text on black GIs in wartime Britain.

15 Ministry of Information, *British Public Feeling about America: A Report by Home Intelligence Division* (London, 1943), FO 371/44601, TNA.

16 Jeffrey Richards, *The Age of the Dream Palace: Cinema and Society in 1930s Britain* (London, 2010); Richard Farmer, *Cinemas and Cinemagoing in Wartime Britain, 1939–45* (Manchester, 2016).

17 Quoted in Sheila Ferguson and Hilde Fitzgerald, *History of the Second World War: Studies in the Social Services* (London, 1954), p. 97. See also Marilyn Lake, 'The desire for a Yank: sexual relations between Australian women and American servicemen during World War II', *Journal of the History of Sexuality*, 2.4 (1991), pp. 621–33.

18 'Notes on Interview with the Adjutant-General War Office: American Army and Air Force. The Colour Bar', July 1942, CO 876/14, TNA.

19 Reynolds, *Rich Relations*, p. 149.

20 Patrick Newley, *You Lucky People! The Tommy Trinder Story* (London, 2008), p. 41.

21 Gail Braybon and Penny Summerfield, *Out of the Cage: Women's Experiences in Two World Wars* (London, 1987), p. 253.

22 PREM 4/26/9, TNA. These and other discussions of the 'coloured' troops were headed 'MOST SECRET' and 'TO BE KEPT UNDER LOCK AND KEY'.

23 FO 954/298, TNA.

24 Anonymous [Major General A. A. B. Dowler], 'Notes on Relations with Coloured Troops', n.d. [7 August 1942], annexed to Secretary for War, 'United States Coloured Troops in the United Kingdom', Memorandum, September 1942, PREM 4/26/9, TNA.

25 'United States Negro Troops in the United Kingdom', n.d. [October 1942], PREM 4/26/9, TNA.

26 Home Secretary, 'United States Coloured Troops in the United Kingdom', Memorandum, 10 October 1942, PREM 4/26/9, TNA.

27 PREM 4/26/9, TNA.

28   Penny Summerfield and Nicola Crockett, '"You weren't taught that with the welding": lessons in sexuality in the Second World War', *Women's History Review*, 1.3 (1992), p. 437.

29   *Home Intelligence Weekly Report*, 17 September 1942, p. 4, INF 1/292, TNA.

30   FO 371/34126, A6556, TNA.

31   Sonya Rose, 'Girls and GIs: race, sex, and diplomacy in Second World War Britain', *International History Review*, 19.1 (1997), p. 157.

32   *Welcome to Britain* (dir. Anthony Asquith, 1943).

33   Quoted in *Sunday Pictorial*, 6 September 1942, p. 3.

34   Ibid.

35   Leonora Eyles, *Woman's Own*, 12 November 1943. Thanks to Claire Langhamer for drawing this to my attention. Langhamer notes that Eyles's advice did not go unchallenged: one critic responded: 'Why aren't they as good as anyone? And why say that they ought not to marry white girls?' Claire Langhamer, *The English in Love* (Oxford, 2013), p. 73.

36   Interview with Cynthia, 12 September 2017.

37   Walter White, *A Rising Wind* (New York, 1945), pp. 16, 138–9, 56.

38   Editorial, 'Black and white rape', *The Crisis*, July 1944, p. 217. Emphasis in the original.

39   See Smith, *When Jim Crow Met John Bull*, pp. 138–51; Liam McCarthy, 'Racism, Violence and Sex: An Alternative History of American Troops in Leicester during the Second World War', unpublished MRes dissertation, University of Leicester, 2016.

40   See J. L. Keith (Colonial Office) to Jefferies (Home Office), 31 July 1942, CO 876/14, TNA; Kenneth Little, letter on 'Treatment of Colour Prejudice in Britain', to J. L. Keith, Colonial Office, n.d., CO 875/19/14, TNA.

41   Smith, *When Jim Crow Met John Bull*, p. 89. My emphasis.

42   Ministry of Information, *British Public Feeling about America*. Emphasis in the original.

43   This is still the case today. Akala, *Natives: Race and Class in the Ruins of Empire* (London, 2018), p. 267.

44   Ministry of Information, *British Public Feeling about America*.

45   Hall, *Familiar Stranger*, p. 104.

46   Harold Moody, *The Colour Bar* (London, 1944), p. 8.

47   'A patriot under colour bar', *Daily Herald*, 3 September 1943, p. 3; Learie Constantine, 'The story of my people', *The Listener*, 9 September 1943, p. 287. In June 1944 Constantine took the case to court and was awarded damages for breach of contract; David Olusoga, *Black and British: A Forgotten History* (London, 2016),

p. 488; Learie Constantine, *Colour Bar* (London, 1954). See also Peter Fryer, *Staying Power: The History of Black People in Britain* (London, 1984), pp. 364–6. Constantine was awarded the MBE in 1945.

48 Robert Kee, 'Is there is British colour bar?', *Picture Post*, 2 July 1949, pp. 23–8.

49 See Wendy Webster, *Englishness and Empire, 1939–1965* (Oxford, 2005); Kathleen Paul, *Whitewashing Britain: Race and Citizenship in the Postwar Era* (New York, 1997).

50 Lee, 'A forgotten legacy', p. 162.

51 Anthony Richmond, *Colour Prejudice in Britain: A Study of West Indian Workers in Liverpool, 1941–1951* (London, 1954), p. 20. St Clair Drake also thought attitudes towards 'Negroes' were tied up with 'the low social status of the Negro population'. John St Clair Drake, 'Significance of the Study', Acc. no. 4910, Liverpool Record Office (hereafter LRO), Liverpool Central Library.

52 'United States Coloured Troops in the United Kingdom', Memorandum by the Home Secretary, 10 October 1942, PREM 4/26/9, TNA.

53 Quoted in Leanne McCormick, *Regulating Sexuality: Women in Twentieth-century Northern Ireland* (Manchester, 2009), p. 163.

54 K. L. Little, 'Coloured troops in Britain', *New Statesman*, 29 April 1942, p. 141.

55 It is impossible to arrive at exact numbers, as the archives generally give no indication of a person's ethnicity. But Ian R. Spencer, *British Immigration Policy since 1939: The Making of Multiracial Britain* (London, 1997), p. 3, estimates 7,000 Asian and black people in 1939; Moody, *Colour Bar*, p. 8 estimates 10,000 before the war. Many thanks to Peter Aspinall for these references. David Reynolds suggests that the number was no more than 8,000; Reynolds, *Rich Relations*, p. 216.

56 See Caroline Bressey, 'Geographies of belonging: white women and black history', *Women's History Review*, 22.4 (2013), pp. 541–58.

57 See, for example, *Home Intelligence Weekly Report*, 23 July 1942, p. 4; 13 August 1942, p. 5; 19 August 1942, p. 5, INF 1/292, TNA. On the setting up of Home Intelligence, see Paul Addison and Jeremy A. Crang (eds), *Listening to Britain* (London, 2010), Introduction.

58 Quoted in Smith, *When Jim Crow Met John Bull*, pp. 118–19. See also Nevil Shute's 1947 novel, in which an 86-year-old pubgoer in Cornwall comments on the black GIs: 'I like them very well, oh, very well indeed. We get on nicely with them here. I don't like those white ones that are coming now, though.' Nevil Shute, *The Chequer Board* (London, 2000), p. 69.

59   'Negro troops' chorus in London's Albert Hall', *Life* magazine, 29 September 1943.

60   Quoted in Hervieux, *Forgotten*, p. 177.

61   White, *A Rising Wind*, p. 21.

62   Ibid., p. 11.

63   Kenneth Little, *Negroes in Britain* (1947) (Oxford, 2010), p. 262, n. 2.

64   *VE Day: First Days of Peace: Race Relations* (dir. Alistair McKee, BBC 2015). Many thanks to Graham Smith for lending me this programme.

65   Email from Bob Farrer, 21 October 2016. Hugh Dalton, the President of the Board of Trade, had anticipated that Britons would be likely to take the side of the black GIs. Christopher Thorne, 'British and the black GI: racial issues and Anglo-American relations in 1942', *New Community*, 111.3 (1974), p. 264.

66   Juliet Gardiner, *Over Here! The GIs in Wartime Britain* (London, 1992), p. 151; Reynolds, *Rich Relations*, centre pages.

67   Telephone conversation with Bob Farrer, 23 October 2016.

68   Ralph Ellison, 'In a strange country', in Dorothy Sterling (ed.), *I Have Seen War: The Story of World War II* (New York, 1960), p. 108.

69   White's detailed report on his visit for the War Department, in which he suggested many ways in which race relations could be improved, such as abolishing the 'pass' system, was largely ignored. Smith, *When Jim Crow Met John Bull*, p. 168.

70   Walter White, *A Man called White* (New York, 1948), p. 3.

71   Smith, *When Jim Crow Met John Bull*, p. 166.

72   White, *A Rising Wind*, p. 21.

73   Hervieux, *Forgotten*, p. 188.

74   Gardiner, *Over Here!*, p. 151.

75   W. E. B. DuBois, 'GIs leave good impression on England', *Chicago Defender*, 24 November 1945.

76   Ormus Davenport, 'U.S. prejudice dooms 1,000 British babies', *Reynolds's News*, 9 February 1947, p. 2.

77   'Fatherless children check the liberalism of British', *Ebony*, 19 November 1946.

78   James Nott, *Going to the Palais: A Social and Cultural History of Dance and Dance Halls in Britain 1918–1960* (Oxford, 2015); Allison Abra, *Dancing in the English Style: Consumption, Americanisation and National Identity in Britain, 1918–50* (Manchester, 2017).

79   Mica Nava, *Visceral Cosmopolitanism* (London, 2007), p. 82.

80   Allison Jean Abra, 'Doing the Lambeth Walk: novelty dances and

the British nation', *Twentieth Century British History*, 20.3 (2009), pp. 346–69.

81 Gardiner, *Over Here!*, p. 114. See also Les Back, 'Syncopated synergy: dance, embodiment and the call of the Jitterbug', in Vron Ware and Les Back, *Out of Whiteness* (Chicago, 2002), pp. 183–4.

82 *Picture Post*, 17 July 1943.

83 Quoted in Gardiner, *Over Here!*, p. 155.

84 Quoted in Leanne McCormick, '"One Yank and they're off": interaction between US troops and Northern Irish Women, 1942–1945', *Journal of the History of Sexuality*, 15.2 (2006), p. 244.

85 Wendy Webster, '"Fit to fight, fit to mix": sexual patriotism in Second World War Britain', *Women's History Review*, 22.4 (2013), pp. 607–24. Similarly, Reynolds points to the distinction made by the British between civil rights and sexual wrongs; Reynolds, *Rich Relations*, p. 307.

86 *Home Intelligence Weekly Report*, 19 August 1942, p. 5.

87 *Home Intelligence Monthly Review*, 8 June 1944.

88 Little, *Negroes in Britain*, pp. 255–6.

89 Ministry of Information, *British Public Feeling about America*, p. 16.

90 See Lucy Bland and Frank Mort, '"Look out for the goodtime girl": dangerous sexualities as a threat to national health', in *Formations of Nation and People* (London, 1984), pp. 131–51.

91 Penny Summerfield, *Women Workers in the Second World War* (London, 1989); Summerfield, *Reconstructing Women's Wartime Lives*.

92 See Claire Langhamer, 'Love and courtship in mid-twentieth century England', *The Historical Journal*, 20.1 (2007), pp. 173–96. See also Lee, 'A forgotten legacy'.

93 Alfred Eris, 'Britain's mulatto "GI" babies', *Liberty*, 7 December 1946.

94 W. E. B. DuBois, 'The winds of change', *Chicago Defender*, 15 June 1946.

95 Sonya Rose, *Which People's War? National Identity and Citizenship in Britain 1939–1945* (Oxford, 2003), pp. 71–90.

96 Quoted in Norman Longmate, *The GIs: The Americans in Britain, 1942–1945* (London, 1975), p. 132.

97 Email from John Carter Wood, summer 2014.

98 Letter from Professor Gilbert Murray to Miss Audrey Richards, CO 876/24, TNA.

99 Ida B. Wells, *Southern Horrors: Lynch Law in All its Phases* (New York, 1892).

100 Interview with James A, 19 April 2016.

101   Interview with Trevor, 15 July 2015.

102   Interview with Pauline Nat, 17 April 2014.

103   See Nick Hubble, *Mass Observation and Everyday Life: Culture, History, Theory* (London, 2006).

104   Quoted in Phil Goodman, '"Patriotic femininity": women's morals and men's morale during the Second World War', *Gender & History*, 10.2 (1998), p. 286.

105   Mass-Observation, *Women in Pubs*, December 1943, file report 1970, p. 3, Mass-Observation Archives, University of Sussex.

106   Interview with Sandra S, 28 October 2014.

107   Interview with Tony H, 19 October 2016.

108   Interview with Monica, 1 September 2014.

109   Interview with Carole T, 9 September 2014.

110   Carole T on *Woman's Hour*, Radio 4, 19 May 2017.

111   Interview with Joyce, 12 August 2014.

112   Interview with Billy, 12 November 2016.

113   Interview with John S, 20 June 2016.

114   Interview with Cynthia, 12 September 2017.

115   Interview with Dave G, 23 June 2016.

116   Margaret Mead, *The American Troops and the British Community* (London, 1944).

117   Henry Lee Moon, 'Army hits Negro babies of soldiers and British mothers', *Chicago Defender*, 28 April 1945, p. 11. On Walter White's inquiry to the US secretary of war about the ban, see Caballero and Aspinall, *Mixed Race Britain*, pp. 213–14.

118   Davenport, 'U.S. prejudice dooms 1,000 British babies'. Caryl Phillips, *Crossing the River* (London, 1993), includes the experience of a British woman who marries a black GI in the war, his having got his commanding officer's permission. This would have been highly unlikely if the woman was white. Thanks to Mary Joannou for drawing my attention to this beautiful novel.

119   Davenport, 'U.S. prejudice dooms 1,000 British babies', p. 2

120   Jenel Virden, *Good-bye, Piccadilly: British War Brides in America* (Urbana, IL, 1996); Duncan Barrett and Nuala Calvi, *GI Brides* (London, 2013); Reynolds, *Rich Relations*, pp. 420–2.

121   See the documentary *Tiger Brides: Memories of Love and War from the GI Brides of Tiger Bay* (dir. Simon and Anthony Campbell, with Valerie Hill-Jackson, 2013).

122   'Problem of Illegitimate Half-Caste Children of US Negro Servicemen and British Girls', FO 371/97/AN668/13/45, TNA; FO Memo, DA Logan, 18 February 1947, FO 371/61017, TNA.

123   Caballero and Aspinall, *Mixed Race Britain*, pp. 229–30.

124 *Hansard House of Commons Debates*, 11 February 1948, Vol. 447, cc.369–70.

125 Reynolds, *Rich Relations*, pp. 231–2.

126 Interview with Carole B, 1 September 2014.

127 Interview with Heather T, 1 September 2016.

128 Interview with Heather T, 1 September 2016.

129 Interview with James A, 19 April 2016.

2

Keeping the 'brown babies'

When Monica's mother gave birth to her in November 1944 she was a 26-year-old single woman still living at home with her father, looking after her six brothers and sisters. They lived in St Helen's, near Liverpool. Her mother had died when she was ten and as the oldest daughter she had had to leave school early to help look after the other children. Monica recalls her mother's account of the situation facing her when she revealed her pregnancy:

> She was pressured horrendously to give me up ... to have me adopted or to have me put in a home ... she wouldn't allow it in the end but she was persuaded a lot because my family was Roman Catholic and the local Catholic priest put a lot of pressure on her ... and on Granddad too ... They arranged a place for Mum in a mother and baby home in Liverpool where she would go in, have the child ... it would be adopted and she would come home and nobody would know about it ... but she refused.

When she came home with a mixed-race baby her father was horrified: 'There was a big row in the house, Granddad threatened that she had to leave, she couldn't stay there no longer.' Although he later forgave her, Monica reflects:

> I think her life was virtually nearly over. She never went out for a long, long time. She sort of stayed at home with me. Granddad was difficult to live with, he'd got used to me, the baby, but never trusted Mum after that and she couldn't go very far, he kept a tight rein on her, I don't think she was probably wanting to go very far after that time because it was a bit of a scandal having a mixed-race child ... Her brothers were particularly cruel to her after she had me. 'You're not going out. We've got to keep an eye on you.' They controlled her.[1]

2.1 Monica as a baby

Monica's story illustrates some of the difficulties facing a woman who bore an illegitimate, mixed-race child in the 1940s: the stigma of illegitimacy, with the concomitant pressure from immediate family and possibly also the Church to give up the baby; the additional stigma and scandal of having a mixed-race child; the constraints often subsequently placed on the mother to control her movements and behaviour. Despite this, of the forty-five mixed-race GI war babies whose stories I am primarily drawing upon, twenty-four were kept by their mothers and/or grandmothers.

The stigma of being illegitimate and 'half-caste'

All forty-five wartime babies were born illegitimate. At least eighteen of their mothers were already married; in eight of these cases, the child was kept by the mother or grandmother. (The uncertainty of the exact number of married mothers is because two of my interviewees, both given up to children's homes, do not know if their mothers were married.) A number of the forty-five black GI fathers were also married, but the exact number is unknown.[2] As explained in the previous chapter, even where both parties were free to marry, marriage between white British women and black GIs was generally forbidden. In *Reynolds's News* in 1947, Ormus Davenport suggested that when a black GI mentioned pregnancy, 'the man was usually transferred to some other county or to a distant part of Britain ... When a girl tried to follow up her claim against the father of her child, the army would invariably find "no evidence of ever having such a man on the records".'[3] Joe, who was put in a children's home, found out later that his maternal grandparents had identified his black GI father to the commanding officer, but when his father said he wished to keep his newborn child, he was told that if he maintained a relationship with the mother he would be charged with rape.[4] The black father of another Joe, who was kept by his mother, was actually charged with rape 'and in the end he was literally handcuffed and shipped out'.[5]

In the eyes of the law, to be 'illegitimate' meant to be born to parents not lawfully married to each other. But this legal definition was accompanied by an ethical one: the mother bearing an illegitimate child was widely perceived as immoral, while the illegitimate child him/herself was thought to be inherently morally tainted. Illegitimacy, or 'bastardy' as it was known, was heavily stigmatised in the 1940s (a stigma that continued into the 1970s). A woman who bore an illegitimate child was frequently pressurised to relinquish it. The pressure came from her immediate family, from local Church authorities and often from a mother and baby home, should she attend one. Such homes, the first of which had been founded in 1871, were generally denominational.[6] If the mother bravely kept the baby and lived in an area where she was known, such as a village or small town, she was unable to hide the child, which frequently led to ostracism, isolation and shame.[7]

It was not just the stigma of having a child out of wedlock, as it was quaintly called, that faced these mothers, but their bearing a mixed-race child. In July 1942 the Chief Constable of Oxford, in a letter to the Home Office, expressed anxiety about the possible consequences of the presence of black GIs: 'every step must be taken to stop British women misconducting themselves with coloured troops, if for no other reason than that we do not desire to have a certain proportion of the population semi-coloured in rural districts in this country in the future'.[8] When children were born to black GIs in Britain they were usually referred to not as 'semi-coloured' but as 'half-caste', although as has been pointed out, the African-American press labelled them descriptively and much more positively as 'brown babies'.[9] There was much ambivalence, even hostility, in Britain towards 'half-castes'. As observed by the visiting African-American anthropologist John St Clair Drake: 'Kindliness to visiting Negro soldiers is one thing. The prospect of a new crop of "half-castes" is another.'[10] In 1937 a polemic entitled *Half-Caste* by the self-defined Eurasian Cedric Dover, while claiming 'the richness of hybrid potentiality', also indicated the extent of prejudice facing those of mixed race:

> The 'half-caste' appears in a prodigal literature. It presents him … mostly as an undersized, scheming and entirely degenerate bastard. His father is a blackguard, his mother a whore … But more than all this, he is a potential menace to Western Civilisation, to everything that is White and Sacred.[11]

The existence of 'half-castes' represented a challenge to national and racial boundaries and to the neat polarity between the white British and the non-white, colonised, racial 'other'. As the historian Sonya Rose suggests, their presence blurred 'the racial lineaments of British national identity'.[12]

The Liverpool University Settlement (a philanthropic organisation focused on helping the poor) had founded the Liverpool Association for the Welfare of Half-Caste Children in 1927. Harold King, honorary secretary of this Association, referred to such children as 'unfortunates'.[13] When in 1938 the official history of the Liverpool University Settlement declared that 'mixed parentage' was 'a handicap comparable to physical deformity', the authors were reiterating what had become a common-sense understanding.[14] For example, the Army Bureau of Public Affairs' educational pamphlet *The Colour Problem as the American Sees It*, produced in late 1942 for the British troops, announced:

> We need not go into a long discussion as to whether mixed marriages between white and coloured are good or bad. What is fairly obvious is that in our present society such unions are not considered desirable, since the children resulting from them are neither one thing nor another and are thus badly handicapped in the struggle for life.[15]

Dr Harold Moody, a Jamaican who had moved to England in 1904 and married a white British woman, was told by acquaintances and even strangers that his children would be social degenerates.[16] But as he pointed out in a 1944 pamphlet: 'Hybridisation is supposed to improve the stock in plants and animals. Why then should not the same thing obtain in the human being?'[17] To Moody's organisation, the League of Coloured Peoples (a civil rights organisation he had founded in Britain in 1931 to help combat and eliminate the 'colour bar'), the answer to the racial discrimination facing mixed-race children was education of 'the British people in the matter of race'.[18] Such an 'education' does not seem to have been widespread. It is interesting to note the attitude of Nella Last, a generally fairly liberal lower-middle-class woman who kept a lively diary for Mass-Observation from the Second World War up until her death in 1968. In January 1950 she registered her shock on reading 'how many half-caste children were the result of the American negro soldiers' short stay in England'; later that year she noted: 'the sight of half-caste children seems to strike at something way deep down in me. I *say* I've no colour bar, but wonder if really I have a very deep-rooted one.'[19] Her recognition of her own 'colour bar' was unusual, but her 'deep-rooted' aversion was possibly fairly common.

How many of these mixed-race GI war babies were there? St Clair Drake came to Britain in 1947 to do fieldwork for his PhD on 'Race Relations in the British Isles' accompanied by his (white) wife, the sociologist Elizabeth Johns.[20] The large number of such children was often pointed out to St Clair Drake. He noted: 'One coloured woman in Cardiff told me to tell the Americans that when the next war breaks out "just keep the coloured troops at home and send along the uniforms. We have the troops here."'[21] And when Johns informed a white woman with mixed-race children, Mrs M, that her husband 'was here studying the children of coloured American soldiers', Mrs M replied, 'They don't need any study for that. American troops? They left plenty. There's thousands of them right here.'[22]

Were there thousands? In January 1946 the League of Coloured Peoples (LCP) published a pamphlet entitled *Illegitimate Children Born in Britain of English Mothers and Coloured Americans* by Jamaican teacher Sylvia McNeill, which addressed this question of numbers.[23] McNeill had written to welfare organisations in each county in England and Wales asking about mothers reporting their 'coloured' children, including seeking their adoption. This led to a list of 545; by 1948 the numbers had risen to 775.[24] The LCP recognised, however, that many babies, if kept by their birth families, would not have fallen within the remit of a welfare agency. In Germany after the war well over half of such children were kept. However, unlike Germany, no centralised demographic statistics were recorded in Britain, so it is impossible to know exactly how many 'brown babies' were born.[25] In 1947 the Trinidadian George Padmore, living in England, estimated 1,700.[26] In 1949 Dr Malcolm Joseph-Mitchell, who was the 'General and Travelling Secretary' of the LCP, estimated the number of children of white women and 'coloured serviceman' to be approximately 2,000, although he might have been including children with West Indian fathers.[27] We can never know exact numbers, but 1,700 to 2,000 seems a fair estimate.

The 'brown babies' were born all over Britain, but predominantly in areas where most black GIs had been stationed: south and south-west England, South Wales, East Anglia and Lancashire. They were brought up in very white locations, the exceptions being Cardiff and Liverpool, with their long-standing black and mixed-race communities.[28] In Tiger Bay, Cardiff, St Clair Drake was informed by a black man that young white women with 'coloured' babies were coming to the area, as

> nobody will let a woman with a coloured baby starve or sleep out of doors ... a coloured baby touches you here [he touches his heart] and these women know it. But now if a fellow takes in a woman that's had a white baby, all the fellows will say: 'Man – you crazy –raising John Bull's baby!'[29]

As already mentioned, Britain at the time was very largely a white country. The numbers of black people rose greatly during the war, not only because of the presence of black GIs, but also because of West Indians coming to contribute to the war effort as service personnel (especially in the RAF) and as munitions workers.[30] Nevertheless, soon after the war numbers shrank again for the next few years, and although they never dropped to the pre-war figure, the Home Counties returned to almost exclusive whiteness.[31] In these geographically white areas, many of the mixed-race GI children suffered racism, an acute sense of difference and a lack of racial 'belonging'. Their mothers were also often treated badly, a number of their children mentioning the hostility and stigma that their mothers faced and the taunt of epithets such as 'nigger lover' and 'nigger's bit'. Monica's mother was often called names in the street:

> I remember one time there was a lady from a couple of doors away, her and mum never got on … I remember one day mum and me was sat on the gate where we lived and this lady came past and … hit my mum and she shouted in the street, 'You nigger lover'.[32]

Terry remembers that some people 'would bang on their metal dustbins whenever my mother walked by. It also became a daily ritual for people to cross the road to avoid my mother rather than speak to her.'[33] Henry's memory of his mother being spat at for having a black child was probably not uncommon.[34]

Davenport wrote three articles about the 'brown babies' for *Reynolds's News* in early 1947; letters of response included those from women describing how determined they were to keep their babies: 'they have fought down prejudice and the hostility of parents and found jobs and homes in which they can build new lives'.[35] Peter's

2.2 Peter with two girls

2.3 Dave G and his mother

unmarried mother Elizabeth got pregnant at seventeen. Her father, a miner, who she lived with, had two other children, and the family survived hand to mouth. When Elizabeth was seven their mother had died and her father had given up her baby sister for adoption, as he simply could not cope. In the circumstances, Elizabeth was pressurised to do the same with Peter, but like Monica's mother, she refused.[36] Dave G's mother also faced familial opposition:

> He [dad] used to visit my grandparents' home. Made welcome there … [but] one of my aunties particularly, and one uncle, were not enamoured with the idea of him associating with my mum … When I was born, those same ones were: 'Really, is this the wisest thing to be doing, keeping this child?' But Mum being my mum, and – I'll say feisty person that she was – strong character that she was, decided that – yeh, she was going to keep me. I mean, who wouldn't want to?! But she was adamant she was going to … The character of my mum, that she was – I'll use this word 'ballsy' enough to actually hang on to me.[37]

When Lloyd's mother, who was working as a machinist in an engineering works in Derby, found she was having me, and she told my grandparents … my grandmother kicked her out of the house. And we lived in a house only about this big [indicating something very small]. But somebody told me that my grandfather didn't know that my grandmother had kicked my mother out of the house. How she got lost in about two rooms, heaven knows!'

Lloyd's grandfather took her back after Lloyd was born.[38] Although his mother had apparently cried out 'It'll be black! It'll be black!' when she was about to give birth, the fact that Lloyd was quite pale and could 'pass' for white might have made the return home easier. Lloyd thinks his relative paleness must have been a great relief to his mother. She never told Lloyd that he had a black father, nor did she tell anyone else.[39]

2.4 Lloyd's mother

2.5 John F

John F's birth led to a rift in the family, but fortunately 'his mother was fiercely protective of him', says John's son Adam, and they were living 'in the little fishing village of Charlestown, Cornwall – a very close and caring community' where John was accepted.[40] Bryn's parents met in Rugeley, a small town in Staffordshire, where his father was based. His father was fully involved at the time of Bryn's birth in 1942, but while the interracial couple had been tolerated by the community, once Bryn was born the couple were subjected to severe community hostility and family shame that left them outcasts. This led to Bryn's mother having a breakdown. She was put into a mental hospital for a couple of years, while Bryn was fostered by a nice couple until her discharge. His mother always told Bryn that his father was black, an RAF pilot who had won a distinguished flying medal for bravery. She encouraged Bryn to be proud of his black heritage and gave him his father's surname at birth. His father was Jamaican but I have included Bryn's story as it parallels those of the mixed-race GI babies.[41]

Many people viewed a white woman giving birth to a mixed-race baby as her having made a terrible mistake, and some of the mothers of these babies felt the same. Gillian's mother, who was twenty, single and a book-keeper also from Rugeley in the Midlands,

> always used to say: 'I've only made one mistake in my life, and I've spent the rest of my life trying to make up for it.' And it must have been so hard for her, never putting a foot wrong, after she had me. But ... we were one of the most respected families in the town.[42]

Jennifer B's mother initially wanted to escape the result of her 'mistake':

> My mother apparently left me in the hospital when I was born. And my grandma and her sister, my Aunt Eileen, had to fetch me. She'd walked home in the snow. They reckon it were near enough knee deep. In her night attire ... I suppose what it was, she'd made this big mistake of getting pregnant, and I suppose she wanted to leave it behind. Wanted it to go away. Which I can understand. Because, as history has it, we all know in them days it was taboo to have a child out of wedlock. And to have a black one would be deemed worse.[43]

Heather T expressed a similar sentiment: 'her having a baby out of wedlock in them days, but for me to be black ... Double whammy, really.'[44] Making this 'mistake' led to white British women being condemned as sluts and subjected to name calling. The maternity of a woman with a black child was thereby simultaneously sexualised and demonised. The widespread view, suggests Carole B, was 'this one has had a baby to a black man because that's how people thought wasn't it? All they see is if you've got a black baby, you've been with a black man.'[45]

The question of the 'brown babies' was raised at the Fifth Pan-African Congress, held in Manchester in October 1945. The Congress, one of seven held between 1919 and 1994, was attended by over ninety delegates, many from Africa and the West Indies, including men who were later to become leading figures in the anti-colonialism movement, such as Kwame Nkrumah, Jomo Kenyatta and Hastings Banda, all three living in England at the time. To some, the Congress marked a turning point in Pan-Africanism, Nkrumah later commenting: 'it brought about the awakening of African political consciousness'.[46] W. E. B. DuBois, who had founded the Congress in 1919, travelled over from the US; Amy Garvey, journalist and widow of Marcus Garvey, travelled from Jamaica. The seven-day Congress was organised by George Padmore, who had been living in London since 1934.[47] Despite the key themes of the Congress relating to political action in Africa, there were three recorded references to British mixed-race babies, all on the Congress's first day, which focused on the 'colour problem in Britain'. The fact that the babies were mentioned at all demonstrates how serious the issue was considered to be by certain black organisations at the time. For example, Edwin Duplan, from the Gold Coast but working for the Negro Welfare Centre (based in Liverpool), referred to 'illegitimate coloured children who had been born to white women … a large problem, in which the Government was taking no hand to provide shelter or assistance for the mothers or children'. Later in the day, Alma LaBadie of the Universal Negro Improvement Association, Jamaica (which had been founded by Marcus Garvey in 1914) returned to this theme, claiming that 'the children left behind by coloured American troops' were 'one of the most vital problems that the Congress is asked to consider'.[48]

DuBois went back to the US after the Congress 'filled with a strange pity for a thousand babies whom I left there facing distress'.[49] In December 1945 Harold Moody, the president of the LCP, wrote to the Minister of Health, Aneurin Bevan, suggesting that Britain and the US should treat each baby as a 'war casualty'.[50] Elsewhere he noted: 'when what public opinion regards as the "taint" of illegitimacy is added to the disadvantage of mixed-race, the chances of these children having a fair opportunity for development and service are much reduced'.[51] But the US refused to give any financial support, despite being willing to pay huge compensation for other war casualties, including to farmers for damage to crops and for sheep that had miscarried. As Sabine Lee suggests: 'As a rule, national governments did not accept responsibilities for their soldiers' conduct and … they did not accept the consequences by way of supporting their soldiers' illegitimate children or those children's mothers.'[52] As for any help from the British state, in October 1943 the Ministry of Health had recommended that welfare authorities should work with moral welfare associations in helping illegitimate children,[53] but at the end of the war Bevan's only policy was the encouragement of mothers to keep their children, with no offer of financial aid.[54] At the time there was no country-wide policy for dealing with unwanted children, for this was prior to the Children Act of 1948, which placed the duty of caring for unwanted children on local authorities, with the Home Office as overall authority.[55]

The mother of a 'brown baby' who tried to keep her child faced not only stigma and prejudice but also problems with accommodation, childcare, employment and finance. The fact that 'landladies definitely discriminate against coloured families' was noted in December 1944 at a conference on 'the position of the illegitimate child whose father is alleged to be a coloured American', jointly organised by the National Council for the Unmarried Mother and her Child and the Church of England Moral Welfare Council.[56] Similarly, the 1949 *Picture Post* report 'Is there a British colour bar?' quoted a 'typical' landlady: 'I wouldn't mind for myself [having "coloured" lodgers]. But there is no telling what the other lodgers might say.'[57] Lack of nurseries, childminders or foster mothers prepared to take 'coloured' children were other obstacles. Miss K of Sevenoaks, Kent, wrote to the LCP in November 1946: 'I have a little coloured boy aged one year and eight months ... I have to earn my living so cannot keep him myself. This is a village where hardly anyone has seen a coloured person ... foster mothers will not take him on account of his colour.'[58] During the war it was possible for some to get babies into residential nurseries run under the government evacuation scheme, provided that mothers accepted essential war work and paid 10 shillings and 6 pence a week, approximately a third of their weekly wages. But this was only a temporary measure, as the nurseries generally closed at the end of the war.[59]

Employment for a mother with a mixed-race baby could also be hard to find.[60] Joy wrote to the LCP in March 1946, stating that she had not worked for fourteen months because 'I find no-one seems to want to employ a girl who has a colored baby with her.'[61] Even if a mother found work, her life might be made unbearable. One example, given in a report of LCP correspondence, noted: 'The news that Queenie has a coloured child has spread, and the girl is constantly taunted, and has on occasion had to leave her employment because of the unpleasant remarks that have been spoken and because of writing on cloakroom walls.'[62] However, at the 1944 conference a social worker mentioned that in a few successful cases the mother had become a domestic servant, 'where the employer wanted to help a girl to make a good home for her baby'.[63] The shortage of domestic servants clearly helped (many women did not want to take on such work if alternatives were available, as they were during the war). Heather T's mother worked as a domestic servant and managed to find people who were prepared to let her bring Heather along: 'wherever she went, I went'.[64]

Some women understandably wanted to bring paternity claims against the fathers of their children. As mentioned, Davenport wrote of what happened during the war when a black GI mentioned pregnancy: he was transferred elsewhere. As the historian Brenda Gayle Plummer suggests: 'US military authorities had considerable difficulty in recognizing the capacity and right of the African-American men under their control to father.' To the American authorities: 'responsible fatherhood … indicated civic entitlement and respectability … the distinction between fathering, as a free man would, and siring, as done by a slave or an animal'.[65] They could not or would not see the black servicemen as truly 'free men', and as with slaves, they denied legitimate black paternity. Despite this, in 1948 the LCP claimed to have helped twenty mothers to file claims, although whether they were successful is unrecorded.[66]

Married mothers

The LCP received a number of letters from unmarried mothers who had the possibility of marriage to (white) boyfriends if they could give up their mixed-race children. Nancy from Birmingham had a baby in December 1944: 'I am sorry that I do not want the child because I am getting married soon and the boy that I am marrying would not like the child to live with us – not only that but we would not be able to get lodgings with it [*sic*].' Another wrote: 'Since my last letter to you I have married a local boy which means it is more important why I should like Dennis to go as soon as possible.' Over a year later she wrote again: 'My husband and I are eager to get away before he gets to the age to understand us. He is just two-years-old and already getting looked down upon just because he is coloured.' Raymond's mother was told by her family that 'a bastard is bad enough but a black bastard is worse'. She wanted the LCP to help get him adopted as she 'has a very nice boyfriend … He wants to get married but will not have Raymond.'[67]

One of my interviewees, Adrian, lived with his mother for nearly four years in Plymouth, and then was taken to a children's home in Liverpool. When she dropped him off, his mother was accompanied by her husband, whom she had presumably chosen over her young child; Adrian can only remember 'a stocky fellow with a limp'.[68] In contrast, the mother of Heather T, who married when Heather was three or four, had no intention of giving up her daughter, and Heather assumed that her stepfather was her actual father until told otherwise by an uncle when she was thirteen.[69] Lloyd also thought that his stepfather, who married his mother when he was about four, was his actual father. Lloyd was born in June 1944 in Derby. 'I always believed, truly, that my stepfather was my real father. Even though they didn't get married till 1948. For some reason, the details before that are blanked. I can't remember being without this father.'[70] The mothers of Dave G and Pauline Nat also married when their children were young. They were both kept, but Dave and Pauline never thought their stepfathers were their biological fathers, as unlike most of the people I have interviewed, they were always told that they had American fathers. It appears that most British GI babies were not told about their birth fathers or else were given misinformation. For example, Monica would ask her mother:

'Where's my dad? Why haven't I got a dad? Tell me about him', and she'd say, 'I can't remember' … In the beginning she just let me think it was granddad, she was quite happy for that to keep me going until I realised that wasn't right … She said, 'Of course you've got a dad but he's dead.' So I said, 'How did he die?' 'Well,' she said, 'he died in the war didn't he?'[71]

Sylvia McNeill estimated that from a third to nearly a half of the babies' mothers were already married to British men when they got pregnant,[72] and some of these women relinquished their children in order to be reconciled with their husbands.[73] This fits with my own research, since of the forty-five whose stories I am drawing on, at least eighteen mothers were already married (and half of these relinquished their babies); casting the net wider to include other accounts, over a third had mothers who were already married.[74] At the 1944 Conference many of the delegates, who were largely social workers and moral reform workers (social workers with a religious affiliation), were keen to keep marriages together where possible. They were not alone in their concern. The Marriage Guidance Council, set up in 1938, received state funding in 1949, the government being shocked by the huge post-war rise in divorce and anxious that marriages be saved.[75] If a married woman bore an illegitimate child, legally the child was that of her husband, and was given the husband's surname. If the illegitimate child was the result of a relationship with a white GI, it was presumably possible to pass it off as the husband's, so long as the dates roughly matched. Or if the husband knew, he could in theory pretend that the child was his. But this was clearly not feasible in the case of a mixed-race baby where the husband was white.

That this problem was common knowledge was underlined by the author of an article in *The Crisis*: 'British men (whether husbands or prospective husbands) would usually be reluctant to accept a child when its illegitimacy could not be hidden.'[76] Implied here is that a husband forgiving his wife an indiscretion was one thing (and he might well have committed adultery himself when away at war), but accepting a child that was obviously not his biologically was a step too far. Iris's mother was married and her husband was away fighting. He was prepared to accept the baby until he saw her skin colour.[77] The mother of Babs (born in October 1944) was also married; her husband 'was in the navy and … when he came back from being at sea he honestly believed that I was his child, I think because my complexion at that time was very fair … It took six months for my complexion to change.' She was sent to a Barnardo's home, one of the many homes run by this large British children's charity.[78] Some husbands apparently believed that children were theirs despite the difference in skin colour. One Oxford woman told the historian Norman Longmate that during the war she knew of a 'none too bright' husband who took his wife's 'dusky baby' as his when assured that it was 'the result of having been startled by a black soldier when out walking one night during her pregnancy'.[79] This theory of 'imprinting' was popular in the early modern period but was generally no longer believed by the nineteenth century, let alone the twentieth.[80]

Where British mothers of 'brown babies' were already married, the couple frequently separated, divorced or stayed together with the mother giving up the child, but an occasional husband would agree to take the child as his own. This was the case with a school acquaintance of the literary critic and author Lorna Sage. In her memoir she writes of a 'dangerously clever' girl of her age at her school in Whitchurch, Shropshire (Sage was born in 1943):

[her] dad had been away in the army during the war, but afterwards went back to work for the railways, and her mother had been a cashier in a proper shop. They'd married early in the war, like my parents, and were colourlessly respectable. So far so unsurprising. But Jean was black ... Her father must have been one of the GIs briefly stationed near Ellesmere. However, no one in Whitchurch, and certainly not at school, ever noticed or mentioned this interesting fact. Jean was her parents' child and attended the high school, and that was that. There were no black people living in Whitchurch then, of course, which in a way may have helped to make her difference invisible.[81]

Another Jean, born and brought up in the village of Evercreech in Somerset, also had a stepfather who took her as his own. Jean's married mother, Lottie, gave birth to Jean when her husband Harold was away at war. Lottie was about forty and she and Harold already had a fifteen-year-old son. Jean's daughter Bec recounts:

When Harold returned home he took my mum on as his own but sadly died when my mum was just two years old. Lottie then raised Mum on her own. They were very poor as she only had menial jobs such as taking in laundry, cleaning and housekeeping, plucking turkeys at Christmas etc. Money was always tight but my mum never recalls this having an adverse effect on her childhood, which was happy. From what Mum told me she was quite a favourite in her neighbourhood and the neighbours certainly looked out for her and helped my Nan out when they could.

Presents would arrive, such as a black doll and a monkey. Bev knows that Jean

did ask her mother about these toys and was presumably told they came from America. When asked why, all my Nan would say was 'I never asked anybody for anything, I brought you up alone, never asked for help.' She would never talk about the mysterious gifts or who sent them. She would never say who Mum's father was when asked outright ... Mum never asked again for fear of upsetting her.[82]

In Janet B's case, her mother's husband also agreed to raise her as his. Janet reflects: 'clearly it must have been a very, very difficult

2.6 Jean

situation for my stepfather ... But he accepted me into the family. In many ways, I don't think he had any choice. It was either that or I think Mum would have left the marriage.' Yet her stepfather, who she called 'Dad', was very protective of Janet:

> Dad used to take us for a walk when he got back [from work as a slater and tiler] ... There was a little sort of pool somewhere that you could look at, and he'd taken us there and we were walking back, and two young lads came – twelve, eleven or twelve ... And one of them called out, as they went by – called me 'blackie'. That was a term that was quite common at that time. Well! [Laughs] Dad whipped round (they'd scuttled off, laughing to themselves, the two boys) – he tore after them, absolutely tore after them, boxed their ears!

When Janet was twelve her mother died and her grandmother told her the truth about her black GI father.[83] Similarly, Michael's mother was married to a man who accepted Michael because he did not want to break up the family; they already had four children. All his childhood Michael thought he was adopted. One day he confronted his mother, who said: 'You are my son and you look just like your father', meaning his birth father.[84]

2.7 Michael

Pauline Nevins, in her wonderful memoir *'Fudge': The Downs and Ups of a Biracial, Half-Irish British War Baby*, relates how she was born in 1944 into a large Irish family living in poverty in Wellingborough, Northamptonshire, the middle of eight children. 'My stepfather never mentioned that he wasn't my father. I called him "Dad" just like the other seven kids.'[85] He was indiscriminately violent towards them all. Terry's mother was already married and had five children when she had twins with a black GI. When her husband came home from the war 'he never held hands, he never cuddled us'. He was always very distant and treated the twins differently from his biological children. Terry called his stepfather 'Dad' and thought that he was his father until he was about eight or nine when told otherwise.[86] The mother of Heather P was also married. Born in March 1946, Heather P, like Janet, Pauline and Terry, was brought up to think that her stepfather was her father. Her stepfather 'apparently totally accepted me and treated me exactly the same as my siblings', but in 1971, at the funeral of her 21-year-old brother, who had died of pneumonia, her stepfather gave a big hint … I happened to find myself standing next to [him]. And I remember putting my arm around him. He just turned round to me and said [aggressively] 'How do you think *I* feel, then?' I thought, 'What does *that* mean?' And so I took it to mean that he would be, naturally, more upset than me because he was a blood relative and I wasn't.[87]

Like Bryn, Heather P is not one of the 'forty-five' mixed-race GI babies whose stories I am mainly drawing upon, since her father, she later discovered, was Jamaican, but her history has many parallels to the forty-five, hence her inclusion.

Carole T's mother was also already married with a child. When her husband returned from the navy and found Carole, born in April 1945, he began divorce proceedings, but stopped when he found out he would not get custody of their daughter.[88] Like Janet B, Pauline Nevins, Heather P and Terry, Carole T also called her stepfather 'Dad'.

2.8 Carole T, her mother and her sister

2.9 John S and his mother

> I was only about five or six … I was out playing and they called me
> in because they used to row a lot about it actually and my stepdad
> was having a rant and he said that it was time I was told. So, my
> mum called me in, sat me down at the kitchen table, explained to
> me what had happened and showed me actually at the time a photo
> and a couple of letters she had, but to be honest at that age I just
> thought, 'Oh good I'm a bit different, I've got an American dad' and
> then with that I was out to play again.

But when her mother and stepfather argued, Carole's birth was often
a point of contention: he would say 'that bastard of yours'. 'I stuck
out like a sore thumb, I was just a reminder I suppose of what mum
had done.'[89] As Carole B suggests, the reminder was that her mother
had adulterously 'been with a black man'. Or in the words of St Clair
Drake: 'The high visibility of the colored illegitimate child made him
so conspicuous that the onlooker could never forget what he symbol-
ized.'[90] Carole B's stepfather sounds similar to Carole T's: 'I was seven
when my mum married him … He'd throw me in my mum's face,
because she had me and yet, if I was out with my mum he'd make a
fuss of me because there were people there but in the house he was
different.'[91]

2.10 John S and his stepfather

If the two Caroles' stepfathers were not very nice, John S's was positively nasty. John was born in May 1945 in Weymouth, Dorset. His mother was married; her husband came back in 1946 to find John. His mother was to suffer something similar to Monica's mother in being kept a virtual prisoner in her house:

> Well, he punished my mum till the day she died. He punished her for what she did. She wasn't allowed out. I look back now, and I think … She was allowed to go shopping from ten to twelve on a Thursday, and that was it … And he punished *me*! … Racist, nasty … when Cassius Clay – 'cause I was an amateur boxer … he was a great hero … Hated him! Hated anything black … whether they were musicians – or anyone … Nat King Cole – didn't like him! … It was tough! It was tough for me with him. And he was violent.

John left school at fifteen and started working for his stepfather on his height and weight machine on Weymouth seafront, but soon left as it was unbearable. The photograph of them reproduced on page 65 illustrates their antagonistic relationship. His stepfather was a compulsive gambler and 'a serial philanderer'. 'He'd win money, but he'd blow it, because the more you win, the bigger the bet that goes on ... She didn't leave him. Divorce was a terrible thing then. They didn't do it, did they?'[92] Another very unpleasant stepfather was Mr R; the case was reported to the LCP. Mr R, who was in the RAF,

> came home frequently to visit his wife and four children. Then she bore a colored child ... He was very cruel to the child and, from the time of its birth, would not let his wife care for it. The climax came when he painted the child's face with whitewash.

The child was put into a children's home.[93]

John S suggests that people did not divorce in the 1940s, but that was not the case for Arlene's mother. She was already married with two children when Arlene was born in October 1943 in Mottram, Lancashire.

> He [Stephen, her mother's husband] didn't come back for quite some time ... Whether he'd been told about me or not, I'm not sure,

2.11 Arlene with her family at her mother's second wedding

but I know that they got divorced very soon after the war … we all grew up without a father … And the twins were just after me as well … And they're all the same father. So he must have come back at some point.

Arlene had a very happy childhood: 'I was the pet of the village, never ostracised',[94] despite her environment being all white, including the village and school. Her mother, a machinist,

> worked every hour – she worked in a sewing factory all day and she made clothes for people at night … I remember her making these big ball gowns, with all the nets. And a tiny little cottage we were in, two bedrooms, living room and a kitchen without hot running water, no bathroom.

Her mother remarried when she was twelve. 'He didn't like me. I was a bit of a thorn, I think, really.' But they moved to a much bigger house: 'A proper bath! A kitchen, with a toilet off there, so we had two toilets suddenly.'[95]

Some married women who bore illegitimate, mixed-race children had very few choices open to them. The desperation felt by such women is illustrated cogently and tragically by the story of Lillian. Lillian's husband was in the RAF and away for over a year. When he returned at the end of the war he found his wife pregnant and threw her out of the house. He sent his two children to Dr Barnardo's; they were simply told that their mother had died. Recently, on receiving documents from Barnardo's, her daughter Mary discovered what had happened to her mother. Lillian had been rejected not only by her husband but also by her parents. She bore a mixed-race child, Malcolm, and in August 1946, living in a very poorly furnished room in Plymouth, she borrowed money for the gas meter from her neighbour and then proceeded to gas both herself and her four-month-old baby. The local paper, the *Western Morning News*, described the child's father as 'an American negro naval rating', and said that she had 'been in desperate financial straits'. The paper relates 'how the woman had worried because neighbours "talked" about her child, which was always well nourished and to which the mother was very devoted'.[96] Her poverty, rejection and the apparent hostility of her neighbours led Lillian to this act of utter desolation. There may well have been other women who acted likewise.

Grandmothers as chief carers

Lillian's mother rejected her and her baby with terrible consequences, but there were other grandmothers who stepped in as prime carers. Some of the letters in response to Davenport's article in *Reynolds's News* were from grandparents who had taken over the care of these children 'in order that their daughters can make a fresh start'.[97] Of the forty-five 'brown babies' whose stories I am drawing on, twenty-four were brought up by their birth families, and of these, ten were cared for predominantly by their grandmothers (and perhaps surprisingly, only in one case, that of John S, was the grandmother looking after a child whose mother was already married).[98] As explained in the introduction, Joyce was looked after by her loving grandparents. Pauline Nat's grandmother also played a huge and important part in her life. 'After I was born, my mother and I lived at my grandparents' home, Granny cared for me when my mum was at work. When I was three-and-a-half Mum married a Southampton man, we moved to a new house and they went on to have two daughters.' Tragically, when Pauline was eight her mother died suddenly of a brain tumour.

> It was decided that Granny would raise me. I went back to my first home where I had previously lived with my grandparents and my youngest aunt, Aunty Diann … My mum was one of five girls and Diann was born sixteen years later … So, she is actually my aunt but we're only five years apart … so she was like a big sister and when I went back home after mum died, it was back sharing a bedroom with Aunty Diann … I loved living with them … Granny once told me when my mum was still single, she, my mum, asked that Granny would raise me, in the event of anything happening to herself. Another time Granny told me that 'If your father Paul had come back for you, we wouldn't have let him have you anyway, you are OUR Pauline!'[99]

Sandra S's mother was eighteen when Sandra was born, living with her parents, sister, and brother of twelve. Sandra lived with her grand-

2.12 Sandra S

mother until the age of ten, when her mother married; her mother, who was a railway guard and painted ships in the dockyard, was not around much in Sandra's early years. Her grandmother worked too, in a hotel, washing up (she once served Frank Sinatra a sandwich); her grandfather was in the merchant navy.[100]

John S lived in Weymouth during the week from the age of five, where he went to school, and then on Friday he would go and stay until Monday morning with his step-grandparents, escaping his abusive stepfather:

From when I was five until I was about twelve, I was brought up by my grandmother at Moonfleet behind Chesil Beach, which was idyllic ... my grandfather was a fisherman on the beach and farmer ... I was out in the country – shut – pushed away – so no-one would see me ... they were fantastic to me. To be brought up by them was a privilege ... And the little church where she was churchwarden is in Holy Trinity in Fleet ... This is the ironic thing! In that church, from when I was a tiny little baby – eighteen months old – hangs the Stars and Stripes. Because all around that church prior to D-Day, the Americans were camped in the woods, everywhere. And … on the Sunday morning, there would be a service for the white troops. And then in the afternoon, there were the black troops. And people used to come from Weymouth and from the village and stand outside to hear these black kids sing Negro spirituals.[101]

Frances Partridge, a writer and member of the Bloomsbury group, wrote in her diary of 5 June 1950: 'To Fleet, in honour of *Moonfleet*, which Burgo [her son] has been reading. We are shown round the church by a cheerful little negro boy in a scarlet jersey, who must have dated from the American army's local presence in 1944.'[102] John S confirms that he would have been that 'cheerful little negro boy'.

When Jennifer B was born in December 1944 in Leicester her mother was nineteen. There had been plans to have Jennifer given up to a children's home. Her aunt's boyfriend peered at her in her pram:

'Aw, ain't she lovely, Daisy [her grandmother]. Oh, if she don't have curly hair nobody will!' He said to her, 'What are you gonna do about her then?' … 'Well', she said, 'the papers are made up, she's going into a home.' 'Oh', he said, 'let's have a look.' And he ripped them up. He said, 'Daisy, you'll manage.' 'Well, I shall have to!' she went. 'Now you've done that, won't I?'

Jennifer B's mother lived at home initially but then she got married and Jennifer was solely looked after by her grandmother, who was in her forties and working as a shoe machinist. 'I loved my grandma. And she loved me too, I know she did. Very much. I miss her.' When Jennifer was nine something terrible happened:

I were playing in the sink, and there was a knock on the door and I thought, 'Who's that?' And my grandma said, 'Who's that?' I said, 'I don't know!' She opened it and there were two detectives there … Well, she'd [her mother] been found on the Friday night. She'd been stabbed.

Her mother had been murdered by an unstable young man. 'It were awful for my grandma, she went white overnight, she did. Well, it were her daughter!' Jennifer remembers what happened next as if it were yesterday:

> I was not allowed to go to the funeral. And … when I'd come back from school … there was an empty chair in the street where a wreath had been laid, and most of the curtains had been closed. 'Cause that's what they used to do years ago. When anybody died in the street, the neighbours would get together and have a collection. And put a wreath there for them. And it really cracked me up, when I'd come home from school, to see that empty chair where my mother's wreath had laid and I couldn't go to the funeral.

When she was fourteen she met Paul Robeson. Her school took them to Stratford-upon-Avon where he was playing Othello:

> He spoke to me! Oh, it were lovely … I said, 'My dad were an American, you know?' He said, [mimics voice] 'Was he?' Like that!

2.13 Jennifer B and her grandmother

… I met Paul Robeson, and had a kiss off him. I don't think I washed my face for weeks. I was absolutely over the moon.[103]

There were also grandmothers who, although they were not the exclusive carers, were nevertheless the chief carers, because their daughters were out at work all day. Dave G remembers that

my grandmother loved me. She looked after me. Because my mum, when she was working, my gran looked after me, and she was also a very strong person. And it's quite strange … but I had two uncles who were the illegitimate offspring of my gran before she met my grandfather.

She was presumably more likely to have been supportive of Dave's mother having an illegitimate baby, given that she had had two herself. Trevor's mother was single, aged nineteen or twenty and living at home with her parents in Worcester when she gave birth. She was out at work all day, at St George's Laundry, so Trevor was effectively raised by his grandmother. But the relationship between this mother and grandparents was not very good, and he remembers a lot of arguing and door-slamming.[104]

Mistaking grandparents for parents

Thinking that their grandparents were their parents was not uncommon at this time for illegitimate children.[105] As Tony H (whose story about being adopted appears in Chapter 4) commented: 'a lot of the people I went to school with, with hindsight, who their mothers were, weren't their mothers, they were their grandmothers or aunties'.[106] Stephen, born in Nottinghamshire, was not wanted by his eighteen-year-old mother, Margaret, so he was adopted by his grandparents, who were in their fifties. He called his grandmother, Annie, 'Mum' and Stan, his grandfather, became his dad. Stan worked in the pit and was respected in the village. Margaret died in her early twenties, but Stephen did not know that she was his birth mother. He remembers that when he was young in school, his class was asked if there was anyone with no grandparents, and he put his hand up and was told 'You're lying, you live with them.' Annie

2.14 Stephen with his grandfather

died when Stephen was about twenty; Stan had died earlier. Years later Stephen learned about Margaret and that he had a younger half-sister, Susan. He tried to trace Susan through the Salvation Army, 'even though he was frightened of rejection due to his colour' (Susan would have been white). Stephen's widow Lesley recounts the story: 'They discovered that she had been put into care when she was about nine years of age following the death of her father but the search ended there.'[107]

Gillian also confused her mother and grandmother. When Gillian was a small child:

> I lived with my grandparents, who I called Mum and Dad. I can't really remember my mum very much at all. Because I called my grandparents Mum and Dad, and Audrey [her aunt] … I called my sister. And David was my brother [only a few years older than her] – who was actually my uncle. Elaine … I called her my sister, but she was really my auntie.

Her mother Hilda 'got married when I was three … They [mother and husband Arthur] … didn't move into their own home, they moved into lodgings.' Perhaps she was not taken with them, suggests Gillian, because of the 'no Irish, no dogs, no blacks' signs in many windows.

2.15 Gillian

Gillian thought her grandparents were her parents; her grandmother was only forty, her grandfather, a coalminer, was not much older.

> I can remember vividly her saying one day to me [fighting tears] 'I want you to be a good girl today. Because your mum's coming to see you.' And I had two thoughts. One was 'I'm always a good girl' [choking back tears]. And the other one was 'But you're my mum.'

She was aged about four. But when her mother and Arthur came to live in the same house, she soon started calling her mother 'Mum' too: 'when I was about five … I was calling two ladies in the same house both "Mum"'. Gillian called her grandmother 'Mum' all her life, such was the bond.[108]

'Jane', from Devon, 'was raised as my grandmother's "daughter", my mother was my "sister". No one ever talked about my father.'[109] Tony B was born in June 1945 and brought up in Huyton, Liverpool. He lived with his grandmother, Hannah, after his mother, Katie, moved out and got married. He thought of Katie (who had had him at about eighteen) as his older sister; his niece, Tabitha, who recounted his story to me, is not sure when he learned of their real relationship. Tony originally went with Katie when she got married, but his aunt remembers that 'he was heartbroken' and wanted to be back with his 'mam' (Hannah).[110]

When she was little Monica initially

> thought my granddad was my dad because we lived in his house and everybody called him 'daddy' ... I remember him taking me for walks ... I became very close to him ... I thought he was my dad until all the kids said things outside and as I grew up and heard different remarks, it dawned on me that he couldn't be.[111]

Experiencing the stigma of illegitimacy, racism and a sense of 'difference'

To Eustace Chesser, a psychiatrist who wrote widely on sex, marriage and childhood from the 1940s through to the 1970s, 'The first little

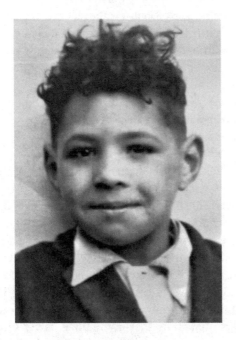

2.16 Tony B

bruise … that factual illegitimacy may make upon a child's mind is the feeling of being shamefully "different".'[112] The stigma of illegitimacy was apparent to some children more than others. Lloyd remembers:

> the woman across the street, who'd got a daughter about the same age as me – we were playing in her garden and … we decided to play indoors. So she asked us in and said, 'But not you, Lloyd' … I felt hurt … And I went home back to my mother, and I said, 'Oh, Mrs A- says I can't go … ' 'That bloody Nelly A-', she said … I don't think it was the colour, but it was the fact that I was illegitimate.[113]

Sandra S was baited when she was little with the word 'illegitimate', but she did not know what it meant. Pauline Nat

> was just aware that I felt different. I looked different from all my English family here. My mum was one of six girls and most of my aunts and cousins were around the Southampton area at the time I was growing up and I was the only one with dark hair, dark eyes, suntan, olive skin whatever you call it but I felt different … [yet] the only thing I was teased about was the fact that my mother wasn't married … When I went to a new school at eleven years old … I ended up with some children around me, almost in a circle … I don't usually use the word but I was a bastard because my parents weren't married and I didn't know what this word was but it was a nasty word, it seemed then, but I can remember being so defensive, I said, 'Oh no I'm not because my parents were married anyway', but obviously they weren't.[114]

Jennifer B was called a 'black bastard', as was Ann. Monica at school feared 'the illegitimacy thing, asking like "were your parents married?" … I used to nearly die in school when you had to fill in these forms.'[115]

Some of the children when they were small did not know that they were not white. As mentioned earlier, Lloyd was relatively pale; he did not have curly hair either, but wavy black hair. He thought he was white and 'didn't know my father was black'.[116] Pauline Nevins notes: 'My mother never mentioned my birth father. The only time she said anything about my birth was when I overheard her and a neighbor woman laughing that my mother wasn't sure what color I was going to be.'[117] Pauline did not get the joke because she saw herself as white: 'Everyone in my family was white – my mother, step-father, seven brothers and sisters, and aunt, uncles and cousins.'[118] 'I grew up thinking I was white until I was reminded otherwise, which was quite often. In terms of recognizing that I was different – I didn't. Obviously when I was called names I was reminded but I didn't internalize this.'[119] Joe, in a children's home, felt that 'being brought up in a predominantly white society, they take the colour off you, they take the colour out of you. You see things through white eyes.'[120] Janet B, when she was little,

> didn't feel different. I wouldn't describe it as different. I knew that when I was out with Mum – and she used to take me almost every-where with her – that people looked at me. But it was usually, 'Oh, isn't she gorgeous! Isn't she … Look at those curls!' And I think I must have been so secure in my belonging in the family that it just didn't occur to me.

However, 'occasionally people would either look at me for too long, or whisper something to whoever they were with as I went by'.[121]

Even today people can grow up with a lack of awareness of their ethnicity. Writing in the *Guardian* in March 2017, Georgina Lawton, who is from an Anglo-Irish family like Pauline Nevins, tells of how 'although I look mixed-race or black, my whole family is white. And until the man I called Dad died two years ago, I did not know the truth about my existence. Now, aged twenty-four, I'm starting to uncover where I come from.' She had been told that she had inherited her looks 'from a dark ancestor who had emigrated to Ireland's west coast years ago, I was a "genetic throwback"'. She did not identify as black or mixed-race until about the age of sixteen, 'because I didn't know anything else'. Finally her mother 'confessed to a one-night stand with a black Irishman she met in a west London pub'.[122] Heather P's darker skin was explained by

> my mother's mother, or my mother's grandmother, having been born in Gibraltar … People would say to me, 'Oh, you've got a nice tan' and somebody would say, 'Go back home where you came from' … 'You don't look English.' And I said, 'Well, no. That's because I've got these forebears who are from Gibraltar.'[123]

When the 'brown babies' became aware of having darker skin and questioned it, some were fobbed off with implausible answers. Monica's mother 'told me once my skin was so brown because I played outside a lot, just anything to pacify me and to quiet me down'.[124] Ann was likewise told by her adoptive parents that 'it was because I was always out in the sun. And one of my brothers, Ivor ... he'd been on holiday and he was there when this conversation went on. And he said, "Look, I'm nearly the same colour as you!"'[125] Janet B's mother, who was very blond, as were her other children, told Janet that her darker skin and hair were due to her (step)father's Celtic inheritance (he was Welsh). Arlene did not realise she was any different until

> suddenly one day, I registered that I was different. And I think I would have been four or five ... Occasionally, I remember going in and saying, 'Mum, they're calling me "blackie"', and she would say, 'Well, go and call them "whitey".' And it doesn't really have the same ring, does it?[126]

Terry, likewise,

> didn't really experience my identity until I was going to junior school, and people were calling me names which I didn't under-stand, because I was brought up predominantly in a white family, so from the inside I was a white person, but the outside, to them, I was a black person. And at that time I couldn't deal with it because I had no measurement of a role model. And even in the classes at school, the teachers themselves didn't help. Because they would refer to things about Africa, as part of being educated in geography. And they'll say something like 'Terry would you like to try and do an African dance?'[127]

Racist name calling was widespread for these mixed-race children. When Jennifer K started school, she was called 'blackie' and 'little chocolate girl' by a girl's mother.[128] Pauline Nevins 'would be skipping along the street, daydreaming as usual, when someone would call out, "blackie" or "nigger"'.[129] Michael and Stephen were both called 'Sambo'.[130] Gillian remembers 'being out with my auntie Ivy and uncle Johnny, and someone walked past and laughed and looked at me and said, "Oh, that must be the milkman's."' In addition to 'blackie' and 'nigger', when Gillian 'got to secondary modern school they used to call me "Gillywog"'. At primary school, aged about seven, she was compared with the other mixed-race GI girl at her school:

> These pretty little white girls put us up against the wall in the playground ... and stood in front of us, discussing us, to decide who was the prettiest ... And then it was awful because they decided I was the prettiest, and the relief ... but then the feelings, because Irene ... I was quite dark, and I'd got black afro hair ... [but] her lips were thicker than mine and her nose was different, and she was darker than I was.[131]

The white girls were judging who fitted best to the white standard of prettiness; Gillian still remembers the horror of that moment and how bad she felt for Irene. Judgements about appearance were widespread. When Jennifer B started school, one teacher looked at her hands and made her scrub them until they bled: her brown skin was read as dirt. Monica remembers:

> There were some other kids who were very cruel: 'You've got to stay on that side of the desk, I'm going to draw a line ... don't you come over my side ... you're not to touch me.' ... 'Where are you from, you're not from our country ... you're not one of us, you wasn't born here!' Shove me sort of thing, 'You can't play with us' and bit by bit it began to dawn on me that this very dark skin that I had was a big problem with other people but nobody explained to me that my dad came from another country, that he was a different race ... I remember having a row with a girl in the street when I was about thirteen, she said to me, 'You should go home, you're not one of us, you're a Yank's kid.' I didn't know what that was ... In 1950 ... I was five or six, to go to school, to walk down the streets in my town was horrendous, people just stopped me, laughed, pointed ... I was made to feel like a complete outcast, like I was contaminated. [132]

That sense of being an outcast was reinforced when these children were barred from friends' homes. As happened with Lloyd, John S remembers that 'there were some people that if you went round to play ... you weren't allowed in the house'.[133] Jennifer B recalls one particular incident:

There was a girl that were very friendly ... Wendy ... And she told me where she lived and I went to call for her one night. And her mother opened the door. Oh, she went bananas. Oh, she went mad! I thought she were gonna have the door off the hinges. It's a good job my fingers weren't in the door, she'd have broke them! She went mad, she did. She were calling me blind, she was. Anyway, when I got to school the next day, Wendy looked at me and I knew she were gonna say something. She went, 'Jenny!' I said, 'I know.' She says, 'Don't call for me again.' I said, 'No, you're alright. I wasn't going to anyway.'

If she actually got into another child's house,

there were probably a grandma there, and the mother, or somebody. And the grandma'd sit there, weighing you up, you know, and her daughter'd come in and she'd go, 'You know she shouldn't be here, you know. She should be in a hot country. She don't belong here you know.' And I used to think, 'Oh, ey up, here we go.'

When she was about eight, in a shop across the road two women in headscarves were talking about her when she walked in: she heard one say 'disgusting'. She remembers that some shops were reluctant to serve her.[134] Similarly, when John F as a teenager went into a shop outside his village, the shopkeeper refused to put the change into his hand.

John S did take not take name calling lying down:

When I was about eight years old, nine years old ... It was a snowy day ... And we were playing football in the playground, and ... I just remember, I don't know, I tripped him [friend Pete] up or something, or he fell over – a foul – and he got up and he called me a 'dirty Nigger'. And ... I punched him right on the nose, and I got a vivid memory of the blood on the snow. Well, my mum was summoned to the school, and we had to go before the headmaster. W. C. Bennett, his name was. Prolific caner. And I remember my mum standing next to me and he said: 'What you have to remember, Mrs. S ... is you *cannot* educate these people.' She shook and went white. And I saw tears coming down her face. Never said anything – don't forget, you respected headmasters ... And then he caned me in front of her.[135]

The lack of role models struck Dave G forcefully:

> One time I think I got a little bit upset, and I just tried to explain that I wasn't angry about being black or being mixed-race … But it was just sometimes I felt a bit lonely, because there was nobody – in spite of how good my mum and Wills, my [step]dad, and the family were with me – it was just I had nobody to recognise as being like me.[136]

As Janet B pointed out: 'The England I grew up in was very white – very white. I very rarely saw a black person.'[137] There was only one other black child at Trevor's secondary modern school of 1,000 children. Monica had the same experience:

> No other mixed-race, brown kids in my area at all or in my school. That was the hardest part. I looked at my family and I didn't look like any one of them. Mum was like blue eyes, she had sort of a reddish, goldie colour hair but she was definitely English complexion, her brothers and sisters was all similar. People literally would turn around if I walked into a shop and stare, it was horrible. It was quite a difficult thing for a child to cope with. I often stayed out of places.[138]

Some of the children developed strategies for coping with racism. In a rugby scrum, Dave G got into an altercation with someone who 'called me a nigger bastard! And I said: "Actually, I think the term you're looking for is "mulatto".'[139] His superior linguistic knowledge snubbed the crude abuser. Arlene coped and still copes through attention to her appearance:

> because I knew I was different, I didn't have a lot of confidence in myself, and I still don't, believe it or not. A lot of people think I'm ultra-confident, but I've developed a way of coping, really, and I'm always unsure going into a place for the first time, as to what reaction I'll get. But my mother always said to me, from being very young, 'Wherever you go, people are always going to look at you, so give them something worth looking at.' So, I never go out looking a mess – still![140]

This is like DuBois's idea of 'double consciousness': the 'sense of always looking at oneself through the eyes of others'.[141]

Terry's way of dealing with the sense of racial difference involved deciding eventually

> to associate myself more with the *black* side than the *white* side. And ... because people like Paul Robeson, people like Winifred Atwell [the well-known Trinidadian pianist] and all these icons in some respects, who'd done well in their life, and I thought if they could do it, I could do it. But, it was at least a start of accepting my identity. I was half-white, and half-black, but it was the black side that became more and more prevalent because ... I wasn't happy with the white side, and the way white people treated black people.

He got in trouble with the law when he was eleven but was nevertheless able to feel some pride when a police sergeant told him that he reminded him of Joe Louis, the leading US heavyweight boxer of the time. And when Terry joined the Royal Marines at sixteen he gained hugely in confidence. 'The Royal Marines, to me, was my surrogate father. They are able to give me something, a sense of belonging. A sense of justice, a sense of feeling, a sense of discipline, a sense of focus ... I was the youngest marine, and the only black marine in the squad, which made it extra special.' He learned how to deal with racism: 'I built up a wall. Somebody'd call me a nigger, you know, it didn't affect me. Inside, it did. But I wouldn't react.'[142]

Jennifer B also learned to ignore abuse:

> I used to bloody hate it when I were a kid. When they used to say, 'Oh, it's that half-caste kid.' ... I used to feel like saying, 'Don't call me that! I'm like you, the same.' But I used to take no notice – my grandma always drove that into me. She used to say, 'Jenny, don't take any notice, because', she said, 'that'll hurt them more ... When you fall for the bait, that's what they like.'[143]

There were a few teachers who well-meaningly tried to combat racism but misread the situation. Arlene relates the story of a new relief teacher for her class when she was about eight:

> there was a boy called David ... who had the most awful stammer. He couldn't get words out at all, and he was asked to sit with me. And he'd said, no, he didn't want to. And this teacher – I can still

2.17 Terry's first day in the Marines

feel the embarrassment – he brought me out to the front, and he sat on a desk and held my hands in both of his, and gave them a lecture on difference, and the fact that because I was a different colour, it shouldn't make any difference, and I can still smell the tweed of his jacket, and he smoked cigars, and when I get that smell, I'm right back into that classroom. And poor David sat there, trying to get it out, and eventually he said, 'I don't know what you're talking about, I just don't want to sit with a girl!'[144]

Racial difference could very occasionally have (dubious) advantages. As a child Trevor was sent round to everyone's house in the neighbourhood on New Year's morning, reflecting the idea that it was good luck to see a 'dark person' first thing; at least he 'got a few bob'.[145] This was one of the very few occasions that his 'exoticness' paid off financially.

Having very different hair texture from white people was another 'difference' that set these children apart. Many of my interviewees commented on how no one seemed able to manage their hair. Janet B reflected on how her mother:

spent a lot of time on my hair, although she despaired of it. Years later … when I was talking to my African-American family, they laughed – they just roared with laughter when I told them about what Mum used to do to try and defrizz my hair, and in the end she used to just have these great huge curls she'd just do up and put a pin in them, and they'd be all over my head. But … my hair is the bane of my life. If there's one thing I regret about my situation, it is that I had this hair … I grew up in the 60s – I was a teenager in the 60s, and if you didn't have dead straight, blond hair, you were absolutely just ignored, and if you had hair like mine you were pitied. Because it was just the worst kind of look. So I really struggled with that for a long time. And, as I say, if I had to name one thing that I hated about … having the background that I've got, I'd say it was my hair. Now isn't that vain?

When Janet found her American relatives, she sent photographs. When she talked to her father's second wife on the telephone:

I said, 'Did you get the photos?' And she said, [in an American accent] 'Janet, what on *earth* was your mother doing letting you go out looking like that?' Like what? I think it was this picture … She

2.18 Janet B

said, 'Your hair, your hair!' I said, 'Well, what was wrong with my hair?' She said, 'Oh, oh – how could she let you go out like *that*?' Mummy used to sit me between her knees, and she'd try and get the comb through, and then she'd try and put little tiny plaits in it to stop it from getting all churned up and ... She tried so hard! [Laughs] ... 'Your dear mother let you go out like *that*!'[146]

Tying bows was apparently a common method of trying to 'control' what was seen as unruly hair. Suzi Hamilton, who has written a memoir about her time at Dr Barnardo's, well remembers 'the ghastly "Shirley Temple" bows that used to be forcibly tied in my hair'.[147] Deborah, who was in a local authority children's home in Somerset, recalled how the nursery nurses 'used to stick these bows on our hair ... they'd *no* idea, *no* idea'.[148] Pauline Nevins

struggled to keep my 'mop', as my mother called it, from looking like I just stuck my finger in an electrical socket. What a cruel trick fate played on me. I was dropped onto an island with an average humidity of 90%, and blessed with hair which, when released from rollers to smooth it, recoiled in protest the minute I stepped outside.[149]

John F used his hair to his advantage: he 'would hide the crusts of toast (which he didn't like) in his afro!'[150] But Heather T 'wanted hair like my sisters'.[151] The 1966 report *Racial Integration and Barnardo's* noted: 'We heard of cases where coloured girls experienced deep distress and a sense of unacceptability until their hair was straightened.'[152] The report suggested that 'local coloured ladies' should be invited into Barnardo's homes to demonstrate the technique. Ironically this was just at the time when black American women were starting to reject straightening, and the 'afro' was about to become fashionable and an assertion of black pride.[153]

Conclusion

Those mixed-race war children who were kept by their mothers or grandmothers faced name calling, racism and an uncertain identity. Their illegitimacy was widely condemned. A lack of openness about ethnicity and of role models contributed to their not recognising or understanding their racial 'difference', not registering their skin tone as part of their sense of self and not feeling pride in their ethnicity. And they were labelled 'half-castes' – 'neither one thing nor another' to quote the pamphlet *The Colour Problem as the American Sees It*. Some of them were ostracised and barred from friends' homes, as if their mere presence threatened people's sense of (racial) order. Everyone referred to them as a 'problem', even those people who were trying to help them. For example, Alma LaBadie of the Universal Negro Improvement Association labelled them 'one of the most vital problems that the [Pan-African] Congress is asked to consider'. Dr Moody wanted each baby to be seen as a 'war casualty', little different from the verdict of the Army Bureau of Public Affairs, which claimed that they were 'badly handicapped in the struggle for life'. But in some rough notes made by St Clair Drake, he wisely argued for the de-centring of the 'brown babies': 'shift the emphasis from Negro babies, throwing it on general problem of war illegitimacy. Help to reinterpret significance of illegitimacy as a war situation and not an index of Negro depravity.'[154] This unfortunately did not generally occur, as the next two chapters will demonstrate.

Notes

1   Interview with Monica, 1 September 2014.
2   Six are known to have been married and nine to have been single, but there is uncertainty about the others.
3   Davenport, 'U.S. prejudice dooms 1,000 British babies', p. 2.
4   Baker, 'Lest We Forget', p. 42. Joe also discovered that the children's home had totally ignored the request from his father's sister in Chicago to adopt him (ibid., p. 47).
5   Joe quoted in McGlade, *Daddy, Where Are You?*, p. 154.
6   Ferguson and Fitzgerald, *Studies in the Social Services*, p. 80.
7   See Pat Thane and Tanya Evans, *Sinners? Scroungers? Saints? Unmarried Motherhood in Twentieth-century England* (Oxford, 2012); Deborah Cohen, *Family Secrets: Living with Shame from the Victorians to the Present Day* (London, 2013), ch. 4; Jane Robinson, *In the Family Way: Illegitimacy between the Great War and the Swinging Sixties* (London, 2015).
8   Letter from T. E. Johnson, Chief Constable of Oxford, to Under Secretary of State, Home Office, 22 July 1942, HO 45/25604, TNA.

9   See *Plain Dealer*, 25 April 1947; *Pittsburgh Courier*, 12 February 1949 and 19 February 1949.

10   John St Clair Drake, 'The Brown Baby Problem', Box 60/15 (n.d., approx. 1948), St Clair Drake Archives, Schomburg Center for Research in Black Culture, New York.

11   Cedric Dover, *Half-Caste* (London, 1937), p. 13.

12   Rose, 'Girls and GIs', p. 155.

13   Harold King to Charles Collet, LCP, 29 October 1937, Acc. no. 4910, LRO. On the Association, see Paul B. Rich, *Race and Empire in British Politics* (Cambridge, 1986), pp. 133–4.

14   Constance King and Harold King, *Two Nations: The Life and Work of the Liverpool University Settlement* (Liverpool, 1938), p. 132. See also Lucy Bland, 'British eugenics and "race crossing": a study of an interwar investigation', *New Formations*, 60 (2007), special issue on 'Eugenics Old and New', pp. 66–78.

15   Quoted in Rose, *Which People's War?*, p. 261. The idea of mixed-raceness being a 'handicap' was still around in the 1950s; for example, in the memoir of Phil Frampton, a mixed-race boy in Dr Barnardo's, he notes a remark in his entry report: 'other physical defects or maladies: half-caste'. In January 1957 the matron wrote that he 'appears intelligent … But is half negro which may be a handicap.' Phil Frampton, *The Golly in the Cupboard* (Manchester, 2004), pp. 58, 82.

16   David Killingray, '"To do something for the race": Harold Moody and the League of Coloured Peoples', in Bill Schwarz (ed.), *West Indian Intellectuals in Britain* (Manchester, 2003), pp. 51–70.

17   Moody, *Colour Bar*, p. 11.

18   P. Cecil Lewis, 'Cardiff Report', *Keys*, 3.2 (1935), p. 61. During the war the LCP produced a pamphlet, *Race Relations and the School*, which advocated radical changes in the school curriculum; Killingray, 'To do something for the race', p. 64. For a eulogy of Moody, see Constantine, *Colour Bar*, p. 169. And see Stephen Bourne, *Mother Country: Britain's Black Community on the Home Front, 1939–45* (Stroud, 2010).

19   Patricia and Robert Malcolmson (eds), *Nella Last in the 1950s* (London, 2010), pp. 88, 86. Emphasis in the original. Thanks to Lucy Delap for drawing my attention to these comments. On Nella Last, see the film with Victoria Wood, *Housewife 49* (dir. Gavin Millar, 2006).

20   For background on St Clair Drake, see Kevin Gaines, 'Scholar-activist St Clair Drake and the transatlantic world of black radicalism', in Robin D. G. Kelly and Stephen Tuck (eds), *The Other Special*

Relationship: Race, Rights and Riots in Britain and the United States (London, 2015), pp. 75–93.

21   St Clair Drake, 'Significance of the Study', LRO.

22   John St Clair Drake, 'Values Systems, Social Structure and Race Relations in the British Isles', unpublished PhD thesis, University of Chicago, 1954, p. 263.

23   Sylvia McNeill, *Illegitimate Children Born in Britain of English Mothers and Coloured Americans: Report of a Survey* (London, 1946).

24   St Clair Drake, 'The Brown Baby Problem', Box 60/15.

25   In Germany the numbers of biracial occupation children were tracked in censuses in 1950, 1951 and 1954. Demonstrating continued concern about racial mixing, these children were also subjected to anthropological studies. As Fuhrenbach points out, such scrutiny would have been inconceivable if it had been proposed to conduct it on Jews after 1945. Fehrenbach, *Race after Hitler*, p. 76.

26   George Padmore, 'British League flays rumor; finds only 1,700 tan GI babies', *Chicago Defender*, 17 May 1947, p. 2.

27   Malcolm Joseph-Mitchell, 'The Colour Problem among Juveniles', talk to Kathleen Tacchi-Morris's International School in Somerset on 9 October 1949, DD/TCM/15/14, pp. 3–4, Somerset Heritage Centre, Taunton. In November 1946 *Afro-American* also estimated 2,000 children (Marika Sherwood, *Pastor Daniels Ekarte and the African Churches Mission* (London, 1994), p. 51), as did Lisa Moynihan, 'Children against the colour bar', *London Magazine*, 29 October 1949, p. 11.

28   See John Belchem, *Before the Windrush: Race Relations in Twentieth-century Liverpool* (Liverpool, 2014); Jacqueline Nassy Brown, *Dropping Anchor, Setting Sail: Geographies of Race in Black Liverpool* (Princeton, NJ, 2005); archives at Butetown History and Arts Centre, Cardiff: www.bhac.org.

29   St Clair Drake, 'Values Systems', p. 259.

30   See Marika Sherwood, *Many Struggles: West Indian Workers and Service Personnel in Britain (1939–45)* (London, 1985); E. Martin Noble, *Jamaican Airman: A Black Airman in Britain 1943 and After* (London, 1984); Allan Wilmot, *Now You Know: The Memories of Allan Charles Wilmot, WWII Serviceman and Post-war Entertainer* (London, 2015).

31   In 1947 St Clair Drake estimated the 'colored' population of Britain to be 10,000–12,000; 'Significance of the Study', LRO.

32   Interview with Monica, 1 September 2014.

33   Kiyotaka Sato, *Life Story of Mr Terry Harrison, MBE: His Identity as a Person of Mixed Heritage* (Tokyo, 2013), p. 26.

34   Baker, 'Lest We Forget', p. 79.

35   Davenport, 'U.S. prejudice dooms 1,000 British babies', p. 2.

36   Telephone interview with Catherine, Edward and Colette, Peter's daughter, son and wife, 15 June 2017. Very recent DNA research indicates that Peter's father may have been Jamaican, not American.

37   Interview with Dave G, 23 June 2016.

38   Interview with Lloyd, 28 June 2017.

39   Telephone conversation with Lloyd, 29 May 2018.

40   Telephone conversation with Adam, John F's son, 22 August 2017.

41   Telephone interviews with Bryn, 8 November 2015, 24 June 2018.

42   Interview with Gillian, 17 February 2017.

43   Interview with Jennifer B, 14 December 2016.

44   Interview with Heather T, 1 September 2016.

45   Interview with Carole B, 1 September 2014.

46   Quoted in Susan Williams, *Colour Bar: The Triumph of Seretse Khama and his Nation* (London, 2006), p. 13.

47   See James, *George Padmore*, ch. 3.

48   Quoted in Hakim Ali and Marika Sherwood, *The 1945 Manchester Pan-African Congress Revisited* (London, 1995), pp. 75–6, 78.

49   DuBois, 'Winds of change', p. 15.

50   Harold Moody to Aneurin Bevan, n.d. [December 1945], appendix 4 of McNeill, *Illegitimate Children*, pp. 11–13. On Moody, see Killingray, 'To do something for the race'.

51   Harold Moody, 'Anglo-American coloured children', appendix 6 of McNeill, *Illegitimate Children*, pp. 15–17.

52   Sabine Lee, *Children Born of War in the Twentieth Century* (Manchester, 2017), p. 246.

53   Ministry of Health to Welfare Authorities (England) and LCC, 1 October 1943, MH 10/150, TNA.

54   See D. E. Sharp (for the Home Office) to Harold Moody, 24 January 1946, appendix 5 of McNeill, *Illegitimate Children*, p. 14.

55   On the Children Act 1948, see Harry Hendrick, *Child Warfare* (Bristol, 2003), pp. 136–40.

56   'Report of Conference on the position of the illegitimate child whose father is alleged to be a coloured American', MH 55/1656, TNA. Joseph-Mitchell of the LCP concurred: an unmarried mother with a mixed-race baby found that 'landladies were not willing to give her accommodation' (Joseph-Mitchell, 'The Colour Problem among Juveniles', DD/TCM/15/14, Somerset Archives). For the history of the National Council for the Unmarried Mother and her Child, see Thane and Evans, *Sinners? Scroungers? Saints?*

57   Kee, 'Is there is British colour bar?', p. 25. See also C. W. W. Greenidge of the Anti-Slavery Society to George Hill, MP, Colonial

Office, 16 November 1945, MSS Brit Emp S19DH/7/14, Rhodes House Library, Oxford (hereafter RHL).

58   'Correspondents and Documents', St Clair Drake Archives, Box 64/3; the 1944 Conference also reported that 'no foster families would take a colored child' ('Report of Conference on the position of the illegitimate child', MH 55/1656, TNA).

59   See Ferguson and Fitzgerald, *Studies in the Social Services*, pp. 124, 131.

60   See Joseph-Mitchell, 'The Colour Problem among Juveniles', DD/TCM/15/14, Somerset Archives.

61   St Clair Drake, 'The Brown Baby Problem', Box 60/15.

62   John St Clair Drake, 'Black Babies – Research Notes', St Clair Drake Archives, Box 63/5.

63   'Report of Conference on the position of the illegitimate child', MH 55/1656, TNA.

64   Interview with Heather T, 1 September 2016.

65   Brenda Gayle Plummer, 'Brown babies: race, gender and policy after World War II', in Brenda Gayle Plummer (ed.), *Window on Freedom: Race, Civil Rights, and Foreign Affairs, 1945–1988* (Chapel Hill, NC, 2003), p. 85.

66   John St Clair Drake, 'The League's Sociological Approach', St Clair Drake Archives, Box 62/12.

67   St Clair Drake, 'Black Babies – Research Notes', Box 63/5.

68   Interview with Adrian, 1 September 2014.

69   Interview with Heather T, 1 September 2016.

70   Interview with Lloyd, 28 June 2017.

71   Interview with Monica, 1 September 2014.

72   McNeill, *Illegitimate Children*, p. 9, found nearly as many married mothers as unmarried mothers with 'brown babies'. A study on illegitimacy in Birmingham for 1944–45 found that over a third of the mothers of illegitimate children were married, while in Southsea the figure was just under half. Ferguson and Fitzgerald, *Studies in the Social Services*, p. 98.

73   At the 1945 Pan African Congress, Alma LaBadie reflected: 'many of these babies were born to married women whose husbands were serving overseas. Now that the husbands were returning the condition of forgiveness was that the children be sent elsewhere.' Quoted in Ali and Sherwood, *1945 Manchester Pan-African Congress*, p. 78.

74   See Winfield, *Bye Bye Baby*, pp. 93–107; McGlade, *Daddy, Where Are You?*, pp. 151–4, 163–8; Baker, 'Lest We Forget'; Smith, *When Jim Crow Met John Bull*, pp. 187–216.

75   Langhamer, *The English in Love*, p. 14. The number of divorces

in England and Wales rose from 9,970 in 1938 to 24,857 in 1945; Ferguson and Fitzgerald, *Studies in the Social Services*, p. 20.

76 *The Crisis*, November 1951, p. 583.

77 Winfield, *Bye Bye Baby*, p. 95.

78 Interview with Babs, 3 June 2014.

79 Longmate, *The GIs*, p. 286.

80 See Laura Gowing, *Common Bodies: Women, Touch, and Power in Seventeenth-Century England* (New Haven, CT, 2003), pp. 111–48.

81 Lorna Sage, *Bad Blood: A Memoir* (London, 2000), pp. 201–2. Thanks to Sarah Waters for drawing this passage to my attention.

82 Telephone conversation with and email from Jean's daughter Bec, 1 June 2018.

83 'GI babies', *Daily Express*, 2 October 1999; interview with Janet B, 29 November 2016.

84 Telephone interview with Janine, Michael's daughter, 8 November 2016.

85 Pauline Nevins, *'Fudge': The Downs and Ups of a Biracial, Half-Irish British War Baby: A Memoir* (self-published, 2015), p. 5.

86 Interview with Terry, 14 December 2016.

87 Interview with Heather P, 7 September 2017.

88 Carole T on *Woman's Hour*, Radio 4, 19 May 2017.

89 Interview with Carole T, 9 September 2014.

90 St Clair Drake, 'The Brown Baby Problem', Box 60/15.

91 Interview with Carole B, 1 September 2014.

92 Interview with John S, 20 June 2016. On John, see also Louisa Adjoa Parker, *Dorset's Hidden Histories* (Dorset, 2007), pp. 76–7; Louisa Adjoa Parker, *1944 We Were Here: African American GIs in Dorset* (Dorset, n.d.), pp. 21–5. See Elizabeth Anionwu, *Mixed Blessings from a Cambridge Union* (self-published, 2016), pp. 64–7: Anionwu, born in 1947, mixed-race, also had a violent stepfather.

93 St Clair Drake, 'The Brown Baby Problem', Box 60/15.

94 Email from Arlene, 21 May 2018.

95 Interview with Arlene, 7 November 2016.

96 Information from Mary, Lillian's daughter, September 2016.

97 Davenport, 'U.S. prejudice dooms 1,000 British babies', p. 2.

98 Out of the additional twenty-five cases, seventeen were kept, seven of whom were raised by grandmothers.

99 Interview with Pauline Nat, 17 April 2014.

100 Interview with Sandra S, 28 October 2014.

101 Interview with John S, 20 June 2016.

102 Frances Partridge, *Everything to Lose: Diaries, May 1945–Dec. 1960* (London, 1985), p. 116. Thanks to Sarah Waters for drawing this to my attention.

103   Interview with Jennifer B, 14 December 2016.
104   Interview with Trevor, 15 July 2015.
105   See Thane and Evans, *Sinners? Scroungers? Saints?*, pp. 35–9, 75; Robinson, *In the Family Way*, pp. 46, 183–4; Kate Adie, *Nobody's Child* (London, 2005), p. 7; Cohen, *Family Secrets*, pp. 124–5.
106   Interview with Tony H, 19 October 2016.
107   Telephone conversation with Lesley, Stephen's widow, 1 November 2016; email from Lesley, 30 May 2018.
108   Interview with Gillian, 17 February 2017.
109   Quoted in Lucy MacKeith, *Local Black History: A Beginning in Devon* (Archives and Museum of Black History, 2003).
110   Email correspondence with Tony B's niece, Tabitha, 7 June 2017.
111   Interview with Monica, 1 September 2014.
112   Eustace Chesser, *Unwanted Child* (London, 1947), p. 18.
113   Interview with Lloyd, 28 June 2017.
114   Interview with Pauline Nat, 17 April 2014.
115   Interview with Monica, 1 September 2014.
116   Interview with Lloyd, 28 June 2017.
117   Email from Pauline Nevins, 12 June 2017.
118   Nevins, *'Fudge'*, p. 4.
119   Emails from Pauline Nevins, 24 May and 12 June 2017.
120   Baker, 'Lest We Forget', p. 45.
121   Interview with Janet B, 29 November 2016.
122   Georgina Lawton, 'Mum always said I was white like her', *Guardian*, 18 March 2017, pp. 1–2.
123   Interview with Heather P, 7 September 2017.
124   Interview with Monica, 1 September 2014.
125   Interview with Ann, 28 November 2016.
126   Interview with Arlene, 7 November 2016.
127   Interview with Terry, 14 December 2016.
128   Telephone interview with Jennifer K, 29 August 2014.
129   Nevins, *'Fudge'*, p. 226.
130   Telephone conversations with Janine, Michael's daughter, 8 November 2016, and Lesley, Stephen's widow, 1 November 2016.
131   Interview with Gillian, 17 February 2017.
132   Interview with Monica, 1 September 2014.
133   Interview with John S, 20 June 2016.
134   Interview with Jennifer B, 14 December 2016.
135   Interview with John S, 20 June 2016.
136   Interview with Dave G, 23 June 2016.
137   Interview with Janet B, 29 November 2016.
138   Interview with Monica, 1 September 2014.
139   Interview with Dave G, 23 June 2016.

140 Interview with Arlene, 7 November 2016.

141 W. E. B. DuBois, *The Souls of Black Folk* (Chicago, 1903), p. 3.

142 Interview with Terry, 14 December 2016.

143 Interview with Jennifer B, 14 December 2016.

144 Interview with Arlene, 7 November 2016.

145 Interview with Trevor, 15 July 2015.

146 Interview with Janet B, 29 November 2016.

147 Suzi Hamilton, *Notice Me! A Barnardo's Child Scrapbook of Memories: 1946 to 1961* (Ely, 2012), p. 10. Shirley Temple was a famous 1930s Hollywood child actress.

148 Interview with Deborah, 17 October 2016.

149 Nevins, 'Fudge', p. 106.

150 Telephone conversation with Adam, John F's son, 22 August 2017.

151 Interview with Heather T, 1 September 2016.

152 Barnardo's, *Racial Integration and Barnardo's: Report of a Working Party* (Hertford, 1966), p. 27.

153 See Kobena Mercer, *Welcome to the Jungle: New Positions in Black Cultural Studies* (New York, 1994), pp. 98–112. See Chimamanda Ngozi Adichie, *Americanah* (London, 2013), pp. 296–7, on white Americans' ignorance about black women's hair.

154 John St Clair Drake, 'Some General Observations', Acc. no. 4910, LRO.

3

'Brown babies' relinquished: experiences of children's homes

In the 1940s, if a mother was unable to keep her child and if neither the child's father nor anyone in the family was willing to take on its care, the only option appeared to be adoption. Many mothers were pressurised to 'get rid of' their babies (akin to the language of abortion), but some managed to resist, as in the case of Monica's mother. Others felt they had no choice or may have actively wished to relinquish their child. Of the forty-five 'brown babies' whose stories I am drawing on, nearly half (twenty-one) were given up for adoption to their local authority or a children's home.[1] Of these babies, fourteen were male, seven female.[2] Yet in the event very few were actually adopted. The vast majority remained in children's homes throughout their childhood and early adolescence, with a number fostered for a period of time. Why was this?

Until late 1947 Dr Barnardo's Homes, Britain's largest children's charity, refused to contemplate adoption. The spring 1946 issue of its magazine *Night and Day* explains its opposition: 'would-be adopters generally ask … for a little girl of tender years, good-looking, with fair, curly hair and blue eyes; healthy … preferably legitimate … and free of … hereditary taint'.[3] According to the historian Deborah Cohen, in 'early-twentieth-century Britain, illegitimacy was imagined as heritable moral weakness' – evidence of 'bad blood'[4] – which would explain the preference for a legitimate child. Yet Barnardo's took in a child 'irrespective of its physical or mental condition … it may be backward mentally, of dusky skin, of homely appearance'.[5] The organisation saw itself as providing a substitute family.[6] Over a third of its children were fostered, however, although this was often a temporary arrangement, with the children's home there to take the child back if necessary. Perhaps surprisingly, given its view that no one would wish to adopt its children, Barnardo's changed its policy in November 1947. In response to the 1946 Curtis Report's recommendation of adoption as preferable to fostering, Barnardo's became a registered adoption society.[7]

The 1946 Report of the Care of Children Committee, known as the Curtis Committee after its chair, Lady Myra Curtis, was the first inquiry into the 'care of children deprived of a normal home life'. It produced sixty-two recommendations, its two key proposals being that responsibility for 'deprived' children should fall under one central authority as opposed to the current five and that all local authorities should set up children's committees to address local needs, with their own children's officer. The 1948 Children Act followed the report's recommendations and stipulated that all children's homes now fell under the authority of the Home Office Children's Department. It also emphasised adoption over fostering (although the ideal was for biological families to be kept together if possible). The Act was part of a sheaf of welfare legislation that came in with the new post-war Labour government, all part of the new welfare state.[8]

Despite this shift in policy on adoption, all bodies involved in the adoption process appeared to assume that black or mixed-race children were 'too hard to place', an attitude that carried on into the 1950s and 1960s. For this reason adoption societies did not like to take a 'half-caste' child on to their books.[9] Presumably a reluctance to adopt a black or mixed-race child related not simply to racist attitudes, but to a desire on behalf of the adopter that the child could pass as their biological child. Up until the Second World War many adopters kept the adoption a secret, including from the adopted children themselves. With the 1939 Adoption Act (which came into effect in 1943, delayed by the war), adoption societies now advised parents to tell their adopted children the truth, where once they had encouraged secrecy. Yet the adoptive parents' desire for a perceived family resemblance remained – the wish to be thought a 'normal' family.[10]

There was another reason why mixed-race children were rarely adopted: child welfare workers' negative attitude towards trans-racial adoption. The LCP came up against this problem when it tried to help some of the mothers find adoptive families. St Clair Drake spent a month in the spring of 1948 working with the children's committee of the LCP; in his report he noted:

There is a tendency on the part of many English people concerned with child welfare to oppose the care of colored children

by non-colored families. The Committee has one case now pend-
ing where after months of tedious negotiations with a very fine
middle-class family, the county authorities, who had the child in a
nursery, refused to allow it to go to a white family.[11]

In fact the LCP found that in 1948 thirteen would-be adopters were
pressured to change their minds by local authorities.[12] Another example of a potential adoption being blocked on 'race' grounds involved
Rosa, who on reading her files in the 1990s discovered that an attempt
in the 1950s by two single unmarried sisters to adopt her, aged twelve,
from a Catholic children's home was vetoed by a social worker, who
condemned the sisters' motives as 'sickly sentimentality'. Rosa was
unhappy at the home and these two women had been taking her for
enjoyable outings; she never saw them again.[13] Clearly, what was
labelled 'race matching' or the 'same race policy' in the 1980s (the idea
that children should only be adopted by those of the same ethnicity/
race) was already in operation in the 1940s and 1950s, although with
a very different impetus. In the 1980s black British social workers and
others began to insist on children being adopted by those of the same
race and ethnicity because of identity problems suffered by some black
and mixed-race children adopted by white families.[14] In the 1940s the
focus was not the child's identity, but the questionable motives of the
adopter: that the desire of a white adopter to take on a black or mixed-
race child could only be suspect.

One issue that was raised in discussions over relinquished 'brown
babies' was what kind of children's home was appropriate: should
they be housed together, in other words segregated, or should they
be in children's homes alongside white children? At the December
1944 conference on 'the illegitimate child whose father is alleged to be
a coloured American' one delegate suggested that it might be better
to place mixed-race children in children's homes 'where the majority
was not white'. The LCP's John Carter, a barrister from British Guiana,
objected, announcing that his organisation was against segregation,
and other conference delegates tended to agree.[15] When Dr Moody
of the LCP wrote to Bevan, the Minister of Health, in December
1945 he emphasised this anti-segregationist stance: children born to
'coloured' Americans who were given up by their mothers 'should be
sent to a large number of homes all over the country, along with white
children'.[16]

There were, however, several homes that prioritised the housing of the mixed-race children of black GIs, not because they necessarily took a segregationist stand so much as that they saw these children as being in greatest need (or in one case having a view of these children as future missionaries). One such home was in Liverpool, the African Churches Mission; another, Rainbow Home, was nearby, in Birkenhead. Both were closed down for health (and possibly political) reasons. I have read of three other private initiatives. There was also a local authority home for these children, Holnicote House, run by Somerset County Council. I now turn to consider these homes in some detail.

The African Churches Mission

In Miss K's 1946 letter to the LCP (where she had mentioned not being able to find a foster mother for her mixed-race son), she also inquired: 'if you know of a Home that will take dark children could you let me know?'[17] The African Churches Mission took in mixed-race children of black GIs and was headed by a remarkable Nigerian, Pastor Daniels Ekarte (known as 'the African Saint'). His date of birth is unknown but he was probably born in the early 1890s.[18] In Nigeria Ekarte was converted to Christianity by a Scottish missionary, Mary Slessor (he referred to himself as 'Mary Slessor's Boy').[19] He was also influenced by Marcus Garvey's project of 'Universal Negro Improvement'.[20] Ekarte worked his passage on a ship, arriving in Liverpool in 1915. Liverpool, which had been Britain's largest slave port, has a history of the presence of black and mixed-race people and of interracial marriage from at least the eighteenth century.[21] By 1922 Ekarte was preaching on its streets, but in 1931 he received an anonymous gift, allowing him to set up his Mission at 122–124 Hill Street, Toxteth, consisting of two knocked-together houses.[22] The Mission held Sunday services with an average attendance of sixty to eighty people who crowded into its chapel. There were also daily services, gospel meetings and much gospel singing. There was a Sunday school and secondary school classes for black children, a bed for the homeless and for women escaping violent partners, and Ekarte worked with black seamen and other black people in the city for their legal rights. He also ran a café, the Cocoa Rooms, near the docks, which was open from 5 a.m. to 9 p.m. and provided free or very cheap meals for the poor (white and black). One local woman remembered his huge generosity: 'Nearly everybody in our community turned up for the morning service at 9.30, when we received free breakfast … There was always food for those needing it and lodgings too.'[23] He was greatly respected by local people; for example, a Mrs Charnod remembered: 'Mr Daniels was a gentleman in everybody's eyes, very polite and had a kind word for everybody.'[24] A woman inspector described him as 'an extremely amiable man … obviously very devoted to his cause'.[25] Other authorities, however, and certain 'philanthropic' bodies saw him as a 'trouble-maker'. For example, Harold King, honorary secretary of the Liverpool Association for the Welfare of Half-Caste Children, wrote to John Harris, secretary of the Anti-Slavery Society: 'Strictly between you and I both I and one or two other people in Liverpool who know Ekarte well, think him an extremely dangerous person.'[26] Harris, a former missionary and a paternalistic segregationist, would have agreed, and his organisation during his lifetime (Harris died in 1940), like King's, refused Ekarte any financial help for his Mission.[27] He described Ekarte to the Colonial Office as a 'vigorous beggar'.[28] Ekarte was clearly thought by Harris and King to be too 'uppidy'.

St Clair Drake first came to Liverpool in August 1947. Prior to meeting Ekarte, St Clair Drake visited Colsea House, a hostel for 'coloured' seamen in Liverpool. The hostel's warden, a mixed-race Liverpudlian (with a West Indian father and a white British mother) was very hostile towards Ekarte: 'That man is a disgrace to the coloured people of Liverpool. He's ignorant and dirty.' He believed that 'coloured people here bring trouble on themselves by not knowing how to behave. These Africans … are rough and untrained.' He claimed to have never experienced any 'colour bar' himself.[29] He accompanied St Clair Drake on his first visit to Ekarte and 'all through the interview sat stiffly without saying a word, and with a look of disdain on his face'. However, St Clair Drake found Ekarte neither dangerous nor dirty, but 'a dignified, kindly, dark brown man who wears a full beard' and who 'dressed neatly although his clothing was very worn'. Less positively, once he learned more about him, he thought him a man of contradictions:

his supporters are continuously bewildered and exasperated by him. They admire his 'selflessness' on the one hand, but deplore what they call his 'irresponsibility' on the other hand ... occasionally using high status names in money-raising campaigns without securing precise permission; of not keeping his accounts in order; of being 'generous to a fault'.[30]

Ekarte explained to St Clair Drake that during the Second World War he had had a call 'to rescue the Negro babies' and to 'make peace between husband and wife'. Following the teachings of Slessor, a missionary zeal informed his work. Slessor had rescued abandoned twins in Nigeria, where their birth had been thought a curse. Ekarte was in effect continuing the work of saving babies, some of whom were left on the doorstep of the Mission, others presented to him by distraught mothers. The African Churches Mission was not big enough to take more than a few children (there were never more than eight or nine at any one time), although he claimed to support another twenty-five, including some fostered nearby, paying a pound a week for each. Where the babies were born to married women, sometimes their husbands would visit Ekarte on his invitation. He told St Clair Drake:

> You have to let the husband talk, to let him 'free' himself ... I say 'then, take the wife. I take the baby. You forgive the wife. Don't rebuke her.' When he say 'How much I have to pay?' I say 'Nuthin'. He says surprise-like 'Why not?' I say 'It will always be a block. It will always remind you of your wife's sin if you must pay.'[31]

Like the 1944 conference of social and moral welfare workers, Ekarte was keen to keep married couples together wherever possible.

Soon after the Mission opened Ekarte found a housekeeper, Mrs Roberts. Her twin daughters also moved to the Mission and helped with the cooking, cleaning and looking after the children, as well as working in the café.[32] R. Whiteway, the woman inspector mentioned above, visited the Mission in February 1946 and described the layout: on the ground floor there were three rooms and a large kitchen. The three rooms were used as Ekarte's study, a dining room, and a bedroom for Mrs Roberts and the children. There was an outside toilet and a separate Mission hall for Ekarte's religious services. On the first floor there were two rooms used as play areas for the children. Whiteway presented it as homely: 'The most appropriate description for this place is that it presents the general appearance of a mother and her eight children in a private household of reduced financial circumstances.'[33]

All reports on the Mission mention that the children were happy and well fed and that Pastor Ekarte was very kind. Roger, a child who lived at the Mission, recalls that 'Pastor Daniels and Mrs Roberts were amazing.'[34] Brian, also a child at the Mission, remembers him well. 'Mr Pastor Ekarte, I mean he would just smile at you … and you'd just do what he said because you knew he had your interests at heart, because you could tell by his facial expressions that he was really concerned about you … a very warm man.' Ekarte would take the children with him when he visited his parishioners:

> we would go with him and I don't know whether you've been to Hill Street where the actual mission was situated but they don't call it Hill Street for nothing … It went from the Cathedral, the Anglican Cathedral right to the docks and it was really steep … he was a great walker and we used to have to follow him but it was all well worth while because every time you got to a home where he was visiting you always got half-a-crown when you left. So, it was good fun really, I mean he was a very nice man.[35]

From 1945 Ekarte tried to get funds for a new building, which he was going to call the 'Booker T. Washington Children's Home', after the famous nineteenth-century African-American educationalist. He hoped the home would accommodate fifty children, for he had a long waiting list: in February 1946 he stated that he had nearly a hundred, a number that had risen to 158 by mid-1948.[36] From 1945 to 1947 Ekarte approached the Anti-Slavery Society several times for a grant but the organisation declined to help, offering no explanation for its refusal, although it gave five pounds annually to the Mission over several years, and its secretary, C. W. W. Greenidge (who had replaced Harris), agreed to become a patron of the proposed home.[37] In April 1946 Ekarte wrote an angry letter to the Ministry of Health's parliamentary secretary, C. T. Southgate. He opened with his usual polite inquiry about Southgate's health, hoping him well 'by the grace of God', but then launched into a furious attack on the ministry's neglect, ending: 'It is about time that your department helped us financially.'[38] (This was prior to the 1948 Children Act, when responsibility for 'unwanted' children shifted to the Home Office.) Ekarte felt that his inability to get funding related to his politics and anti-racist stance. He conveyed these in his sermons, Brian remembering them as very impressive and as 'Christian Socialism really':

> It was one of the things that hit you when you went to church and you heard him preach … when he warmed to his message he was very animated and I used to really enjoy going and in fact when we left the Mission I used to always go back on Sundays to listen to him because I was so enthralled. I mean, he wasn't making a doctrinal statement, it was a social one, a political one but he had this problem, this racist problem with the city council which he felt were racist towards him and if he would help a white person, bringing up white children, he would have got all the funds he wanted and he felt that it was because it was a black community that he didn't get the funds.[39]

After Ekarte died in 1964, a local woman reflected on his sermons: 'Mr Daniels, as we knew the Pastor, preached sermons full of fire and brimstone, but how impressive he was.'[40]

Given that Ekarte was having difficulties raising funds in Britain for his projected children's home, he turned to the US. He told St Clair Drake that in his opinion: 'There is no rich black man in England … Now in America there are all kinds and black men with big mansions and motor cars.'[41] By late 1946 his African Churches Mission was getting some excellent US publicity, with two African-American magazines, *Ebony* and *Liberty*, presenting sympathetic articles accompanied by photographs, thereby raising awareness of the plight of the children.[42] In January 1947 Ekarte sent Edwin Duplan of Liverpool's Negro Welfare Centre to the US to raise funds.[43] Ekarte may not have been aware of the political tension between the Negro Welfare Centre, under West African leadership, and the LCP, headed by the Jamaican Moody: Moody saw the Centre as attempting to claim leadership of 'the Negroes in the United Kingdom'. Accordingly, soon after Duplan left England, Moody followed him to New York, and in March publicly cautioned against supporting him, suggesting that the funds would not be used wisely.[44] Moody spoke of the LCP as the only '*bone fide* agency dealing with the Brown Baby problem' and encouraged financial support for his organisation instead.[45] The NAACP rallied round Moody, seeing the LCP as its English counterpart, and support for

Duplan and Ekarte's Mission quickly waned. The NAACP, founded in 1909, was by this time one of the most influential black organisations, whose membership of 50,000 in 1940 had multiplied ten times by the end of the war.[46]

The following month Duplan's credibility was undermined still further, for on 5 April 1947 a highly sensational story in the *Daily Mail* claimed that 'Five thousand dusky "problem babies" ... left behind by coloured US troops' were going to be shipped to America. The solicitor of the 'Negro Welfare Society' (presumably the Negro Welfare Centre) was quoted as saying: 'There are 10,000 illegitimate coloured children in this country ... we propose to send half of them to America. We have been promised a liner in nine months' time.'[47] The story was widely circulated in the US. The Home Office denied that any application for a liner had been made and stated categorically that there were no plans to ship children to the US. It was unclear where the figures had come from or the intent of those who had propagated the rumour.

This question of the British 'brown babies' being sent to the US to be adopted will be considered in the next chapter, but the relevance of mentioning the *Daily Mail* article here is that it had a bearing on Ekarte's subsequent (diminishing) US donations. A group of upper-middle-class black women in Chicago had formed a 'Brown Babies Organizing Committee' the previous year and were sending Ekarte money and Christmas presents for the children; they do not appear to have been unduly worried by Moody's speeches in New York or the newspaper rumours. Indeed Mrs Spalding, a prominent member of the Committee, told St Clair Drake that 'her group will continue to support Ekarte even if there is no rigid control of accounting and inspection ... when someone is trying to do good and is untrained, you just have to expect some irregularities'.[48] Yet these rumours misled others about the situation in Liverpool, as did the reporting of Duplan's speeches. *The Sun*, a respected New York newspaper, stated in January 1947 that according to Duplan there were about a hundred children at the Mission.[49] The Brown Babies Organizing Committee asked Marva Louis, the wife of the boxing champion Joe Louis, to visit the African Churches Mission in early 1948, as her husband would be visiting Britain for a series of bouts.[50] But Marva Louis's visit to the Mission led to a damning report in the African-American paper the *Chicago Defender*. In a front-page article headed 'JOE'S VISIT BARES WAR-BABY SWINDLE', the second strap-line summed up the visit's outcome: 'Gift Held Up After Marva Visits Mission: Champ's Wife Finds Five Dirty Tots in Unkempt Quarters'. Marva Louis had expected at least a hundred children but instead found 'five ragged and undernourished tots in an unkempt place with none of the facilities you'd expect to find in a nursery'. Joe Louis withdrew his intended $1,000 donation for the new home,[51] and Duplan came back from the US empty-handed, or so he said. If there had been any donations it is possible that he had appropriated them, for he was already known to the police as a fraudster, and according to George Padmore had run some 'dubious bottle parties and night clubs' during the war.[52] Before meeting Ekarte, St Clair Drake had been warned about Duplan by a police inspector visiting the Colsea House hostel: 'I think the old man [Ekarte] tries to be honest. But Duplan has duped him. We were just about to arrest him when he got away to America.' He had been swindling African seamen, and he very probably swindled Ekarte too.[53]

In 1949 the Mission home was ordered to be closed by Liverpool City Council on health grounds. There had been spot checks on the Mission and while the children had been found to be happy and healthy, the house was condemned as unsuitable. In February 1949 Home Office inspectors found broken windows and insufficient chairs for the children; Jim H, who was a child at the Mission, remembers that 'there were holes through the ceiling. We had a bed upstairs and we could see into one of the rooms where they held the services.'[54] On 31 May 1949 the Home Office issued a 28-day notice. The following day Ekarte appealed to the Home Office: he pointed out that neither he nor the children's mothers had ever received any money from the government or from charities. (He had been refused a local authority grant on the grounds of overcrowding and was informed that if he reduced his numbers to four children, the matter would be considered, but Ekarte had felt unable to comply.)[55] On 3 June, eleven days *before* the period of appeal had expired, local officials and the police pounced. Brian, just turned five at the time, recounts the story:

> They came at about seven o'clock in the morning and I remember it as though it was yesterday ... They came up and tried to catch us but these were big buildings and they had a cellar, they had an annex and then when you put that together as two houses, then these people didn't know where we were. We gave them the run-around you know. They'd locked Pastor Daniels in his office ... and they had

to bring in reinforcements to get us because they just couldn't catch us ... I remember biting one official.[56]

Brian reflects that 'You always remember that kind of trauma.' The *Sunday Pictorial* wrote a heart-rending feature entitled '"Black Saint" fights for his children', describing the incident and Ekarte's grief, his 'tears trickling down his ebony cheeks'.[57] Brian thinks the closure of the home was political: 'Mr Ekarte would always champion the likes of the black seaman and so on to the council and he made himself a nuisance and I think this was their way of getting back at him.'[58] Given the authorities' view of Ekarte as a 'trouble-maker', Brian's verdict was no doubt correct.

The children were eventually forcibly removed; they loved Pastor Ekarte, they had never known another father figure, they had no desire to leave what for many of them was the only home they knew. To Jim H, 'as far as I was concerned there was no one else in the world apart from the Pastor, Pastor Ekarte who looked after us and Mrs Roberts'.[59] The four men I have interviewed who were there as small children, Brian, Jim H, Adrian and Roger, all remember the Mission and Ekarte with deep affection. Brian, born in May 1944, had been taken to the Mission aged three months; his mother had had him when she was sixteen. She was living at home in a two-bedroom house with her own mother who already had two children and was expecting a third.[60] Jim H, born in September 1943, had also been given up as a small baby. His mother and his aunt Joan, who had epilepsy and learning difficulties, had had babies at almost the same time (nine days apart); his mother took her sister's baby (who was white) as her own child and Jim was taken to the Mission. 'I think that the stumbling block from what I can gather was that my grandfather didn't want me home because I was a black baby.' When Jim learned as an adult that he had been swapped with his cousin, he was understandably angry and upset.[61]

Most of the children removed from the Mission ended up at Fazakerley Cottage Homes, also in Liverpool, comprising over twenty detached villas for about 700 children. (The Curtis Report's recommendation that homes accommodate no more than twelve children was clearly ignored.) Brian remembers the initial loneliness:

when I got there on the first day, I mean I was parted from what I called my cousins from the African Churches Mission ... so I was in this huge world and nobody I knew and you fended for yourself quite a lot and I remember sitting on the pavement one day just sobbing my eyes out because you were in such a big place.

While Brian called his friends from the African Churches Mission 'cousins', to Jim H the boys that came with him were like brothers. Either way, they were the only 'family' they had at the time. Did they get visitors? Brian remembers 'you saw people having visitors and I never got a visitor. So you ask yourself … they've got their family, where's mine?' But Adrian says there were a few: 'Mrs Roberts … a Mrs Carruthers [who helped Ekarte and fostered some of the Mission children for short periods]. They were really brilliant. They took an interest in us.' Jim also remembers that 'Mrs Roberts came up a couple of times but Pastor didn't come.' Brian later found out that 'he wasn't allowed to come'.[62] However, Adrian thinks that they, the children, were allowed to visit the Pastor and Mrs Roberts.

There were some good memories of Fazakerley Cottage Homes. Brian recalls that 'eventually I did settle down and got interested in sport and things like that'. The highlight of the year was their annual visit to the Isle of Man. Adrian looks back enthusiastically on these holidays:

[I]t was brilliant, brilliant and … we used to go out in the morning, we wouldn't come back to maybe four or five o-clock at night … for our tea … we just went out in the Isle of Man, we'd been there so often we knew everywhere and we used to go on coach tours to Douglas, Ramsey, Port Erin, Laxey, Ramsey … it was brilliant, absolutely brilliant. We used to go fishing off the pier and if any boats used to come in … French fishing boats, we used to jump on them and try to talk to them.[63]

The facilities at Fazakerley Cottage Homes were clearly of a higher standard than at the Mission, and they had the wonderful annual holiday, but the Cottage Homes lacked the warmth and love of Pastor Ekarte and Mrs Roberts. It was not just the children who had stayed at the Mission that loved Ekarte; when he died in 1964, one local tribute to him in the *Liverpool Post* recalled:

Pastor Ekarte has been described as 'the African saint' and I can truly say that to a great many coloured people and 'half-castes' in

3.1 Children in the Isle of Man football team

Liverpool he was just that … Words can never describe the loss the coloured people have suffered by his death. He will never be forgotten among us.[64]

The men I interviewed who had lived at the Mission have certainly not forgotten him either, such was the deep impression left by his personality, great kindness and warmth.

The disaster of Rainbow Home

Four years prior to the children being snatched from the African Churches Mission, Mr and Mrs Russell, a philanthropic white couple in their early fifties from Worcester, had also wanted to help what they referred to as 'little unwanted strangers'. In May 1945 Ruth Russell wrote to the National Council of Unmarried Mothers and the LCP about the babies: 'their existence in this country may be somewhat unhappy on account of the dual handicap of the colour-bar and illegitimacy'.[65] Once she heard about the African Churches Mission, she offered to work in collaboration with Ekarte to raise funds for a larger building. In October 1945 Russell wrote to the magistrate and prison reformer Margery Fry appealing for financial help. She explained the situation facing Pastor Ekarte:

> His small house is much over-crowded with a very long waiting list, and it is for this reason the local authority cannot help him, on the grounds that it would only encourage him to keep these little mites ... in a congested and squalid locality ... My husband is quite willing to give all his small capital to help this cause (he only has a few hundred pounds) but we are appealing to others to help us ... Please assist us to enable these children to grow up to be good and worthy citizens.[66]

Margery Fry, who knew nothing of Russell or Ekarte, approached the Anti-Slavery Society for advice; they in turn forwarded the letter to Ekarte asking for more information. He confirmed that he was indeed working in collaboration with the Russells and he sent the Society a circular letter about his proposed home, with the names of the Trinidadians George Padmore and Learie Constantine as chairman and secretary respectively of his fundraising committee. The Anti-Slavery Society then replied to Fry dismissing the enterprise, although with no reference to the Russells:

> I am not convinced that the three people who are appealing for funds would be the most suitable to organise such an institution ... The late Bishop of Liverpool, who supported him [Ekarte] for some time, afterwards withdrew his support. George Padmore is a coloured journalist in London of the extreme left ... Constantine inspires more confidence but I think it would be better if they had some well-known English people associated with them.[67]

In effect the Anti-Slavery Society was arguing against supporting an organisation that was only headed by black people, as the reference to 'well-known English people' assumed whiteness. In December 1945 the Russells then turned to the Ministry of Health about setting up a home for the children but were also rebuffed: 'these people are not to be encouraged ... hardly the people to run such a home successfully and keep trained staff'. The Ministry had prior knowledge of Russell: she had been interviewed by them in August the previous year concerning a care home she had been running in Stockton-on-Teme from which the majority of the patients had been removed, presumably because of inadequate care.[68]

In 1946 the Russells produced a pamphlet, *The Rainbow Children's Homes*, which managed to offend everyone else trying to help the 'brown babies'. The pamphlet claimed that the home that the Russells were establishing in Birkenhead was 'the first practical move towards providing shelter' for 'children of mixed descent'. This erased the work of Ekarte. The pamphlet also listed an all-white provisional management committee (they had possibly taken advice from the Anti-Slavery Society) which, as St Clair Drake pointed out, alienated 'coloured' leaders, including the LCP. And it stated that homes were to be set up around the country with 'the ultimate aim of arranging for special training for those children suitable to undertake professional or other valuable work in the Colonies, where … they … may form a useful link of friendship between the peoples there and those in this country'. St Clair Drake, who meticulously charted the developments in what he termed the 'Rainbow Homes fiasco', reflected:

> For a British white group to even suggest a program for training colored children as a 'useful link' between Britain and the colonies was to open up old sores. Pan-Africanists and League leaders alike were suspicious of anything that sounded 'deportationist' … Pan-Africanists wanted them [the children] trained by Negroes and in a Pan-African and nationalist atmosphere – not as 'useful links'. To them the Russell plan smacked of 'an imperialist plot' while their own advocacy … was 'devotion to Mother Africa'.[69]

In alienating Ekarte on the one hand and the LCP on the other, the Russells now had no access to a list of children to move into their home. Through May 1946 bargaining letters went back and forth between the Russells and the LCP. The Russells finally agreed to an LCP member sitting on their board and in return the League immediately sent a list with twenty-three names. But in July the Russells reneged on their promise: according to St Clair Drake they 'suggested that since they were negotiating for a house it might be better not to have coloured people on the board until the deal was closed'. The Russells bought their house the following month and the local press gave the project extensive coverage, stressing that the children would be trained for the colonies. Despite the betrayal of board membership and this repeated talk of training 'for the colonies', in late September Learie Constantine and the Pan-African leader Ras Makonnen generously donated £100 and £150 respectively. The LCP and the Pan-African Federation were added to the Russells' board in November.[70]

In early November 1946 the first child arrived at Rainbow Home; by December there were twenty-five. During November Birkenhead's infant protection visitor found 'conditions very unsatisfactory from the point of view of cleanliness and management'. She did, however, add that 'The children appear to be receiving reasonable care.'[71] In December an inspector from the Ministry of Health had a good look round. The interior was dilapidated, 'the kitchen and pantry are filthy ... The house is bitterly cold ... [but] the twenty-five inmates in themselves appeared to be clean and healthy.' He found the matron 'extremely pleasant'. The Russells were up in Scotland collecting funds for the home at a football match.[72] Despite these critical reports, Rainbow Home was formally opened the following day (21 December) by the wife of Birkenhead's Lord Mayor, the Russells presumably having returned from Scotland. In a letter that month to Greenidge of the Anti-Slavery Society, Ekarte noted: 'the Russells are no longer with us ... As we could not pull together, our connection was severed.'[73] The Russells had rebuilt bridges with the LCP but not it seems with the African Churches Mission.

By January 1947 the Russells were having difficulties: 'We have made every effort to obtain money by means of flag days, football match collections, dances etc during the past year. We have either found permission to hold these refused, the expenses and difficulties of organising them too heavy, or the results very small.' By February, not only were twenty of the children ill with gastro-enteritis, whooping cough and measles, but the 'extremely pleasant' matron had resigned, fed up with the lack of heating and the Russells' interference. On 1 April 1947 a Home Office inspector from London arrived and was

> horrified at the state of the house ... I could find no adequate food or fuel ... I could find no proper clothing for the children. The state of the children caused one great alarm. I thought they were extremely thin and emaciated and very listless ... On a general level of cleanliness it was filthy.[74]

Six of the children were sent to Birkenhead's Public Assistance Committee institution (which had replaced the workhouse); thirteen were sent to hospital, of whom two died.[75] In July the home was officially closed.

In September the Russells were charged with negligence. Mrs Russell said she had done her best: 'I sold all my furniture and all my rings [!] to keep the children going.' She had not been involved in looking after the children and blamed the matron and the nurses: 'The children should have done very well if the staff had looked after them. I don't know whether twenty-seven children could have eaten all of that tinned food but *we* didn't eat it.' The chairman of the Rainbow Homes Society defended them:

> Mr and Mrs Russell were never neglectful in their duty to the children. They failed in their duty to raise funds … The Home was not the Ritz Hotel … The great need was to get the children into the Home as soon as possible. Most of them were in physical and moral danger.[76]

The children had certainly been in physical danger of starvation at Rainbow Home. The Russells were initially given a prison sentence which was converted to a fine on appeal.[77] The Curtis Committee had been set up following the death in January 1945 of thirteen-year-old Dennis O'Neill, beaten and starved to death by his foster father. While the Committee's report formed the basis for the 1948 Children Act, the philanthropic chaos and tragic deaths of two small children at Rainbow Home may have been a further impetus to the Act's enactment.

Three other proposed private homes for 'coloured' children

On 2 October 1946, two months before the Russells' home opened, the Minister of Health received a letter from an Alexander Montgomery of Huddersfield who announced: 'I have purchased a thirty-five-room hostel in Hudd [*sic*] … My intentions are to give homes to black children and train them to trades or as missionary workers then send them back to their own land.' He said he was 'a supporter of the World-Wide Evangelical Crusade Missions Society'. He asserted that they 'will only be a burden to our country unless something is done for them. Can you give me your blessing to my plans by giving me advice and support on getting this work started?' He informed the Ministry that he was a married man with children. The Ministry of Health consulted Huddersfield's town clerk, who replied that their Medical Officer of Health knew Montgomery slightly and thought 'his feet are not very firmly planted on *terra firma*'. Southgate of the Ministry of Health wrote back to Montgomery discouragingly: 'it is the consid-ered view of this Department that their [the children's] best interests are not served by their segregation from the rest of the community'.[78]

Two years later there was news of another home for the 'brown babies' when *Crisis* magazine recorded that 'Dr Malcolm Joseph-Mitchell of the less well-publicized League of Colored Peoples (Britain's NAACP) is caring for about fifty children.'[79] Apparently Joseph-Mitchell had bought a house in Purley, South London, but it lacked funding and had to close.[80] In March 1949 the African-American paper the *Pittsburgh Courier* carried an article about a home set up by a Mrs Cornwall in the village of Newdigate, near Dorking, Surrey. Married to a Jamaican who had served in the RAF during the war, and with a mixed-race child of her own, Cornwall had recently taken out a 21-year lease on a mansion to house some of the 'brown babies' of England. The article claimed that she 'is determined to give her life' to help them. However, Cornwall was insistent that while the home was principally for these children 'because theirs is the chief need, white children shall be admitted to the home too, for I don't believe in segregation of any kind'.[81] (Ekarte also had one white child at his home, Gladys, whose mother was Jewish but whose father was a white American Gentile. To quote Brian: 'Ekarte took her in because the Jewish community wouldn't accept her.')[82] Like the Russells, Cornwall needed a great deal of money to convert the house and was seeking funding. Also like the Russells and Montgomery, she had a plan for training these children 'for positions in the colonies'. But her perspective was rather different to the Russells' and more akin to that of Ekarte. On occasion, according to St Clair Drake, Ekarte expressed a desire to 'gather together all the babies, train them in industrial education and then send them forth at adolescence to help redeem his beloved Africa'.[83] Marcus Garvey, who Ekarte revered, wanted people of African descent to recover Africa from the white man.[84] To Cornwall: 'The colonies offer nice, fat jobs for white Englishmen ... These colonies are inhabited by coloured people and coloured people should have these jobs ... When I see how Englishmen grab for these jobs, my blood boils.'[85] Frustratingly I have been unable to discover anything more about Montgomery's or Cornwall's homes. While there may have been other private homes set up for the children, I have not come across them.

The private children's homes discussed above – the African Churches Mission, Rainbow Home, the proposed homes of Cornwall and Montgomery – all visualised the children having a special mission in life: either to regain Africa in some way (the view of Ekarte and Cornwall), to act as a 'useful link' between Africans and the British (the view of the Russells, which was regarded by Pan-Africanists as an 'imperialist plot') or to be trained in 'trades or as missionary workers then send them back to their own land', the fantasy of Montgomery.[86] Joseph-Mitchell's objectives are unknown. While Ekarte did not always argue that the children, once adults, should go back to Africa and generally believed that they should have a place in Britain, the others did not seem to consider that there was a future for the children anywhere but Africa. They appeared to have seen these mixed-race children, who had white British mothers and black American fathers, as alien and non-British, with Montgomery thinking them 'a burden to our country'. At least Cornwall wanted the children to replace 'white Englishmen' in Africa, but like the Russells and Montgomery she thought they 'needed' a helping hand to get them 'back' to their 'true' homeland.

Holnicote House: a Somerset County Council initiative

Holnicote House, a beautiful National Trust building near Minehead in Somerset, was requisitioned in 1943 by Somerset County Council, initially for use as a nursery for children evacuated from cities. However, the council increasingly took mixed-race GI children from their mothers, possibly as an intentional policy, often when they were only two weeks old or even younger; at least two-thirds of the babies had married mothers. By 1948 Somerset had forty-five such children, of whom nearly half were placed in Holnicote House.[87] I have not found any other county council which provided homes explicitly for babies born to black GIs, although it is of course possible that there were some. Holnicote House was used as a nursery, so it was only for children up to five years old, after which they were fostered, adopted or sent to homes for older children.

Deborah, born in March 1945, was given up by her recently widowed schoolteacher mother, who when pregnant had been taken in by the local vicar to hide her pregnancy:

> Because of her position in the community, and because I was going to come out black, it was decided that she wouldn't keep me ... I was ... immediately placed in the care of the Somerset County Council children's department and placed in the children's home called Holnicote House ... I should imagine she was relieved, because she had two little girls, and she was a reasonably important figure in her local community and the disgrace or the shame of it would have been quite difficult for her to deal with.[88]

Ann's mother was engaged to be married when she got pregnant; her fiancé was serving in France:

> And she lets him know that she's become pregnant, so they bring him home in order to marry her. She got married in October of '44, they send him back then to his regiment. And I was born in the February of '45, and of course, because of the colour, she knew I wasn't her husband's. So what she told him of where I'd gone ... goodness knows.

Ann wonders 'how she managed to lose me somewhere along the line'; she thinks a miscarriage was probably mentioned. 'Within a week of me being born, I was down at Holnicote House ... she had to get rid of me somehow, didn't she, 'cause she didn't know when he was going to get back.'[89] Carol E's mother was also married and had five children; her husband was away fighting in Italy. Carol was born in February 1945 and she too was quickly put in Holnicote House, nine days after her birth.[90]

All the accounts of living at the home portray it as a very happy place, with the children looked after by loving young nursery nurses. Carol E has

> [l]ovely memories. Beautiful place, beautiful place for all the children, really, really nice. The children were happy, we went on lots

of walks, we played. Well looked after … I can remember all the children … We were all brothers and sisters … I'd go back there tomorrow if I could. If my children ended up in a nursery home, that's where they would go, down there. Absolutely loved it.[91]

Deborah's and Ann's memories of Holnicote House are similar to Carol's. Deborah recollects: 'We were always together. We were always like a little family … It was lovely … all I felt was – safe … you just think you're being cared for, and we were.'[92] Ann comments:

I don't ever recall anything being nasty. Just a lot of care, really … we were all there in the same position. No-one had a mother and father, all we had around us were nurses … We were all very close … Christmas Day in the home, we had gifts, Christmas morning. Christmas afternoon we shared them with everyone. No-one ever had anything that was their own.[93]

The Christmas after she was fostered and taken to Wales, Ann recalls receiving gifts and feeling a sense of sadness about those at the home:

Christmas of '49 I got up Christmas morning and got all these gifts. And in no time at all I was thinking of my friends at Holnicote. Whatever they had, they had to share, but all that I'd had I didn't have to share with anyone. I felt quite sad and missed the other children.[94]

The three nursery nurses I have talked to who were at the home are also very positive about the place: Barbara C declared that 'I loved it. There was never any smacking and all the matrons were good women.' The nurses were in their teens (the home was a training nursery for nursery nurses), and according to Margaret B they went to local dances in Porlock. Elizabeth also remembers taking the children to the beach at Minehead – 'a very happy time'. All three women look back on their time there nostalgically.[95] The 1946 Curtis Report indeed found nurseries to be more progressive than residential accommodation for older children.[96]

Deborah remembers that there were often times when people would visit and look at them all lined up in a row:

3.2 Leon Y at the back, then Carol E, Deborah and Ann at the front

> I can remember the situation of being lined up ... for people visit-
> ing. And that was starting to happen quite regularly ... The matron
> apparently had been very instrumental in trying to find families for
> us. I think she was very genuinely fearful of our future – knowing
> that once we left there and went to other children's homes, it might
> not be such a cosseted, safe place.[97]

Leon Y, one of the mixed-race children in Deborah's friendship group,
'always used to come out and say: "Oh, have you come to take me to
your house? Have you come to be my mummy?" or "Have you come to
be my daddy?"'[98] Sadly no one adopted Leon. Three of the people from
Holnicote House who I have interviewed – Ann, Deborah and Janet J
– were all adopted at the age of about five and will be considered in
the next chapter, as too will the attempts by Somerset's superintendent
health visitor to get the children adopted in the US.

Like Leon Y, Carol E was not adopted. When she was nearly five she
was sent to another children's home – Chadwell House in Wellington
(also in Somerset); one or two of the children from Holnicote went
with her. It was much smaller, with about twelve to fourteen children.
She was happy there too, but at twelve she was sent to a third home, in
High Wycombe, Buckinghamshire, which she did not like because she

missed all the children she had been with for the last seven years. 'I just felt like I'd been abandoned, basically.' She was there only about a year and then was happily fostered by a couple, who became her family.[99] Although Leon Y was not chosen for adoption, he had a happy time in the boys' home he was sent on to, Whitewell Home in Frome, run by a very kind couple, although he did not receive much of an education.[100] Somerset County Council's deputy children's officer in the 1950s, who had known Leon, told David Stanley, the former deputy director of Somerset social services, that 'mixed-race boys were assessed as not fosterable and so far as I know no attempts were made to find alternative homes for them'.[101] This appears to have been the case for the boys at Fazakerley Cottage Homes in Liverpool too. Not only was it thought hard to find adoptive parents for mixed-race children, but apparently 'the great majority' of all adoptive parents wanted girls.[102] There are a host of possible reasons for this preference: girls were seen as more pliable and less troublesome, they could be used as domestic servants as well as future carers for their adoptive parents, and they were thought to be more easily integrated into white society than a mixed-race boy.

Other local authority homes

Richard was born in May 1945 in Totnes, Devon; his mother was married and already had four children. The fourth had not been her husband's and while the husband had accepted this first illegitimate child, who was white, when he got back from fighting in Sicily he said he was not prepared to accept a second one. Richard was first sent to a local authority baby home in South Devon and then, aged two-and-a-half, he was transferred to a children's home in Barnstaple, North Devon: 'there must have been about thirty children in there … I was the only mixed-race child.' The home was run by a couple called Hicks, and according to Richard, Mrs Hicks was wonderful:

> I had my tea one night. And I had it too fast. And I had a stomach ache that night. And then I was moaning and groaning, when I was in bed. Mrs Hicks took me out of my dormitory, and took me into her bed, and rubbed my belly all until I went to sleep.

He called her 'mum' and wanted her to adopt him. She never did adopt him, but she did later adopt another child from the home. The children were taken out by visiting 'aunts' and 'uncles', but Richard tended not to be chosen:

> Now this woman came into the children's home, and she said to Mrs Hicks, 'Do you have anybody?' And she said … 'Nobody wants him over there.' … And she's pointing to me … And she said, 'I'll have him.' And she was called Chichester. Joanne Chichester. The sister of Francis Chichester … I used to go and stay with her at weekends. She used to have cups … tea and everything. And talk to me. About life. She lived alone. She was a spinster … And never raised her voice to me. If I had done something wrong, she would say, 'That's wrong. And this is the reason.' … We had a beautiful relationship … And I called her Auntie … I learned so much from her. Especially kindness.[103]

Dave B was born in March 1945 in Pontypool, South Wales. His mother was married with a daughter; her husband was away fighting. His father, he found out later, was in the 320th Barrage Balloon Battalion, an all-black US unit based in South Wales. The unit played a crucial part in the D-Day landings, the barrage balloons forming a

3.3 Richard with Mrs Hicks

defensive barrier on the Normandy beaches, keeping enemy planes at bay.[104] Dave was taken into care in 1946 by Monmouthshire County Council.[105] He was in three different children's homes, all local:

> There were times in my life where I felt almost privileged ... Everything was fun, you know. The grounds were big and you could go out and play ... I've had probably one of the happiest childhoods. I have no complaints about my childhood, I was looked after, cared for.[106]

His experience of being fostered will be considered in the next chapter.

The Waifs and Strays' Society and Dr Barnardo's: two of Britain's leading children's homes

The three main British children's charities providing homes in the late nineteenth and twentieth centuries were the Waifs and Strays' Society, Dr Barnardo's Homes and the National Children's Home.[107] There was no guarantee that these charities would agree to take a child. The LCP got an anxious letter from a married woman whose mixed-race child had been refused entry to the homes of all three organisations. Her husband was prepared to take her back should she get rid of the baby.[108] This was not the only case; the LCP mentioned that 'we have letters from distressed mothers telling us that matrons of leading homes are not willing to admit coloured children'.[109] Some were admitted, however. None of my interviewees was taken in by the National Children's Home, but several were placed in homes run by the other two. Dr Barnardo's first children's home was established in 1870 in East London; the Waifs and Strays' Society, founded in 1881 by Edward Rudolf, opened its first home in South London. Both Barnardo and Rudolf were inspired by religious conviction – evangelicalism and Anglicanism respectively.

The Waifs and Strays' Society

Five of my interviewees were placed in homes run by the Waifs and Strays' Society (which changed its name to the Church of England

3.4 Billy

Children's Society in 1946, presumably thinking that 'waifs and strays' sounded too Dickensian). Billy was born in June 1945 in Plymouth. His mother was married with a three-year-old daughter and a husband in the RAF fighting in Africa. She had met Billy's black GI father in early 1944 in Callington, North Cornwall, as mentioned in Chapter 1. After his birth, someone suggested the Waifs and Strays' Society; they told his mother 'We'll let you know'. She decided that if they had not got back to her within six months, she would keep Billy. They came for him after five months. After a brief stay in Knoyle House Nursery in Wiltshire, Billy was moved to a beautiful mansion called Clouds, also in Wiltshire. This was a Waifs and Strays nursery for thirty children and sounds rather like Holnicote House: the nurses were sixteen- to eighteen-year-old trainees and very loving.

My earliest memories are all of Clouds. The first is of a large bedroom and looking out of the window on to rolling downland, lovely trees, a sort of Capability Brown landscape, and seeing a fox cross the park. The dormitories were named after flowers – Tulip, Daffodil and Primrose. We each had a nurse who looked after us the whole time we were there to give us a continuity of care.[110]

There were a few mixed-race children, one of whom was David M, born in September 1945 to a girl who had met his 22-year-old father at the age of fifteen; she was pressurised to give David up, while his father was imprisoned, possibly for underage sex. David saw his time at Clouds as 'the best part of my childhood … The house itself, the grounds around it, absolutely wonderful … And our experience, you know, as children, was really nice.'[111] At six, David and Billy were sent to St Luke's Boys Home, a large house with an acre of ground in the centre of Burgess Hill, Sussex. Everyone in the area knew they were from the home and called them 'Lukeys'. There were fewer children at St Luke's (twenty-one) and it was very institutional (for example, the dormitories were numbered 1, 2, 3, 4) and quite strict. Like other children's homes, they had 'aunts' and 'uncles' who took them out. Billy would stay with one nice woman for a week every September; similar to Richard's experience of Joanne Chichester, this 'aunt' taught Billy 'manners, how to hold a knife and fork, to say please and thank you, to pass round the butter'.[112]

When he was about twelve, Billy suddenly asked about his parents. The matron replied: 'Your parents are dead', which he accepted.[113] Telling children in children's homes that their parents were dead or that their mother did not want them appears to have been common. (Some adopters likewise wiped out the biological parents of their adopted children, one woman confessing of her adopted child's mother: 'We have killed her off in a bus accident.')[114] Children's homes up until the mid-to-late 1960s tended to reveal nothing of the children's past to them. The idea that a 'fresh' start was beneficial and that the past could be upsetting meant that the staff entered a conspiracy of silence.[115] The anonymity of the birth mother was protected, but the child was subjected to the emotional harm of a regime of secrets and lies.

David M and Billy were the only mixed-race boys at St Luke's and had a very close relationship. They were like brothers; David remembers 'a boy coming up to me in the home and saying, "Is Billy your brother?" And [not wanting to deny it] I said, "Well, he's not my sister, is he!"' But after sixteen months, David was inexplicably moved to another home. He cannot believe the insensitivity of this parting:

> what actually really still gets at me is that in the report … it was, like, 'David appears to be very fond of Billy.' So the staff knew it. They knew there was a great affection between us … yet they parted us. They could have sent both of us together.[116]

Children's homes were against children getting too attached to each other partly because it would make their separation harder when they were placed for adoption or fostering.[117] Two or three years prior to the separating of Billy and David, John Bowlby's 1951 *Maternal Care and Mental Health* stressed the importance of attachment for a child's development – a theory soon to become very influential.[118] Even had St Luke's known of Bowlby's work, the fact that it was two small boys who were emotionally attached to each other, as opposed to a mother (or mother substitute) and child, would have contributed to the discounting of the boys' relationship. The maternal bond and the dangers of maternal deprivation were Bowlby's focus. However, there was another piece of research published in the same year as Bowlby's on six three-year-olds who had come to England from Terezin concentration camp in German-occupied Czechoslovakia. This study by Anna Freud and Sophie Dann found that the children, who had been together without their parents (who were all killed), were devoted to each other and had close, supportive and loving relationships: 'companions of the same age were their real love objects'. The study demonstrates the power of attachment to other children where parents or caring adults are absent.[119] British children's voluntary homes, largely staffed by untrained, poorly paid workers, were very unlikely to have had knowledge of new psychological and psychoanalytical theories and findings.

David M was sent to a reception centre in Balham, then to a home in Hull. At one point he was ill in the isolation ward with a mixed-race girl and a younger mixed-race boy:

> it was almost like a little family situation. And I felt … in charge, almost dad, you know. And there's mum, and the little kid … I remember that with quite some affection. And then one day, about a year later, we were all in the playroom. The master came in and said, 'Oh David, by the way, you're going to down to Balham next week.' And walked out.

3.5 David M

After being back in Balham, David was sent to Rudolf Memorial Home, in Dulwich, South London, his fourth children's home.

> It was for maladjusted children. And I look back and think, 'Maladjusted? How was I?' The only thing that was actually wrong with me was the rocking of the bed, at night-time. [He used to get on his knees and rock back and forth when asleep.] Now, I'd been seeing psychiatrists, a psychiatrist who eventually had said, 'Look, I think this is all about anxiety.' Because it was a period when I was really wanting a mother.

He had a bad time at the home: 'It was a very restricted home. It was a home where they had their own school ... we never actually met other children. So that was for three years ... you're in this institution ... in the one building ... And the education was horrific.' He was also subjected to a lot of corporal punishment from two sadistic matrons. Miss Legg would hit children in the face: 'She would come up to you and talk to you, and then, bang!' Miss Inchley would cane children or beat them with a hairbrush, for little or no reason.[120] The Curtis Committee had looked at institutions' 'excessive discipline' and its report commented on the danger of 'harsh or repressive tendencies', which were particularly evident in voluntary children's homes. Corporal punishment was legally addressed in 1951 (extending the 1948 Children Act) and applied to all local authority and voluntary homes. It stipulated that 'no corporal punishment shall be administered to a child under ten years of age except by smacking his hands with the bare hand'.[121] David's home clearly breached this regulation. The Curtis Report also noted 'a lack of personal interest in and affection for the children which we found shocking'.[122] In David's homes there was indeed no affection: 'having left the nursery, and from then on throughout my life, until much later when I was older, I never had a cuddle … you'd like a mum … But for me, also, it was like, I'd like Billy again.' Later he saw a psychiatrist's report of the time which read: 'There's nothing wrong with David. What he needs is love.'[123]

When David M was eleven he was fostered for a time by a couple, the Ws, but it was not a success: 'there was never *love* there'. Mrs W even said to David: 'I've never loved you.' When David was about forty he thought he would try and find Billy again, the one person he had loved and who had shown him love. The Children's Society (formerly the Church of England Children's Society) was unable to help but encouraged him to look through the telephone book, as Billy has a very unusual surname. David found Billy's telephone number, but 'then it was like a little bit of a dread, because you think, well, we could be so incompatible. We could hate each other, and there's all my dreams gone.' But their meeting was a great success and they are still close friends and in regular contact. However, forming a family has been harder, due, David thinks, to not having lived as a child in a family and having been torn from Billy and then from his little 'family' group in the home in Hull:

I had two [adult] relationships where … I've been part of the family. You know, I'm with my girl, and we've lived together, and funnily enough both of them had children, as it happened. But … I felt everything closing in on me … I have realised that family life is very difficult. I can't cope with it. I really can't. And lovely people, but I couldn't.[124]

Joe, who also spent his childhood in a 'brutal' Children's Society home, likewise had 'no role model as a child for a long-term relationship'.[125]

The third person I interviewed who was sent to a Waifs and Strays' home was James A. When James was born in November 1944, his mother, a hairdresser, was already married with four children aged between two and ten. His skin colour made it obvious that he was not the son of her husband (who had not enlisted to fight due to ill-health), and James and his mother were forced to leave the marital home; further, 'she was told that she couldn't have anything to do with the [other four] children'. His grandmother and her husband (James's step-grandfather) eventually took in James and his mother, but insisted that James be put in a home. His mother approached the Waifs and Strays' Society when James was five months old. In October 1945, when James was eleven months old, and after a lot of paperwork, including a statement of recommendation from the local vicar, he was accepted at one of the Society's homes near Leeds – over seventy-five miles from where his mother lived in Long Eaton, Derbyshire. James's mother only ever saw this as a short-term measure (as was the case with many children placed in care by parents). She visited James regularly and was very keen to have him back, but a number of obstacles stood in the way. One problem was that she had poor health, not helped by her ex-husband refusing to be reconciled despite her being 'very repentant', which had 'left her a very broken and nerve-wracked woman', according to Miss Wilden, a welfare officer.[126] She also had to look after her own mother, who was frequently ill. The biggest barrier was her difficulty in getting a house of her own, even when she remarried in 1949. She and her new husband Reg had to live with her mother and stepfather, as she informed the Church of England Children's Society in a letter in February 1950:

I live in my mother's house and she does *not* agree to James coming home. Recently she was very upset by remarks made by people living near as her heart is very bad, in fact the Dr [*sic*] told me any excitement or worry bringing on an attack could prove fatal. We have been to the specialist, there is no cure. For months we have been trying to get a house in another district. You see I have four other children living in the same town [Long Eaton] and it is thought it would not be fair to either James or them. My only hope of happiness with James would be if I could get a home of my own as when any dispute arises I am also told to get rooms of my own; you see how difficult it is.[127]

Her mother had angina, and one can imagine the threat of death through worry being used as a powerful argument against James ever coming to live with them. James would have been the reason for his grandmother being 'very upset by remarks made by people living near' – her desire for respectability and acceptance intermingled with racism.

While James's mother was having a difficult time with her mother, she was not being treated well by the Church of England Children's Society either. There are two recorded occasions (in the Society's files on James, copies of which are now in his possession) of his mother being refused permission to take James away from the home for a short holiday. She wrote to the secretary of the Society on 6 December 1948 asking to have James to stay over the Christmas period. She assures him that 'I am a frequent visitor to the Nursery at Meanwood [near Leeds] where he is placed. I feel sure that Matron Hoggarth would approve.'[128] She clearly was not given permission, as on 6 January 1949 she wrote again, saying that 'it is the first time I have

3.6 James A

not seen him at Xmas time, I thought I could make the journey and so bring him back home with me. I trust you will now be able to see if he can have the promised holiday with me. Matron Hoggarth says he is quite thrilled with the idea.'[129] Permission had been refused because although she had given his full name, she had omitted his age in the previous letter. It is hard not to see this refusal as a petty response to a minor oversight.

In July 1950 Mr Flynn, the master of the Society home in Wakefield that James was moved to that year, wrote to Colonel Birnie, the director of the Society, asking permission for James's mother 'to have him for two weeks Aug 21 to Sept 2 – of course she would fetch him and bring him back, would you kindly let me know if this is all right'.[130] Permission was refused. James's mother subsequently wrote to Birnie:

> I understand from Miss Turner [a welfare officer] that you are puzzled by the application ... for me to have him [James] for a holiday ... My husband and I still haven't got any other accommodation, I wish with all my heart we had. My mother's objections are still the same, though I'm pleased to say her health has improved since she recently had an operation. When I went to see my son a few weeks ago (I try to see him whenever I possibly can) it was suggested that I might like to take him for a holiday. I wrote to my sister who lives in Hillingdon in Middlesex and she thought it was a wonderful opportunity for me to have a few days at her house with him. I am sorry I did not write and explain all this to you.[131]

There may have been other, unrecorded examples of high-handed refusals of reasonable requests. James's mother was made to feel beholden to the Society, while it appeared to treat her – and possibly all the parents of 'its' children – with barely concealed contempt.

It was not until May 1953, when James was eight-and-a-half, that his mother finally managed to get her son permanently away from the children's home.[132] In fact he had been in hospital for over a year with TB. Although his mother and stepfather were still living with his grandmother, a council house of their own was imminent and his grandmother appears to have acquiesced to a short stay. It was just as well that James did not have to return to the Society home in Wakefield run by Flynn, for James well remembers how 'he wasn't a particularly nice man, and he had a walking stick and I knew how he used to use it'. James suggestively misremembers his name as 'Flint', a hard, sharp piece of rock; Flynn/Flint sounds like a hard man who in his six-monthly reports on James always described him as 'stubborn'. In contrast, earlier reports from the nursery were all positive: when he was four, under 'conduct' James was described as a 'normal mischievous boy; very active and intelligent … James is a grand little boy.' When five the report said of his conduct: 'James is a delightful child and I think he shows promise of being very intelligent. He has a very affectionate nature and is extremely fond of his mother.'[133] But in October 1950 Flynn suggested that James 'needs a firm hand, he is a very stubborn boy',[134] which to Flynn presumably justified the beatings. James's mother persevered and finally reclaimed her son. Flynn agreed to James's return to his mother because James would have a bedroom of his own, the mother's new bungalow was nearly ready and 'he will need very careful nursing and individual care [since he was still convalescing from illness]'.[135] It helped that Colonel Birnie, the head of the Society since November 1949, had revised its aims and objectives in 1952, emphasising that where possible a child should remain with its mother, in line with the Children Act.[136] Thankfully James had been under Flynn's 'care' for only two years – from February 1950 until March 1952, when he had been admitted to hospital.

James got on very well with his new stepfather, although he was not happy at school. He did not start school until the age of eight because of being in hospital and was behind the other children: 'I put it down to not picking up the early building blocks of knowledge when you're younger.' But he also hated going to school 'because I would get groups of lads following me around, calling me names … "Sambo", "Blackie", "Chocolate drop".' 'I used to get into a lot of fights when I was younger … one of the worst things, and this is what I got into fights for a lot, is, the worst word I could ever think of, "Nigger". I *hated* that.' There was only one other mixed-race child in the area. 'I rather embarrassed my mother one day when I was on this bus with her. And I stood up and looked around, and I says: "Why are all these people white and I'm black?"'[137]

My fourth interviewee from a Church of England Children's Society home, Sandi H, was in Downend, owned by Bristol City Council but run by the Society. She had a bad time at the home where every one of the hundred children except her had mothers and was there temporarily; this meant that a lot of children were coming and going, and there was no sense of family or continuity. Sandi was told in the home that her father had died in the war and her mother did not want her or could not look after her. When she was thirteen she was unhappily fostered.[138] Her story will be considered in the next chapter.

I have not been able to talk directly to my fifth Children's Society home resident, Colin, as he is unwell, but I have talked to his ex-wife, Celia. Colin's mother was single, nineteen and from Cheltenham, living at home. Her sister also lived there with her husband and children; there was no room for Colin, born in December 1946. His grandfather was a labourer but often ill and unable to work and the family was consequently very poor. Colin was placed in a Church of England Children's Society home in the village of Clent in Gloucestershire and was never fostered. Celia does not think he had a bad time in the home, which was fairly small with about twelve children, and the reports on him were good, but 'He has never been a communicator. He was very reluctant to talk about his early life.' As an adult, according to Celia, he 'found family life difficult and suffocating'.[139] It is possible that this was partly due to his having spent all his childhood and adolescence in a children's home, similar to David M's and Joe's experiences.

Dr Barnardo's

By the late 1940s Dr Barnardo's was enormous, with ninety-six homes catering for 7,000–8,000 children. In its Annual Report of 1951 there was a note made of the 'special problem' of mixed-race children: 'When Dr Barnardo's was named "the Father of Nobody's Children" the title was never more appropriate than for those little ones in our care of mixed parentage. The bringing up, and more particularly, the launching into life of coloured boys and girls in the homes is a special problem.'[140] Whereas with white Barnardo's children there had been a shift from seeing them as 'Nobody's Children' to 'Somebody's Bairns' as early as 1916,[141] it appears that this shift did not apply to non-white children. White British women who bore mixed-race children were widely thought to have acted so inappropriately and unpatriotically that their children, thought to be the product of sin and lust rather than love, were effectively the children of 'nobody'. Differentiating according to 'race' was not new or exclusive to Barnardo's: child reformers had deployed racialised language in relation to certain children for many years. From the nineteenth century into the early twentieth, 'street arab' had been used as a term for poor street children, perceived as dirty, nomadic, homeless and parentless.[142] The urban poor generally were seen as a 'race apart', with the 'heathen' poor of 'darkest London' akin to the natives of 'darkest Africa'.[143] This racialised language separated the 'street arabs' from the 'civilised' British population. But unlike the mixed-race children of the mid-twentieth century, the 'street arabs' were white, or rather their whiteness could be restored, their racial 'difference' being temporary: through the intervention of the care system, they could be transformed into clean and productive British workers.[144] Whether mixed-race children in the 1940s and 1950s could likewise be transformed into useful British citizens was a question that child-care workers seemed unsure about, including the question of whether these children were truly 'British'.

Suzi Hamilton, who has written a memoir of her time at Dr Barnardo's, always felt that she was treated as a 'problem'. She was born in April 1945 to a married mother. She quotes her Barnardo's report, which she at last got access to in 1995:[145] 'Husband … has been told of the circumstances of Susan's birth and he has forgiven the woman for her lapse [with a black GI], but he has refused to allow the child to remain in his home.' The marriage was 'saved' through the mother/wife shunting off the 'problem' child. After a brief stay in a Barnardo's home in Berkshire, Suzi was transferred to the Girls' Village Home in Barkingside, East London. The labelling of it as a 'village', and indeed the name 'cottage homes' as in the case of Fazakerley, were attempts to give a more 'homely' feel to an institution.[146] Attempts to have Suzi fostered or adopted failed:

> Whilst I was very young I was 'put out for adoption' on at least three occasions … I was collected, very much like a parcel, by an 'aunty' and 'uncle' … However, I was never kept long at these places. According to the matrons, I was sent back to the Village almost immediately for 'bad behaviour'. Apparently I started to spit and wet the bed – two things I *never* did in the Cottage![147]

The psychoanalysts Melanie Klein, Anna Freud and Susan Isaac, writing in the 1930s and 1940s, argue that enuresis (bed-wetting) is connected to two things: 'the relationship with the mother and the disruption of domestic and familial relations'.[148] Suzi's bed-wetting was likely to have been due to the disruptions and anxieties of moving to a new home. Suzi had a lasting image

> forever etched upon my memory, I remember that I had been given a little brown shoulder bag ... I must have been about eight years old. I loathed bags and other girlie trappings ... So, right in the middle of the village street (somewhere in Wiltshire, I was told later), I swung the hated bag round and round my head until the strap broke! Actually, I might have been trying to keep name-calling children away from me. Summary punishment was administered upon my return to the Village. I was not put out again for adoption.[149]

Suzi's resistance to adoption or fostering was very probably due to insecurity about change.[150] The two women who ran her 'cottage' were not kind to her: she had 'a tough time' at the home. While there were no more attempts to get her fostered or adopted, she did still go for holidays with 'aunts' and 'uncles'. Her menstrual period came for the first time on one of these holidays and the 'aunt' 'told me that I must be *extra* careful about washing, as I would "smell more than white girls"'.[151] The racist idea that black people are intrinsically dirtier than whites was propagated through adverts for soap in the nineteenth and twentieth centuries – the notion was that soap would 'cleanse' the dark, impure body.[152] Unlike Richard and Billy's positive experiences with 'aunts', this 'aunt' experience of Suzi's was not good. This was not the first time that she had faced racism; she experienced a lot of name calling, exacerbated by her (then) surname Plumb, so she was not only called 'little black Sambo' and worse, but also names like 'plum pudding'.

The 1966 report *Racial Integration and Barnardo's* noted that the organisation had experienced a huge growth in 'coloured' children under its care. Before the Second World War it had had very few such children; towards the end of the war, 'we admitted many children of English mothers and coloured American Servicemen stationed in this country; more recently the main increase has stemmed from the growing numbers of immigrants'.[153] The proportion had risen from under 8 per cent of the overall numbers in 1955 to 20 per cent in 1965, with 40 per cent of children in its nurseries that year being 'coloured' (a term which was extended to those of mixed-race). Compared to its

1950s' attitude, Barnardo's appears to have shifted its view of these children: 'we are emphatic that we should, in all but exceptional circumstances, do everything in our power to make these children feel that they belong to British society, which is historically multi-racial'.[154] The report admitted that as an incentive, foster parents were being paid a higher rate for fostering 'coloured' children, but now recommended that in the future the rates should be the same as for white children, and 'colour should not be regarded in itself as a "difficulty"'.

On leaving the homes

However good or bad the experience of being in a children's home, nearly all the homes appear to have been inadequate in helping the children's transition into the outside world. Even Dave B, who speaks well of his time in care, commented that 'you almost felt like you were … *dumped*. There was no "after". At the end of it all, you're sent out to the world.' This was when he was fifteen or sixteen. 'I think for about a year they did keep a check on me. After that, no.'[155] On leaving school at fifteen, Adrian was also made to leave Fazakerley Cottage Homes, which was managed by Liverpool City Council, and he was put in lodgings with other teenagers run by a couple called Cole:

> I had the impression we were just dumped there by the council … but we didn't know anything else … they weren't the best and they knew it. It was money … we were like a money thing for them … nine or ten of us in there … it was three rounds of bread and one sugar in your tea. But like I say, bad as it was I had to stay there because I … had nothing, I didn't know how to live or anything. I hadn't had that experience of living out of this home … I stayed there until I was about thirty … I had to … nobody told us nothing about how to do this, how to do that, how to go and get a flat … I mean, if I had have left there, I would have been on the streets. I wouldn't be where I am today. Oh definitely, it was horrible, it was horrible but yeah, I had to put up with it and what got me, the social services knew as well what was going on.[156]

Roger also had a bad time after leaving Fazakerley Cottage Homes at fifteen, so he went and lived at the Mission with Pastor Ekarte for a

short period, although the building was now very dilapidated.[157] Joe
was thrown out of his home too with no after-care. He soon discovered that his institutional upbringing had not prepared him for living
in the outside world: 'I had no idea about money – I had no idea
about anything.'[158] Unlike Adrian, Roger or Jim, Brian was fostered
when he was fourteen. Fazakerley was closing down and this led to
'the children being off-loaded to any Tom, Dick and Harry'. He was
allocated someone unsuitable:

> Most of the children up for fostering were institutionalised for many
> years, they were reaching their teens, a very difficult time in the life
> of any child. Yet Mrs Brown was a widow, in full time employment,
> was a town councillor in her free time, yet she was expected to take
> charge of a boy who had not yet made any adjustment to normal
> family life. It was bound to fail and it did. The arrangement lasted six
> months when Mrs Brown made a request to the social services that
> I be fostered with another family.

Mrs Brown was a Salvationist and a fellow Salvationist couple offered
to take Brian; it 'proved to be a very good move'.[159]

Billy was unusual among my interviewees in having had a good
after-care experience. He was at St Luke's until 1960, which he thinks
was 'one of the better homes, although there was no love'. Aged fifteen
he was asked what he wanted to do; he was always reading so he chose
printing. The Church of England Children's Society owned St Alban's
Press in Frome, Somerset, where he was apprenticed for two years.
They then decided to close the place and start up in London with offset
lithography. Billy had the option of joining a local printer or going to
London; he chose London and remained a printer for the rest of his
working life.[160] Billy's experience was, however, atypical. The report
Racial Integration and Barnardo's was well aware of the need for better
after-care, presenting shocking figures on 'coloured' Barnardo's boys
who had entered employment between 1956 and 1960: of eighty-
one boys, of whom nearly half (thirty-nine) had 'American Negro'
fathers, twenty-one had 'known social difficulties in lodgings, work,
sex, mental health etc.' (including two suicides) and an additional
twenty-five had 'known social difficulties including convictions'.

Conclusion

The accounts given here of a number of mixed-race children's experiences give a poor impression of the British care system. It appears that the 1948 Children Act's guidelines were not always followed. First, many children carried on being housed in large numbers, despite the Act proposing small homes.[161] Fazakerley Cottage Homes from the 1940s into the early 1960s, for example, placed 700 children in twenty cottages, in other words, thirty-five children per cottage. Secondly, the Curtis Committee had recommended the lessening of punishment; this was enacted in 1951 but clearly not adhered to by the Church of England Children's Society's Rudolf Memorial Home, where David M suffered many sadistic beatings, or the home where James A was whacked by Mr Flynn. Thirdly, few helpful structures appear to have been put in place to help care-leavers, a situation that is a problem to this day, with children leaving care in the twenty-first century not necessarily much better prepared for the future than those of the 1950s and 1960s. The columnist Sali Hughes, writing in the *Guardian* about contemporary Britain's scandalously high level of homelessness, notes: 'There is a high chance they [homeless people] come from a care system that consistently fails to prepare them for ejection at the onset of young adulthood.'[162] However, at least the age of eligibility for support for care-leavers has recently been increased to twenty-five. Fourthly, the 1948 Act's emphasis on prioritising adoption was very largely ignored in relation to mixed-race children. We can conclude that apart from two wonderful nurseries, namely Holnicote House and Clouds, where the children were loved and cherished, and Dave B's fairly positive experience of Monmouthshire homes, the care system very largely failed the wartime 'brown babies'. That so many have nevertheless done well and have lived fulfilling lives is a testament to their strength of character and determination.

Notes

1   Children's homes were either voluntary or run by a local authority. Of the twenty-five additional people that I know a little about, only eight were relinquished, i.e. one third. This suggests that between

a third and nearly half of Britain's mixed-race GI war babies were given up for adoption.

2   This chimes with Dr Barnardo's study of 'coloured' children in its care in 1965, of which the number of boys was nearly double that of girls; Barnardo's, *Racial Integration and Barnardo's*, p. 11.

3   'Should they be adopted?', *Night and Day: The Barnardo's Magazine*, spring 1946, pp. 5–6.

4   Cohen, *Family Secrets*, pp. 113–14.

5   'Should they be adopted?'

6   Peter Higginbotham, *Children's Homes: A History of Institutional Care for Britain's Young* (Barnsley, 2017), p. 86.

7   June Rose, *For the Sake of the Children: Inside Dr Barnardo's* (London, 1987), p. 199.

8   Nicholas Timmins, *The Five Giants: A Biography of the Welfare State* (London, 2001).

9   Celia Bangham, Somerset's superintendent health visitor, discussing the abandoned 'half-caste' child: 'On account of its colour, there was no possibility of getting such a child adopted'; 13 December 1945, FO 371/51617, AN3/3/45, TNA. Another example of this difficulty comes from the memoir of Phil Frampton, a mixed-race boy at Dr Barnardo's. His mother was told in 26 May 1955: 'I fear a Nigerian half-caste is almost impossible to find adopters for'; Frampton, *The Golly*, p. 77. Hilary Halperin, general secretary of the National Adoption Association, in a letter to Graham Smith, 16 February 1978 noted: 'Sadly very few babies of White/Negro parentage were ever found adoptive homes. I remember from my work as Chairman of the old LCC Children's Committee (1952–58).' Letter in David Stanley's possession. Even in 1966 Barnardo's claimed that 'prospective adopters willing to take coloured children are scarce' (Barnardo's, *Racial Integration and Barnardo's*, p. 9).

10 See Cohen, *Family Secrets*, pp. 113–42.

11 St Clair Drake, 'The League's Sociological Approach', Box 62/12.

12 Moynihan, 'Children against the colour bar'.

13 Baker, 'Lest We Forget', p. 74.

14 On 'same race' policy, see Ivor Gaber and Jane Aldridge (eds), *In the Best Interests of the Child* (London, 1994); Derek Kirton, *'Race', Ethnicity and Adoption* (Buckingham, 2000).

15 'Report of Conference on the position of the illegitimate child', MH 55/1656, TNA.

16 Moody to Bevan, 12 December 1945, reprinted as appendix 4 in McNeill, *Illegitimate Children*, p. 12. The Ministry of Health also appeared to be against segregation. See notes on meeting with Alma LaBadie, 6 February 1946, Acc. no. 4910, LRO.

17   'Correspondents and Documents', St Clair Drake Archives, Box 64/3.

18   Sherwood, *Pastor Daniels Ekarte*, p. 24.

19   St Clair Drake commented that it was 'a term that outrages higher status Negro sentiments'; 'The Brown Baby Problem', Box 60/15.

20   On Garvey, see Colin Grant, *Negro with a Hat: The Rise and Fall of Marcus Garvey and His Dream of Mother Africa* (London, 2008).

21   See Fryer, *Staying Power*; Brown, *Dropping Anchor*; Belchem, *Before the Windrush*.

22   Carlton E. Wilson, 'Racism and private assistance: the support of the West Indian and African missions in Liverpool, England, during the inter-war years', *African Studies Review*, 35.2 (1992), p. 57; Sherwood, *Pastor Daniels Ekarte*, p. 29.

23   *Liverpool Echo*, 23 July 1964.

24   Sherwood, *Pastor Daniels Ekarte*, pp. 32–7, 104.

25   Report by R. W. Whiteway, woman inspector, 13 February 1946, MH 55/1656, TNA.

26   John Harris to Harold King, 29 October 1937, Acc. no. 4910, LRO.

27   See Rich, *Race and Empire*, pp. 37–41.

28   John Harris to Colonial Office, 22 October 1937, quoted in Sherwood, *Pastor Daniels Ekarte*, p. 101.

29   John St Clair Drake, 'Observer's report on his first visit to Liverpool', 25 August 1947, St Clair Drake Archives, Box 62/12.

30   St Clair Drake, 'The Brown Baby Problem', Box 60/15.

31   Ibid.

32   Sherwood, *Pastor Daniels Ekarte*, pp. 38–9.

33   Report by Whiteway, 13 February 1946, MH 55/1656, TNA.

34   Telephone interview with Roger, 1 September 2014.

35   Interview with Brian, 24 March 2014.

36   Report by Whiteway, 13 February 1946, MH 55/1656, TNA; Ekarte to Greenidge, Anti-Slavery Society, 23 August 1948, MSS Brit Emp S19DH/7/14, RHL.

37   See Greenidge to Ekarte, 9 April 1946, Greenidge to Ekarte, 5 December 1947, MSS Brit Emp S19DH/7/14, RHL; Sherwood, *Pastor Daniels Ekarte*, pp. 99–100.

38   Ekarte to Southgate, Ministry of Health, MH 55/1656, TNA. With the Children Act 1948, responsibility for unwanted children moved to the Home Office rather than the Ministry of Health.

39   Interview with Brian, 24 March 2014.

40   *Liverpool Echo*, 23 July 1964.

41   St Clair Drake, 'The Brown Baby Problem', Box 60/15.

42   'Fatherless children test racial liberalism of British', *Ebony*, 19

November 1946; Alfred Eris, 'Britain's mulatto "GI" babies', *Liberty*, 7 December 1946.

43   Letter from Ekarte to Foreign Secretary, Ernest Bevin, 20 January 1947, FO3H/61016, TNA.

44   'The "American Campaign" Debacle, 1946–47', St Clair Drake Archives, Box 61/2.

45   St Clair Drake suggested that this inter-organisational struggle had started two years earlier and was apparent at the October 1945 Pan-African Congress, where emphasis was put on the Negro Welfare Centre as the champion of the 'brown babies', with no mention of the LCP. However, in the second edition of the Congress report the LCP and the African Churches Mission replaced 'other African organisations' when referring to those doing 'legitimate welfare work among coloured children'. St Clair Drake, 'The Brown Baby Problem', Box 60/15.

46   Hervieux, *Forgotten*, p. 43.

47   'Britain "exports" 5,000 babies', *Daily Mail*, 5 April 1947.

48   St Clair Drake to Joseph-Mitchell, 41 January 1948, St Clair Drake Archives, Box 64/3.

49   *The Sun* (New York), 22 January 1947. In January 1947 the *New York Amsterdam News* reported Duplan as claiming that there were eighty children in the Mission. Sherwood, *Pastor Daniels Ekarte*, p. 58.

50   Wynn, *The African American Experience*, p. 22. Joe Louis, known as the 'Brown Bomber', had been declared world heavyweight champion in 1937; the following year he had beaten the German Max Schmeling in a fight that was widely perceived as democracy versus Nazism.

51   *Chicago Defender*, 24 April 1948, p. 1. Apparently Marva Louis advised her husband to keep the money in reserve until he got an explanation from Ekarte. In a footnote, Sherwood comments that it is unknown whether such an explanation was forthcoming. Sherwood, *Pastor Daniels Ekarte*, p. 74.

52   George Padmore to Walter White, 29 April 1947, Acc. no. 4910, LRO.

53   St Clair Drake, 'Observer's report on his first visit to Liverpool', Box 62/12. See also Sherwood, *Pastor Daniels Ekarte*, pp. 56–8 on Duplan.

54   Interview with Jim H, 16 August 2014.

55   Report by Whiteway, 13 February 1946, MH 55/1656, TNA.

56   Interview with Brian, 24 March 2014.

57   'Black saint fights for his children', *Sunday Pictorial*, 12 June 1949, p. 2.

58 Interview with Brian, 24 March 2014. See also Sherwood, *Pastor Daniels Ekarte*, ch. 4; Belchem, *Before the Windrush*, chs 2 and 3, which substantiate this claim.

59 Interview with Jim H, 16 August 2014.

60 Interview with Brian, 24 March 2014.

61 Interview with Jim H, 16 August 2014.

62 Interview with Brian, 24 March 2014; interview with Jim H, 16 August 2014; interview with Adrian, 1 September 2014.

63 Interview with Adrian, 1 September 2014.

64 *Liverpool Echo*, 23 July 1964.

65 Quoted in 'The Rainbow Homes Fiasco: 1946–1947', St Clair Drake Archives, Box 61/2.

66 Ruth Russell to S. M. Fry, 5 October 1945, Mss Brit Emp S19DH/7/14, RHL.

67 Anti-Slavery Society to Ekarte, 9 October 1945; Ekarte to Anti-Slavery Society, 13 October 1945; Anti-Slavery Society to Fry, 15 October 1945; Mss Brit Emp S19DH/7/14, RHL.

68 Caballero and Aspinall, *Mixed Race Britain*, pp. 224–5.

69 'The Rainbow Homes Fiasco', St Clair Drake Archives, Box 61/2.

70 Ibid.

71 Ibid.

72 James Woodward, Public Assistance Committee, Birkenhead, to General Inspector, Ministry of Health, Manchester, 20 December 1946, Acc. no. 4910, LRO.

73 Ekarte to Greenidge, 2 December 1946, Mss Brit Emp S19DH/7/14, RHL.

74 'The Rainbow Homes Fiasco', St Clair Drake Archives, Box 61/2.

75 'Neglect at a children's home', *Guardian*, 17 September 1947. Deaths in the care system were not unusual. Forty-eight children died in Lambeth's care system between 1970 and 1989; Raymond Stevenson, *Interim Report on Child Abuse: Shirley Oaks Children's Home 'Looking for a Place Called Home'* (London, 2016). Thanks to Lucy Delap for lending me this disturbing report.

76 'The Rainbow Homes Fiasco', St Clair Drake Archives, Box 61/2.

77 'Rainbow Home: fines instead of gaol', *Daily Mail*, 24 October 1947, p. 3.

78 Montgomery to Minister of Health, n.d., received 2 October 1946; Ministry of Health to Harry Bann, 12 November 1946; Southgate to Montgomery, 25 November 1946; MH 93216/7/16, TNA.

79 Quoted in Caballero and Aspinall, *Mixed Race Britain*, p. 223.

80 Isha McKenzie-Mavinga and Thelma Perkins, *In Search of Mr McKenzie: Two Sisters' Quest for an Unknown Father* (London, 1991), p. 92.

81   *Pittburgh Courier*, 19 March 1949, p. 3.

82   Interview with Brian, 24 March 2014.

83   St Clair Drake, 'The Brown Baby Problem', Box 60/15, noted that the LCP pressurised him to downplay this call for 'training for work in the colonies'.

84   Grant, *Negro with a Hat*.

85   *Pittburgh Courier*, 19 March 1949, p. 3.

86   Dr Barnardo had a missionary fantasy in relation to three black girls from Sierra Leone who were in his Village Home. See Caroline Bressey, 'Forgotten histories: three stories of black girls from Barnardo's Victorian archive', *Women's History Review*, 11.3 (2002), pp. 351–74 (p. 367).

87   Somerset County Council, minutes of the Children's Committee, 27 July 1948–2 December 1952, CH1/1, p. 77, Somerset Heritage Centre, Taunton, Somerset; FO 371/51617, AN3/3/45. The Children's Committee existed from 1948 as a result of the Children Act. The house had previously been leased to the Holiday Fellowship (an organisation similar to the Youth Hostels Association) by the National Trust, and after the war the Fellowship was keen to reclaim it. But the county council could not find other premises for the children and held on to the property until 1951. Somerset County Council, minutes of the Children's Committee, 27 July 1948–2 December 1952, CH1/1, pp. 16, 385.

88   Interview with Deborah, 17 October 2016.

89   Interview with Ann, 28 November 2016.

90   Holnicote House Revised Register, November 1947, in possession of David Stanley.

91   Interview with Carol E, 3 May 2017.

92   Interview with Deborah, 17 October 2016.

93   Interview with Ann, 28 November 2016.

94   Email from Ann, 11 June 2018.

95   Telephone conversations with Barbara C, 9 November 2016; Margaret B, 21 October 2016; Elizabeth S, 8 June 2017.

96   Hendrick, *Child Welfare*, p. 133.

97   Interview with Deborah, 17 October 2016.

98   Ibid.

99   Interview with Carol E, 3 May 2017.

100   Interview with Leon's widow, Lesley, and daughter, Amy, 25 November 2016; *No Mother, No Father, No Uncle Sam* (dir. Sebastian Robinson, West HTV, 1988). Thanks to Ann for lending me this programme.

101   Letter from Elizabeth Mapstone to David Stanley, 25 February 1997, in possession of David Stanley. Ann, how-

ever, told me that one boy from Holnicote House was adopted, Norman.

102   Notes of meeting held at Home Office, 27 August 1945, quoted in Jenny Keating, *A Child for Keeps: The History of Adoption in England, 1918–45* (London, 2009), p. 187.

103   Interview with Richard, 31 March 2017.

104   See Hervieux, *Forgotten*.

105   Since 1974 Monmouthshire has been incorporated into Gwent Country Council.

106   Interview with Dave B, 13 April 2017. Claudia Soares points out in her study of the Waifs and Strays' Society, 1881–1914, that individual childcare homes had relative autonomy, and some of these homes did manage to convey a sense of homeliness. Claudia Soares, 'Neither Waif nor Stray: Home, Family and Belonging in the Victorian Children's Institution, 1881–1914', unpublished PhD thesis, University of Manchester, 2014.

107   See Higginbotham, *Children's Homes*. On the Waifs and Strays' Society, see Soares, 'Neither Waif nor Stray'. On Dr Barnardo's, see Rose, *For the Sake of the Children*.

108   St Clair Drake, 'The Brown Baby Problem', Box 60/15.

109   LCP quoted in Ronald Bedford, 'Coloured-barred babies', *Daily Mirror*, 22 July 1947.

110   Billy in John Burningham, *When We Were Young: A Compendium of Childhood* (London, 2004), pp. 259–60.

111   Interview with David M, 8 December 2016.

112   Burningham, *When We Were Young*, p. 261.

113   Interview with Billy, 12 November 2016.

114   Margaret Kornitzer, *Adoption & Family Life* (London, 1968), p. 131.

115   Rose, *For the Sake of the Children*, pp. 262–3.

116   Interview with David M, 8 December 2016.

117   Thanks to Denise Riley for pointing this out.

118   *Maternal Care and Mental Health* was a 1951 report for the World Health Organization. On the influence of Bowlby's ideas after the Second World War, see Denise Riley, *War in the Nursery: Theories of the Child and Mother* (London, 1983).

119   Anna Freud and Sophie Dann, 'An experiment in group upbringing', *Psychoanalytic Study of the Child*, 6 (1951), pp. 127–8. Thanks to Angela Joyce for sending me this.

120   Interview with David M, 8 December 2016. Abuse in children's homes was not, of course, unique to this period. See Higginbotham, *Children's Homes*, pp. 257–69; Stevenson, *Interim Report on Child Abuse*.

121   *The Administration of Children's Homes Regulations* (1951) no.

1217, regulation 11.

122   Quoted in Hendrick, *Child Welfare*, p. 134.

123   Interview with David M, 8 December 2016.

124   Interview with David M, 8 December 2016.

125   Baker, 'Lest We Forget', p. 46. Chesser writes about 'love starvation' leading to 'retarded emotional growth' as one of the disabilities suffered by children brought up in institutions; Chesser, *Unwanted Child*, pp. 15, 47.

126   Letter from E. Wilden to A. R. Vaughan, secretary of the Church of England Children's Society, 6 May 1948, Archives of the Church of England Children's Society (in James's possession, as are all the correspondence and reports mentioned below relating to James).

127   Letter from James's mother to the Church of England Children's Society, 1 February 1950.

128   Letter from James's mother to the Society, 6 December 1948.

129   Letter from James's mother to the Society, 6 January 1949.

130   Letter from G. F. Flynn to Colonel E. St J. Birnie, 13 July 1950.

131   Letter from James's mother to Colonel E. St J. Birnie, 22 August 1950.

132   There is a parallel here with Elizabeth Anionwu, born in 1947, the daughter of a Nigerian man and a white British woman, who was placed in a children's home until her mother got married (not to Elizabeth's father) and reclaimed her, aged nine. Anionwu, *Mixed Blessings*.

133   April and November 1949, Church of England Children's Society Reports, signed by J. Hoggarth, Beckett Nursery, Meanwood.

134   14 October 1950, Church of England Children's Society Report, signed G. F. Flynn, Bede House, Wakefield, and see reports of March 1950, March and October 1951 and March 1952.

135   Letter from G. F. Flynn to Mr Board, 11 May 1953.

136   Higginbotham, *Children's Homes*, p. 117.

137   Interview with James A, 19 April 2016.

138   Telephone interview with Sandi H, 21 February 2015; interview, 29 April 2016.

139   Telephone conversations with Celia, 15 February and 23 March 2017.

140   Rose, *For the Sake of the Children*, pp. 203, 252.

141   Lydia Murdoch, *Imagined Orphans* (New Brunswick, NJ, 2006), p. 149.

142   Ibid., pp. 25–32.

143   See Bressey, 'Forgotten histories'. For the extensive literature on the

racialisation of the British poor, see Murdoch, *Imagined Orphans*, p. 177, n. 66.

144   For the presence of black girls in Barnardo's Victorian records, see Bressey, 'Forgotten histories'. In an archive of 40,000 portrait images, she found twenty-six young black girls. On 'washing' white, see Shurlee Swain and Margo Hillel, *Child, Nation, Race and Empire* (Manchester, 2010), p. 83.

145   Phil Frampton was another Barnardo's mixed-race child who struggled to get access to his files. He was born in 1953. 'It took a year of anger, MPs' letters, several solicitors' notes and a near-fatal illness in November 1998 to force Barnardo's into agreeing to hand over my files'; Frampton, *The Golly*, p. 1. Under 1987 legislation children who have been in local authority care are entitled to see their files, but this does not apply to voluntary organisations such as Barnardo's.

146   See Soares, 'Neither Waif nor Stray'.

147   Hamilton, *Notice Me!*, p. 10.

148   Amanda Jones, 'The Wartime Child in Women's Fiction and Psychoanalysis 1930–1960', unpublished PhD thesis, Anglia Ruskin University, 2015, p. 194.

149   Hamilton, *Notice Me!*, p. 10.

150   Similarly, when 'brown baby' Beatrice was fostered, she behaved badly, which Pamela Winfield suggests was due to a sense of insecurity; Winfield, *Bye Bye Baby*, p. 96.

151   Hamilton, *Notice Me!*, pp. 16, 10, 149, 31.

152   Referred to as 'commodity racism' in Anne McClintock, *Imperial Leather: Race, Gender and Sexuality in the Colonial Context* (New York, 1995), pp. 207–31. See also Anandi Ramamurthy, *Imperial Persuaders: Images of Africa and Asia in British Advertising* (Manchester, 2003), pp. 24–62.

153   Barnardo's, *Racial Integration and Barnardo's*, p. 4. According to Barnardo's Mr Wellbank, in 1944 they were getting 'about one ["coloured" child] every other day'. 'Report of Conference on position of illegitimate child', MH 55/1656, TNA.

154   Barnardo's, *Racial Integration and Barnardo's*, p. 5.

155   Interview with Dave B, 13 April 2017.

156   Interview with Adrian, 1 September 2014.

157   Telephone interview with Roger, 1 September 2014.

158   Baker, 'Lest We Forget', p. 43.

159   From Brian L's website: www.muskogee.007.com.

160   Interview with Billy, 12 November 2016.

161   'Secretary of State to give directions limiting the number of children who may at any one time be accommodated in any particular home',

Children Act 1948, p. 873.

162   Sali Hughes, 'Homelessness is not a free choice: I know it's miserable and exhausting', *The Guardian*, 9 December 2017, p. 16. See recent Barnardo's initiatives to address this problem: http://www.barnardos.org.uk/what_we_do/policy_research_unit/resea rch_and_publications/leaving_care_research.htm   (accessed   14 December 2018). Thanks to Annie Hudson for this link.

4

Adoption, fostering and attempts to send the babies to the US

The last chapter indicated that the adoption of British 'brown babies' was relatively unusual. Adoption societies assumed that no one would want such children, so presumably did not make much effort to find adopters. Further, a kind of 'same race' policy was effectively in operation, with white people's attempts to adopt a mixed-race child deemed inappropriate and 'sentimental'. In addition, everyone involved in the adoption process noted that most adopters preferred girls, so it was even harder for mixed-race boys to find adopters. Of the forty-five 'brown babies' that I am primarily focusing on, only four were adopted by non-relatives, one was adopted by his US father and several were adopted by their grandparents, while a few were fostered.

Fosterings good and bad and a scuppered adoption

Tony M, born in May 1946, was placed as a baby in a Barnardo's home in Essex, of which he has no memory, but aged five he was taken to Balsham, a village in Cambridgeshire, and fostered by a white couple who had already fostered twelve other Barnardo's children. Tony was never adopted but stayed very happily with this big family throughout his childhood. He called the couple 'Mum' and 'Dad' and the other children were his brothers and sisters: 'I just went for a holiday and it went on for fifteen years.' His wife Mari elaborates: 'I think you were an angry little child … and you used to sit under the table and scream … and the dad actually picked you up … and just hugged you and said, "This little boy just needs loving".' Tony was the only mixed-race child in the family and indeed in the village, but he says he did not feel different at the time. He has never wanted to find his birth mother or father: 'I just want them [his children] to know their father had a happy upbringing in Balsham … Why bring other complications into it?'[1]

Babs was not so fortunate in her fostering. She was born in October 1944 in Ipswich, Suffolk. Her father worked in the US Airforce's Engineer Battalion and was based in East Anglia for up to eighteen months. As mentioned in Chapter 2, when Babs was born her married mother was able to pass her off as her husband's because she initially had light skin, but after six months she darkened. Of the photograph shown here Babs comments: 'I think the only way that I can describe the look on my face is one of surliness and mistrust'. She was sent to a Barnardo's home in Long Melford, Suffolk for four years.

> Then this family came to foster me and what happened there was my foster mother was married to a widower and he'd had six children and after the birth of his last child his wife had actually developed post-natal depression and she committed suicide … he asked if she [the foster mother] would be willing to marry him but it was really he wanted a house parent thing for his children, and so it was a marriage not based on affection but on convenience and so she raised all these children. What happened then was when the sixth one was approaching school-leaving age, she had been married to him for quite some time and there was no sign of her having any children and I think she began to feel that the home was going to be very empty and so they decided that they would foster.

Babs's new brothers and sisters were nice to her, as initially were her foster parents, but she was subjected to racism in the neighbourhood and in her school. 'I'd never seen anyone that looked like me in the area and sometimes when I wanted to play outside with other children their parents wouldn't let them play with me and the kids would tell me "My dad says I'm not to play with you".' This was a familiar story for many of the 'brown babies'. The school was particularly awful:

> there was a teacher in the school when I was in Sudbury, he was obviously very racist and I hated this school and one day … he sat me at the back of the school classroom and he gave me a box of jigsaw pieces to play with and turned around and announced to the rest of the children that I didn't have the same ability to learn and so all I knew what to do was to play and they could be taught … I

4.1 Babs

was about six or seven … Then there was a geography class and the children had to put together this … it was like a plasticine model of a desert island scene which they made out of pipe cleaners and made palm trees … and created climbers that were climbing for coconuts and he turned around and he said to these children when it was time to have a classroom break, we should go out and they should ask me to show them how I can climb a pole like a monkey … I was quite angry with him then and I just said to them 'I am not coming back to this school again.'[2]

Such underestimation in British schools of black children's intelligence continues to this day.[3]

All was not well at Babs's foster home either. She remembers always being hungry and losing weight; she was not fed properly and ate other children's leftovers at school. Yet her foster parents were paid well by Dr Barnardo's to look after her. Then there was her foster father: 'he used to make a fuss of me' but when she was ten 'there came an occasion when I was sitting on his lap and he attempted to molest me'.[4] It was very probably more than simply an 'attempt'. One day at school a child slapped her playfully on the backside and it hurt much more than it should have. A doctor examined her and discovered an abscess. Babs cannot remember her foster father actually abusing her, but her abscess points to it, and she later found out that he sexually abused his birth children. What is more, he had been under suspicion for the drowning of his first wife in the river Stour; it was possibly not suicide at all.[5]

Aged ten-and-a-half Babs was taken away from her foster home:

the social worker for Barnado's that used to come and do periodic visits … one day she just came and she said to me, 'You've never been away to the seaside for a holiday have you?' and I said, 'No' because we lived very much in farmland [her foster father was a farm labourer] … she said to me, 'Would you like to go on this holiday to the seaside, it's a camp with lots of other boys and girls?' and she said, 'It's for three weeks.' So of course naturally who wouldn't want to go? … I had a really, really good time.

She was made to work though: 'I don't think I've washed so many pairs of knickers as I have on that holiday … there used to be about thirty pairs every morning.' Then on the last day of the holiday, 'the house parents called me and they told me that the following day I wasn't going home any more you see, and I looked at them and couldn't understand why not and then I thought I must have done something wrong'. She was taken to another Barnardo's home: 'it had seven feet high walls round the perimeter'.

All of the lovely clothes that my foster mother had suddenly bestowed upon me [before she left for her holiday], they were all taken from me and I was just put in grey socks and very coarse clothes with no kind of personality about the dress sense or anything and that happened to every child, not just to me, and you weren't allowed to have anything of your own … so it was very depersonalising really.

Years later she found out that she had been taken away from her foster parents because

when the social worker came to visit the house they found me on my own and of course they were being paid quite a generous sum and I think with retrospect … it was probably a good thing that I was taken away when I was because of the behaviour of my foster father.[6]

Babs now wonders if in fact his behaviour was known about by Barnardo's and that was the real reason for her removal.[7]

Richard also had an unsuccessful fostering. He was in a local authority children's home in Barnstaple, North Devon, but when he was eight he was fostered by a couple living on a farm, the Bs, where he was used as unpaid child labour, working with chickens, cows, pigs and sheep.

> I wasn't allowed to speak until I was told to … they fed me … there wasn't no love there … They wanted somebody to work the farm. And I was so tired … I really didn't take much notice of school at all. Not at all. Never passed a *thing* in school.

He ran away when he was fourteen: 'I was told to go into the field in the middle of the village and pick up the swedes from the ground. Well it was freezing. It was cold and it was ice. And my hands were just dropping off, my legs were just freezing.' So he retreated indoors but the farmer found him and 'he kicked me. And when he kicked me that was the end of it. It was raining. And I ran all the way into Barnstaple, to the Victoria Chambers. To the children's services place.'[8] However, Richard went back to the farm after about six weeks as he was worried about Mrs B's safety, since her husband used to hit her. Despite being only fourteen, Richard felt protective towards her. The following year, when he left school, they refused to pay him anything, and as he was never treated as a family member, he left them for good.

Sandi H was in a children's home in Bristol. When she was thirteen she was fostered by a white family in Gloucestershire.

> They had two other daughters, and I was in between them. I was three years older than the youngest, and seven years younger than the oldest. So, I didn't even gel with either of them. But I'm sure they done it for the right reasons, and I think I was there … till I was about seventeen … And I *knew* I didn't fit in – I knew I didn't belong there.

She got blamed for the youngest child's actions. She never called her foster parents Mum and Dad. They used to say to her: 'After all we've done for you.' Sandi would run away back to the children's home, as she missed her friends. The fostering was not a success.

The year after she was fostered she suddenly realised that she was black.

> In this [children's] home, there was two other black kids there. The rest of the hundred kids were white. So, I knew I was different, but I couldn't understand what it was … I didn't know I was black till I was about fourteen … One morning I looked in the mirror and I saw a black face looking back at me … and I was shocked. And I went running round to me mates. And I said: 'Why didn't you *tell* me? I'm black, aren't I?' And that's how dumb – 'dumb' might not be the right word, but that's how uninformed I was about anything.

People had said racist things to her throughout her childhood: 'But it was just a word that you knew had an effect on me … "blackie" was the term in them days. They used to say it to me, and I'd say it back – yeah – "*You're* the blackie as well".' Her experience was similar to that of Pauline Nevins, discussed in Chapter 2. Sandi experienced the name calling but like Pauline she did not internalise it, and did not recognise the nature of her 'difference' until she was older. When Sandi was nearly seventeen, she wanted to leave the foster home so she joined the navy.[9]

Dave B was fostered several times, but

> I didn't want to leave the home, you know? I liked it so much … I was a bit of a problem. I used to bed-wet … when I was taken away … Maybe it was me saying, 'I don't want to stay here. I want to make life as difficult as possible.' And I used to scream.[10]

However, looking at the records of his children's homes, which Dave has recently obtained, a rather different picture emerges. It appears that in two cases out of four the placements broke down for reasons that were nothing to do with his behaviour. He was first fostered when he was six by the Wilkses, who were Baptists and asked specifically for a boy, 'preferably coloured', for 'Mrs Wilks is very keen on a boy to bring up and train as a missionary or to train for the ministry'. This sounds similar to the objectives of Montgomery, discussed in the previous chapter. Despite initially having asked for a permanent placement, the Wilkses returned Dave to the home after three months because they could not cope with the 'temper tantrums' that had arisen in the previous two weeks. There was no attempt to address what was behind these tantrums. Dave's second fostering placement was when he was nearly nine. Mrs Davies, who he called 'Gran', also a Baptist, unfortunately became ill after three months and Dave was moved to her friends, the Wises, for six months. This was again a success until the Wises had to move in with Mrs Wise's mother, who 'is a semi-invalid and seems to be extraordinarily jealous of David'. He was then back in the children's home for two years, although he stayed with Mrs Davies in the summer holidays and for both Christmases. Then in September 1956, when he was aged eleven-and-a-half, he moved back to Mrs Davies, who pronounced that she 'would like to have David permanently ... He is no trouble at all.' But the following September she said she could no longer cope. The boarding-out officer, who visited all fostered children monthly, reported that during the fortnight away in a caravan with Mrs Davies and two of her grandchildren, 'David spent most of the fortnight crying and being difficult and is growing persistently enuretic.' The boarding-out officer was worried: 'David's relationship with his "gran" is the only emotional relationship of any depth he has experienced and the breakdown of this home is severe in its implications.'[11] Rather than his time in the children's homes, Dave now thinks back to this period with Mrs Davies as 'probably my happiest time ... I remember those days fondly ... she was so patient and caring'.[12] So what had gone wrong?

How are we to understand Dave's crying and bed-wetting, given that he loved living with Mrs Davies? His three previous fosterings had ended abruptly. This is likely to have contributed to a sense of insecurity on Dave's part. He was surely struggling with feelings of rejection – rejected by both his biological and foster parents. His sense of being unwanted along with a sense of being different – one of the few children of colour in the area – must have contributed to his despair. He would have wanted to stay with Mrs Davies but could not believe it possible, so he made it not possible – a self-fulfilling prophecy. As for the bed-wetting, the fact that it came about towards the end of a year with Mrs Davies suggests anxiety that the new home would not continue – it was 'too good to be true', so it could not be true. After all, he had been returned to the children's home after all his other summer holidays with Mrs Davies. Despite the disruption of the different fostering placements, Dave did very well at school; when he left at fifteen he was second overall out of a class of thirty-nine.

Jim H, who was in Fazakerley Cottage Homes in Liverpool, was never fostered, and although he had the chance of being adopted, the adoption was scuppered by the reappearance of his grandmother. When he was fourteen, in May 1958, his photograph appeared in a local newspaper because he had found a wallet full of money in a telephone box and handed it in to the police. He was living in the children's home but went to school outside: 'I made friends in school with one particularly good friend ... his mum and dad wanted to adopt me ... I was quite happy to do that ... and then obviously my grandmother had seen the picture [in the newspaper] ... and made a claim.' He had to go and live with her: 'I didn't have any option really.' His grandmother wanted Jim now that he had nearly reached school-leaving age (he was fifteen in September) because he could start to earn.[13] He would have much preferred to have been adopted: 'I wanted to go with the people who were going to adopt me ... They cared about me.' Jim had discovered that he had a talent for playing golf: 'I'd started my golf in the home and I'd wanted to get into golf ... I'd been offered a job at Bootle Golf Course as an assistant then on a wage of one pound seventeen shillings and sixpence.' But his grandmother insisted that he get

> a proper job and my first job was working in ... Collingson Cutsole factory on a wage of three pounds, nineteen shillings and sixpence ... I had the nineteen shillings and sixpence and of course the three pounds went towards my keep. So, I couldn't do what I wanted to do.

He left his grandparents and went to live with an aunt and her children, and then joined the army.[14]

Adoption success

Unlike Jim H, Tony H was very happily adopted. His married mother, who already had two boys, had an affair with a black GI who was based at Burtonwood air base, near Warrington in Cheshire, working as a driver for the station commander. They met in the Bluebell pub in Burtonwood while her husband was away fighting and she gave birth to Tony in January 1945. 'He [Tony's father, Harold] had been to the hospital at Whiston and saw me there … He said to my mother: "Would you call him Raymond?" Because that's his [Harold's] father's name.' (Tony uses his second name, Anthony.) Harold came to Tony's christening, but after that he never saw Tony again. On his return, the husband 'took his two sons away from his wife and they were brought up by an aunty or their grandmother, I believe … She [Tony's mother] was ostracised … From what I gather, I was taken off her. It was a case of "You can't look after it yourself."'

Until the age of seven Tony was in children's homes in Bury in Lancashire and then in Newcastle. Preston Children's Department moved him from Bury to Newcastle because he minded being the only non-white child, though the Newcastle home was also exclusively white. The homes economised on clothes, as was similarly experienced by Babs:

> They had this system where they would virtually farm you out on weekends from the orphanages and they'd send you out with any old clothes. The local good people, the citizens – there was clothing rationing, and the likes of that – they would take the children for the weekend, local from where you lived – they would obviously kit you up with clothes that their children had … And when I was taken back to the orphanage … all the new clothes I had was taken off me. I do remember that. I had an issue with clothes. Because then I was given my old clothes back, and so, from what people I've spoken to … I was a thief, I was. And *I* think I was taking back my own clothes!

The home also economised on haircuts:

> They used to put this pudding basin over your head … you'd line up and cut your hair. And I had woolly hair and I used to look stupid after this. You know, most people look stupid with a pudding hair-cut, but in an orphanage, as you can imagine, you know, you just got chh-chh – guy's doing it for free, so they're happy, and I used to get upset about it. And one particular time there was a coloured guy there … I wouldn't let him go![15]

This was one of the first black people Tony had seen and he immediately identified with him, but the man was only there briefly.

In October 1951, when Tony was six, his mother wrote to the Newcastle home that she 'longed to keep him and work for him, but it was so difficult … I have been thinking if he could be adopted it would be better for himself.'[16] Since the 1939 Adoption Act, which came into effect in 1943, only local authorities and adoption societies could legally arrange adoptions. The government was aware of the difficulties in procuring adoptions for mixed-race children. For example, an April 1947 Foreign Office memo noted:

> legally of course the position of girls who had half-caste bastards is no different to that of the ones who had white ones. In practice of course, it is much harder for the HO [Home Office] to get the children adopted, which is in many cases the best solution, or even to get them into children's homes.[17]

Recognising this difficulty led Preston Children's Department to seek help from the LCP in finding an adoptive family for Tony. The reply was discouraging:

> Unfortunately, the coloured people in Great Britain, with few exceptions, fall into two groups: the students, who are young and unmarried, and who will return to their homes in the colonies … when they have completed their studies, and the manual workers or artisan class, who are living with their wives and families, who are not, as a rule, in a position to feed another child. The bulk of the coloured middle class remain … in their own colony. Thus, you see, the difficulty in getting the little boy adopted by those of his own colour. As regards adoption by white people, this does happen from time to time and from all that we hear it has been successful to date, but here again the call is for orphan girl babies and not for boys, as any adoption society can tell you.[18]

Despite this gloomy forecast, in December 1952 a potential adoptive couple were found for Tony. Eugene had come over from Jamaica during the war to join the RAF and had stayed; Iva had travelled with their young son Bobby on the *Empire Windrush* in June 1948 to join him, and they were living in Nelson, Lancashire. Once the cricketer Learie Constantine left in 1949, they were the town's only black family. Tony arrived with ill-fitting shoes: 'When I went to live with the Hs, at seven years of age, I had a pair of shoes that were size nine. They were that big, they didn't fit me until I was twelve, and that's a fact … that's one of the standing jokes.' Another issue was 'I was enuretic … wet the bed *continuously* – I did that until about eleven … and that was a *problem*.' But his adoptive mother was very relaxed about it: 'she was more: "Oh well, maybe tomorrow"'. (If the potential adoptees of Suzi, mentioned in the last chapter, had also been relaxed about the bed-wetting, perhaps the placements might have been a success.) The Hs, who already had a son a year older than Tony (Bobby) but wanted another child, treated the boys exactly the same: 'a typical example: the first bike we got was a tandem!' His new parents were strict but very loving; when they applied to adopt Tony in March 1959 (having fostered him for the previous six years), the reason they gave was that 'they love the lad and want to do what is best for him'.[19] Tony defines himself as African-Caribbean, not African-American, because of his strong identification with his Jamaican family.[20]

Preston Children's Department was not the only organisation to write to the LCP to ask advice about finding adoptive and foster

4.2 Tony H on the right with his adoptive mother and brother

families. The *Daily Mirror* collaborated with the LCP on an article in July 1947 entitled 'Colour-barred babies'. The article opened by declaring: 'There are 750 happy, healthy boy and girl babies in Britain that nobody wants. They are the children born during the war years to married and unmarried British women and American Negro soldiers.' The article ends with the rousing challenge: 'Won't YOU take a coloured kiddie into your home?'[21] For many the answer was 'Yes' as letters (over a hundred) began to stream into the LCP office. A year later the LCP had arranged three cases of fostering and thirteen successful adoptions, with a further two under way.[22] By this time they had received nearly 300 requests.[23] However, as was pointed out in the last chapter, the LCP's attempts to find adoptive families for the babies came up against what I have suggested was a form of 'same race' policy. The organisation was also not helped by the negative attitude of 'one of the most important social workers in Britain', who 'believed that *any* coloured child in an otherwise white community is virtually unassimilable'.[24] 'Assimilation' in relation to people in Britain is generally used to refer to *cultural* assimilation, but here the idea appears to have been that a child of colour, despite not bringing with her/him any specific cultural attributes, could not be absorbed into, or become part of, British society – a 'white community' – simply because of skin colour.

It was not just the social workers who were a problem: one LCP official was worried that some families were 'just seeking to train up a docile servant'. This appears to have been the case with Richard. The LCP official felt that 'many of the white families would "cool off" after more serious reflection'.[25] It did not help that 'some people have a very rigid concept of the type of child they want. Most people prefer girls … Very young children are seldom desired.'[26] This latter point is in stark contrast to today, where the younger the child the more desirable he or she is to adopters, due to an emphasis on the need for early attachment. I do not know how many of the nearly three hundred people asking to adopt were successful, the LCP's three fosterings and fifteen adoptions meeting only a fraction of the overall requests.

Holnicote House adoptions

By 1949 Somerset County Council had thirty-one 'brown babies' in its care (the previous year it had had forty-five, so possibly it had managed to get fourteen adopted or fostered); about half of these were at Holnicote House. In April that year Somerset County Council's children's committee minuted that well over a hundred applications had been received to adopt or foster the children. Six months later, according to the journalist Lisa Moynihan, not one child had been placed with any of these British families. The Somerset children's committee officer gave his views to Moynihan – views which he believed were 'shared by at least 90% "of middle class people" and 75% of "the working classes"'. According to Moynihan, the officer claimed that:

> It is impossible to deny that a colour bar exists in England ... I like many coloured people but I wouldn't want my own children to marry them ... Even the small numbers who profess to have no colour bar and offer to adopt children may, I feel, often do so rather as a child would choose a quaint and unusual toy.[27]

There is a similarity here to labelling as 'sickly sentimentality' the motives of Rosa's potential adopters, mentioned in the last chapter.

In March 1949 Kathleen Tacchi-Morris, a dancer who ran a progressive, international school in North Curry, Somerset, offered to educate twelve of Somerset's 'brown babies' in exchange for the cost of their keep. A wide-ranging education would be offered free of charge, including music, horse-riding, languages and the opportunity to travel abroad. To quote the cultural critic Hazel Carby: 'She believed in an education which integrated the body and mind, that enabled artistic expression of the highest order built upon an intellectual foundation free from religious dogma and punishment.'[28] Tacchi-Morris told the *Daily Mirror* in March 1949 that 'I have not heard the result of my offer, but it looks as if I might have to fight to get the children.'[29] The clerk of the county council, having seen the article, wrote to her that very day to say that 'no application had been received and can't be considered until one has'. She also received abusive letters; for example, an anonymous one verbally spat at her: 'So you want to keep in this country the nigger bastards of near-prostitutes? You are the kind of woman who is making England unfit for white people!'[30] The council turned her application down with no explanation. She did not give up and a year later offered to foster one of the children, but this too was dismissed. Active in the anti-nuclear warfare movement, in the 1950s she founded Women for World Disarmament. She was a remarkable woman but her radicalism was clearly too much for the conservative Somerset County Council.

A number of adoptions from Holnicote House did, however, occur. One such was Ann, who was happily fostered by a couple in South Wales when she was five; a few years later the couple adopted her. They already had four boys.

> My mum had had a little girl, and she had spina bifida and fluid to the brain [and died at six months], and she was desperate for a girl. And her parents said, 'There's a photograph in the paper of all these little babies that had been left behind with the GIs. If you want a girl that bad, why don't you adopt one of those?' And one [of the sons] who was in the army at the time doing his National Service, he picked me out the same as Mam picked me ... out of the newspaper.

Ann 'couldn't have asked for better parents' and her four much older brothers were also lovely. Her parents never told her that she was adopted.

> They never told me a thing ... Until I was thirteen and this elderly lady said to me about how I should go back where I belong, and then I said, 'And where is that supposed to be?' 'You niggers are all the same', she said. 'And Mr. and Mrs. G are not your mother and father.' So I went home and told my parents, and ... my father said, 'I really think it's time we sat down and talked to Ann.' And my mother said, 'No. No, I can't do that,' she said. I think she was afraid she'd lose me ... And I went down to my grandmother and told her. She sat me down. Oh – she sat me on her lap, actually. And she said, 'Does it really matter? Does it really matter?' she said. 'We all love you. And we wouldn't be without you for anything. So it doesn't really matter.'

Ann's experience was not atypical: a study of people adopted in the period from the 1920s to the 1950s found that the majority learned of their adoptions not from their parents but from other people.[31] Ann's mother never wanted to admit to Ann that she was adopted: 'when I got married at eighteen, my father gave me my adoption papers, and my mother took them off me and said: "The day you don't want to call me 'Mam' will be the day you can have these back." And I said,

"That will never be."' When Ann was about to marry, the neighbour who had shouted 'You niggers are all the same' at her 'asked me about an invitation to my wedding: "Where's my invitation?" I said, "What invitation?" "You're getting married." "Yes," I said, "well, you haven't got one." I thought, "Over my dead body you're having an invitation!"' There were a few racist neighbours like this woman, but Ann never experienced any racism in her family until she married a miner and they had to live initially with his parents:

> Well, his mother didn't like me because I was the wrong colour … She said: 'Well, you should marry people of your own race and colour.' … She said that she didn't want no niggers as grandchildren … When I told her I was pregnant [she said]: 'I hope you die, *and* the baby.' And when I had the baby, the baby was stillborn. And I said, 'Well she's had her wish. Only thing is, I'm still here.'

Ann went on to have four other children and her mother-in-law was loving towards them but never accepted Ann.[32]

Another child of Holnicote House, Deborah, was adopted when she was nearly five. Deborah, along with a younger girl from the home, was taken on a long journey:

> I was just absolutely baffled and confused. I had no idea what was happening or why it was happening. All I know is that I was leaving Holnicote House … And there was another girl going with me as well … The actual process of going from Holnicote House to Leigh [in Essex] was very traumatic to me emotionally – very. And I can recall that very clearly. I remember not knowing who I was with – and this man, who was my adopted father … and one of the nurses came with us as well, and we went on this incredible journey. I mean, I think the only train journey we'd been on before was to Minehead or Weston-Super-Mare … I'd never been on a train for so long. And it just seemed endless, endless … And I remember getting more and more anxious about it all.

Her adoptive parents were Sid and Queenie.

> Queen Elizabeth her name was, and that's absolutely true. She was a seamstress – a very good one. And he was in, broadly speaking,

4.3 Deborah

sales and wholesale. They lived in a nice, three-bedroomed semi in Leigh-on-Sea, which post-war was pretty nice. But the interesting thing, which you'll find amazing, was that she was black! And she was the daughter of a merchant seaman. The family didn't really approve of her, being black … She was in show business … Dancing on stage – all that kind of thing. But the sad thing about Queenie – she absolutely hated being black. She hated her colour … she hated being black. She was ashamed of it … which was very sad, actually, because it made me ashamed of it for a while.

Holnicote House's matron, Miss Bowerman, visited them soon after their arrival at their new home, commenting that 'it is wonderful to see them so happily settled'.[33] But Deborah was not happily settled at all.

I had the advantage of being brought up in a family I looked as if I could have belonged to, whereas a lot didn't … but … I didn't get a sense of love ... And I suppose for the first time in my life I started to feel anxious, in fact I had nightmares, apparently, for months and months and months.

The anxiety was partly to do with her new sister, Corinne, also from Holnicote House but nearly two years younger, who 'just seemed to do everything to hurt me'.

It must have been hard for my mum and dad. Because here were these two girls that were supposed to be nice little siblings – sisters together, and we were just at each other all the time. Well, she was at me. She used to beat me, she used to throw me, chase me round the garden, she used to threaten me with dead mice because, you know, I was terrified of them – everything! It was horrible![34]

Then there was school:

The first time I ever heard the 'N' word was at school ... unfortunately Sid and Queenie – again they must have had good intentions – they sent us to a private school. That was probably the worst thing they could have done. Because I can remember other mothers telling their daughters not to play with us. I can remember that, you know? I can remember other kids looking and saying: 'Why are you black?' and then the 'N' word.

After about a year they were taken out and sent to an ordinary state school.

There was still name calling. Whether I'd toughened up by then, I don't know. But do you know the hardest thing was not knowing why I was different ... if you've got an identity that includes being black, you should be proud of it – proud of that. She [her mother] was in denial or trying to reject it. So, I had no explanation ... The thing I never used to get used to was ... being pointed at in shops ... 'Mummy, why is that girl black?' 'Mummy look at that black girl over there!' or 'Mummy, look at that "N"!'

She was devastated not to pass her 11-plus:

I wanted to be clever. But at the same time, I spent my childhood existence learning just to be accepted. I can remember in a playground situation once – you know how girls sit around … And somebody was asking me: 'Why is your hair like that? Why are you coloured?' We didn't call each other 'black' in those days … I said: 'Oh, 'cause I'm from Peru.' [Laughs] And I got a bit of cred for that, you know? 'I'm from Peru.' And I did well! I mean, I became a prefect, I did well at being accepted, and gained in popularity.

To be from Peru sounded special: she was not a British 'colonial' or a 'negro' but from a South American country that had been home to the Incas. But things were not good with her parents:

There was a lot of nastiness. I mean you'd call it abuse now, but it was punishment, really. But they were pretty nasty things they did, my mum – and my father, even nastier. [Laughs nervously] And I know that's not uncommon, but it was still horrid. I think he started on Corinne first, and, I don't know why, but then he moved onto me. And … ugh … just … ugh … hated it.[35]

Janet J, also at Holnicote House, was born in October 1945 and adopted at four-and-a-half by a couple who lived in Leytonstone, East London. Holnicote House's matron was delighted at the adoption: she wrote to the couple: 'I just could not bear the thought of my lovely little Jan being brought up in a children's home … with grateful thanks for all you are doing for Janet.'[36] Her adoptive parents, both white, told Janet she was adopted when she was about seven. 'And that was the end. Nothing was ever spoke again.' According to the historian Deborah Cohen, telling a child once about adoption and then never mentioning it again was fairly common in the 1950s.[37] Janet's adoptive parents were home-owners and both worked as managers, her father in a furniture store, her mother in a pie-and-eel shop, having worked her way up from being in service at the age of thirteen. Janet was given lots of presents. 'I remember dolls being bought. I remember my first doll was a doll that stood up, and it was taller than me! … I can remember another time when I had … twin black dolls. Not many black dolls in that time.' Her mother took great pride in her own and Janet's appearance. 'Ages she would take, to get my hair like that … It's not tight-curly … [it's like] Shirley Temple.' (The

1930s Hollywood child actress had ringlets as well as the bows that
Suzi Hamilton so detested.) From the photograph reproduced here,
it looks as if Janet's mother tried to align their hairstyles so that there
would be a visual similarity. Janet was a shy child, but 'my mother
liked to put me on show'. 'I didn't want to get out of the car [when
they arrived anywhere] because people always were staring.' Unlike
Deborah, she did not experience the stares as hostile. Janet's daughter
Karen suggests that people

> might not have actually known that Mum was black. Because even
> now some people don't know. Well, lots of people will never guess
> where Mum is from. And that's all to do with hair … [she] has wavy,

4.4 Janet J with her adoptive mother

wavy hair that is not afro … And therefore you didn't get the name calling. Whereas I did as a child [Karen is black with tighter-curled hair] … They had an image of what a black person looked like, and it's to do with hair.

This issue of 'what a black person looked like' came up a lot in relation to the 'brown babies' as well as their children. For example, when Carole T's daughter, who has light brown skin and curly hair, was at nursery school in the 1960s, she was called racist names. Carole

went to the head mistress and she said, 'Oh Mrs T … I'm sorry to hear that … but to be honest … I've never even thought of you like that … I would never have known.' You know, a lot of people say that to me now: 'I didn't even think of you as directly black. We just think you've got a nice colour.'[38]

This issue of 'what a black person looked like' and how it was/is centrally related to a combination of skin tone and hair will be returned to in the last chapter.

Janet J's adoptive mother was over-protective, while her father was more easygoing. 'My mother was very … strict … and OCD [obsessive–compulsive disorder].'

I never had friends home. I was the little girl that played in the back garden … Never can play on the street, never encouraged friends to come to the house … Everybody's riding bikes. But 'No, you can't have a bike.' And I did manage to get a pair of roller skates, but, 'You can't go on the road with it.' So I used to go up and down the path in my little back garden … being an only child and not being allowed to socialise with other children.

Her mother fostered Nigerian babies, but only until they were about three years old, and so too young to become Janet's playmates. 'And then they [the parents] finished their studies … and then obviously they go back home. So they would come and they go.'[39] But her mother made friends with another local white family (they were then living in Romford) whose daughter Pauline was also adopted and mixed-race. Although eight years Janet's junior, they became friends; Pauline was Pauline Black, later the singer in the ska band The Selecter.[40]

Attempts to send the 'brown babies' to the US

Given the difficulties in finding homes for mixed-race children in Britain, Somerset's superintendent health visitor Celia Bangham was keen to arrange their adoption by their putative fathers, near relatives or other 'coloured' families in the US. As far as I can discover, Somerset was the only council to attempt to seek adoptions in the US. Why it was alone in this is unclear, but Bangham appears to have taken this on as her special mission. On 13 December 1945 the Home Secretary, James Chuter Ede, met with Bangham and Victor Collins, MP for Taunton, to discuss the US adoption possibility. Chuter Ede was unenthusiastic: he worried about 'the appalling discrimination made in many parts of the US against coloured people'. He also explained the legal position on adoption: under British law (the 1939 Adoption Act) children were only allowed to be sent abroad to live with British subjects or relatives. African-American couples who came forward to adopt were thus excluded from consideration, and since they were only deemed 'putative' fathers (DNA testing for paternity did not come into being until the 1960s), the black GIs were not considered to be relatives. Sending the children to the US would thus necessitate an amendment to the Act. The Home Secretary simply announced that he 'would consider what could be done constructively to deal with the matter', thereby putting it on hold.[41]

The possibility of sending mixed-race GI babies to the US had been raised at the December 1944 conference. Miss Steel of the Church of England Moral Welfare Council thought the suggestion 'very cruel … it would add to their sense of being unwanted, not only the sense that their mothers had given them up but the country where they were born'. Mr Wellbank of Dr Barnardo's agreed: 'It is not a good idea that they should be exported. We should get over the colour problem.'[42] In February 1945 a Sarah Moyse sent a letter to the wife of the US president, Eleanor Roosevelt, suggesting that some of the children could be schooled in the US. Eleanor Roosevelt approached her husband, who abruptly replied: 'This is a British problem – not American.'[43] As Plummer rightly suggests, 'the shedding of paternal responsibility was a proxy for the shedding of national responsibility'.[44] Certain British government officials appear to have agreed with the American president. After the meeting with Chuter Ede in December 1945 correspondence went back and forth between government officials, and in February 1946 it was stated in a memo from the Foreign Office to the British Embassy that 'the Home Office is not altogether sure that it is desirable to give a degree of official sanction to the view that there is no place for these coloured children in the United Kingdom'.[45] The Home Office was laboriously admitting at least some responsibility for the children.

Alma LaBadie from Jamaica met with representatives of the Home Office and the Ministry of Health in February 1946. She suggested that 'the half-caste illegitimate children of coloured American and West Indian servicemen and British women' could be adopted by people in the West Indies, and she had already heard of interest there. Miss Well of the Home Office was encouraging: given that adopters in the West Indies would be British subjects, it would be far easier than sending the children to the US.[46] LaBadie also wrote to Lady Molly Huggins, the wife of the governor of Jamaica, and asked her how funds could be raised in Jamaica for these children. Lady Huggins passed on the query about funding to Eleanor Roosevelt.[47] Unfortunately I have been unable to find out whether any children were ever sent to the West Indies.

British officials may have initially opposed the 'brown babies' being sent abroad, but in the US moves were afoot to receive these children. The Chicago 'Brown Babies Organizing Committee', mentioned in the last chapter, had compiled a list of over 500 individuals wishing to adopt.[48] But the US adoption endeavour experienced a massive setback when the highly sensational story in the *Daily Mail* claiming the imminent arrival of a ship with 'five thousand dusky "problem babies"' hit the headlines in April 1947. In Andrea Levy's novel *Small Island*, set in the 1940s, Queenie, a white woman who has recently had a baby with Jamaican former RAF pilot Michael, tries to persuade a Jamaican couple to take the baby as theirs: 'I'd have to give him away, you see ... In the newspaper they said they were going to send all the half-caste babies that had been born since the war – sons, daughters of coloured GIs mostly – they were going to send them to live in America.'[49] Despite Home Office denials of such a ship, the rumour spread widely through the States and triggered a strong reaction. The issue was addressed in Congress, where Congressman John Rankin of Mississippi declared that he was 'unalterably opposed to bringing to this country a lot of illegitimate half-breed negro children from

England … the offspring of the scum of the British Isles'.[50] He also suggested that they 'probably inherit the vices of both [races] and the virtues of neither'.[51] Herbert Munroe, head of the information bureau of the State Department's visa division, referred to these children as 'little black apes'.[52] A letter from the New York legal advisor to Daniels Ekarte's solicitor in May stated that 'I have today discussed the entire matter with the British Consulate General, New York, and find it necessary to eliminate possibilities of adoption … the issue of bringing children here has received a very strong opposition.'[53]

Certain African Americans also opposed the arrival of these children. Bishop Emory J. Cain from North Carolina announced:

> The intelligent Negroes of America are trying to discourage the mongrel in our race. We feel there is something about our race we want to preserve. We lifted ourselves out of slavery in eighty years and are proud of such leaders as Booker T Washington and George Washington Carver [the botanist and inventor]. We couldn't be proud of these children.[54]

DuBois had come across a rather different reaction when he had brought the problem of the 'brown babies' 'before a group of people, white and colored, intelligent, liberal': 'I sensed among the colored ones a certain feeling of vengeance accomplished upon white womanhood in retaliation for what colored women had suffered.'[55] Yet vengeance and hostility towards 'mongrelisation' were not the only reactions from African Americans: many wanted to help the children. For example, the *Chicago Defender* announced that on 8 June 1947, 'many stars and the public will do their part to help the "Brown Babies of Briton" [*sic*] with a gala cocktail Sip [party] at the Club Sudan in Harlem'. The event had 'the sanction of the NAACP'. It also noted that 'contrary to reports there are not 5000 "brown babies" but barely 400, and these children will receive the proceeds through their representative H Duplagne [*sic*] of the British Dept. of Social Welfare in London'.[56] Not only did the report greatly underestimate the children's numbers but somehow Duplan had been transformed into an important government official. It is tempting to surmise that Duplan had been party to his own 'promotion'.

US adoptions realised

Through 1947 interest from black Americans in adopting the babies continued. Many letters were sent to the NAACP from people wishing to adopt, despite the organisation not having the resources to organise adoptions.[57] By late 1947 the fantasy of a ship arriving in the US from Britain with 5,000 'brown babies' was still being cited in American newspapers[58] and articles about the children of Holnicote House appeared in widely circulated American magazines: one in late December 1947 in *Newsweek*, the other the following August in *Life*, which claimed that 'British authorities are now considering offers of adoption received from US Negro families.'[59] This claim was indeed true because there had recently been a change in Home Office policy.

Through 1946 the Home Office had been in a quandary about the babies, unsure whether it was advisable to send them to the US or not. In December 1945 Chuter Ede had been against such an action, but a year later the Ministry of Health was informed that the Home Office was now in favour, so long as 'the mother does not want the child and there is a reasonably satisfactory home in the United States'.[60] By November 1947, another year on, an agreement had been arrived at with the Americans: a child would be permitted to travel to its putative father (or the father's relatives) in the US, dependent on the arrangements being 'in the best interests of the child'. What the 'best interests of the child' might be at any point in time depended (and depends) on who had/has the power to decide. Ideas about child welfare were in fact undergoing a shift in the late 1940s in the face of the enormous disruptions of the war.[61] The arrangements for these particular transatlantic adoptions were to be undertaken by the International Social Service in the US in cooperation with the Family Welfare Association in Britain.[62] In December 1947 the Home Office and the Foreign Office agreed that the scheme would come into effect on 1 January 1948.[63] The policy applied to 'coloured' children only, according to the Foreign Office, since white children were 'an entirely different problem'.[64] In what way they were 'an entirely different problem' was not spelled out, but this no doubt referred both to the greater ease in getting white children adopted in Britain and the lesser likelihood that white American fathers would want to adopt their own children, since unlike black GIs they had had the possibility of marrying the child's mother. However, the Home Office became worried about this overt exclusion of white children: there was 'the need to avoid any suggestion that we in this country are trying to get rid of the coloured waifs left behind by the American occupation'.[65] And yet getting 'rid of the coloured waifs' appears to have been precisely what they were intending.

In January 1948, during parliamentary question time, Chuter Ede announced the government's policy change: 'no obstacle should be put in the way of emigration of the children to the United States for adoption by relatives, if it is established in a particular case that this would be in the child's interests'.[66] He neither mentioned that this countered the Adoption Act, nor clarified whether the children were to be exclusively mixed-race. Presumably Chuter Ede was consciously trying to avoid implying that they were 'trying to get rid of the coloured waifs'. US adoptions appeared at last to be happening: in March Somerset County Council minuted arranging 'the transfer of coloured illegitimate children [numbers unspecified] ... to America'.[67] Celia Bangham tried to get Eleanor Roosevelt to sponsor the children's adoption by approaching a relative of Roosevelt's, Mrs Herbert, who lived in Somerset. Mrs Herbert in turn got in touch with Mrs Roosevelt who passed her on to Walter White (White and Eleanor Roosevelt were close friends), who then passed her on to the Russell Sage Foundation. White was worried that he had sent her on a 'wild goose chase'.[68] It is unclear if anything came from these pass-the-parcel inquiries. Independently of all this, by the end of the year the LCP had liaised with the American Embassy to help secure visas, transport and guardians for seven children travelling out to fathers or relatives in the US. But this was a drop in the ocean, as the League had received 172 letters from black Americans willing to adopt (another report, by St Clair Drake, gives the number as over 200).[69]

Some of the black GI fathers were also trying to get their children over to America. Denise, who spent her childhood in a small Buckinghamshire children's home, was amazed to discover, on reading her files in 1997, that her father had written to the home for six years requesting a photograph and asking about the possibility of her travelling to America:

I have addressed several letters regarding Denise but have received no answer. I would thank you very much to know where she is, and how she's getting along. I'd like to send her something. I also

wrote asking if it was possible to please send a photograph of Denise
… How old will Denise have to be before she's able to journey
to America without an escort? I do hope to hear from you soon
regarding this matter.

The home never replied. A letter from her maternal grandmother to
the home's matron indicates that he wrote to her too, but she also
never replied. Denise's mother had married a white GI and gone to
live in the US; the grandmother was determined that 'he won't have
my poor little Denise … he wants her over there and that would not be
for her good so I did not answer his letter'.[70] But she was no one's 'little
Denise', and heartbreakingly recounts how she longed to be adopted:
'People would come to the home and choose the pretty blonde children
for adoption; they never looked at me. I used to try and scrub my skin
white. We were clothed and fed but there was no affection.'[71] Carole
M, who was born to a black GI and a white British woman in 1956 and
will be discussed in the concluding chapter, similarly tried to scrub
herself white with Vim. And like Denise, she 'longed to be blond and
blue-eyed'.[72] The soap adverts mentioned in the last chapter, showing
black people turning white, must have contributed to this dangerous
fallacy that black skin could be whitened by soap. John S, kept by his
mother, found some milk of magnesia in his grandmother's larder
when he was about seven, and drank it in the hope that it would turn
him white. He also ate chalk.[73]

The adoption of Leon Lomax

One father who was successful in getting his child over to the US
was Corporal Leon Lomax. His son is the only 'brown baby' I have
interviewed who was adopted by his African-American father. This
was not arranged by either Somerset County Council or the LCP.
Corporal Lomax, an African-American soldier, arrived back in Ohio
at the end of the war; he had been stationed in England for much of his
time away. He had a confession to make to his wife, Betty. In February
1949 she recounted their exchange to the *Pittsburgh Courier*:

He said: 'I've been gone a long time … about three years … that's
a long time for a fellow to be away from his wife. In the meantime

I met a girl. She was nice, she was friendly, and Betty, I was very lonesome, so … what I'm trying to say is that there's to be a child. Betty, you don't have to answer right away, but would you agree to take this child?'[74]

The baby had been born in December 1945 and was given the name by which his father was known: Leon. (His father was in fact Oscar Leon but always called Leon.) Leon junior was put into a children's home in East Anglia by his single mother. With great difficulty, Leon senior eventually managed to have his son flown out to the US, and he arrived in January 1949. The *Pittsburgh Courier* called his arrival 'the story of the year!'[75] To the *Pittsburgh Courier*, 'the entire "Brown Baby" question is one of the most controversial subjects in this country today. It is a question that involves two great nations – the United States of America and Great Britain.'[76] When Leon arrived in the US he was heralded as 'the first "Brown Baby" adopted by an American couple to reach America'. Many readers subsequently sent letters to the *Pittsburgh Courier* asking if they too could adopt one of these babies.[77]

Leon's adoption had been a lengthy process. His father and his father's wife had first tried to adopt him back in January 1946; neither the British Embassy nor the American State Department replied to

4.5 Leon L arriving in the US

the couple's letters. In June that year they wrote to the American Red Cross and again got no reply; they asked the child's mother to get the British Welfare Department to help but to no avail. Then in December 1946 or early 1947 – reports vary – they read in an American magazine about a Dr Wingate in Britain, who as a church minister 'had opened his parish to some of the "brown babies"'.[78] Wingate was able to help the couple, and in March 1947 the Lomaxes' local welfare department in Ohio paid them a visit. After the Lomaxes paid out $200 for the child's travel expenses, Leon Lomax junior finally left London for the US on 31 December 1948.[79] Despite the fanfare of publicity that greeted his arrival in the States, Leon had a fairly difficult childhood. His stepmother was hard on him at times, punishing him for the philandering of his father. She died of a heart attack when Leon was eight and he was looked after by various uncles and aunts. His father married two or three more times and was hardly around. Leon junior recounts that at the age of nine he once ran to hug his father, who he had not seen for some time, but his father simply stuck out his hand.[80]

US adoptions closed

By 1951, according to Margaret Kornitzer, the press officer for the Standing Conference of Societies Registered for Adoption, only twenty or thirty of the 'brown babies' had emigrated to North America. She explains the low numbers as being due to the costliness of the process for the adoptive families and its lengthiness, given that it was surrounded by checks and balances.[81] However, she fails to mention the most crucial reason: a further about-face in Home Office policy in the intervening period. In March 1949, after meeting with a deputation from Somerset County Council, the Home Office ruled that the thirty-one children under the council's care would not now be allowed to emigrate.[82] It refused to amend the Children Act of 1948, which had incorporated the regulations about prohibiting adoption overseas by non-relatives. An official statement of explanation was released: 'any implication that there is not a place in this country for coloured children who have not a normal life would cause controversy and give offense in some quarters'.[83] Somerset County Council's children's committee had received eighty-five adoption applications from the US, partly in response to a brief article and photograph of some of the children in *Life* magazine.[84] As an alternative to adoption, the committee now chose suitable 'uncles' and 'aunts' from among the eighty-five and asked them to write and send presents.[85]

Why in 1949 did the Home Office shift its position yet again? In its newsletter at the end of 1948, the LCP suggested that the publicity concerning the transporting of 5,000 children had 'stirred up a storm of controversy in the United States ... there is considerable sensitiveness on both sides of the Atlantic about any action that might give the impression of a mass migration of coloured children from Britain to America'.[86] George Padmore pointed out the role of British campaigning:

> Ever since it became known that certain reactionary anti-Negro natives of Somerset were bringing pressure ... to try to get rid of coloured orphans left behind by American Negro soldiers, the League of Coloured Peoples and the Pan-African Federation in Manchester have protested to the British government against the plan to ship the unwanted orphans.[87]

It was perhaps unfair to refer to Celia Bangham as one of the 'anti-Negro natives of Somerset', as she may have truly cared for the children's future, referring to them as 'healthy, intelligent and charming ... I am so anxious for them to have the best possible chance in life.'[88] However, she had not stopped her county council from rejecting Tacchi-Morris's offer. Was it the combination of US and UK opposition that led to a change in Home Office policy?[89] The Home Office had denied the existence of the chartered ship, but it appears that through 1948 it had become increasingly concerned about being seen as shirking responsibility and dumping the mixed-race children of British subjects on to the Americans. Of significance too was the passing of the British Nationality Act that year. Citizenship was granted to citizens of British colonies and former colonies, giving them the right to come to Britain and stay indefinitely.[90] While the government was clearly ambivalent about the arrival of many West Indians in June 1948 on the *Empire Windrush*,[91] when debating the British Nationality Act the following month Chuter Ede pronounced: 'we recognize the right of the colonial peoples to be treated as men and brothers with the people of this country'.[92] How could he then effectively deport the 'brown babies' who, as the children of British mothers, had automatic

British nationality? For birth on British soil, regardless of parentage, conferred British nationality.[93]

Conclusion

The case of Dave B, who was moved from children's homes into foster homes and then back again on a number of occasions, is one example of how such constant moving created huge instability. As we saw in the last chapter, David M, although only fostered once (unsuccessfully), was moved from children's home to children's home numerous times. Again it was very disruptive. Today there is greater awareness that children who are moved constantly tend to have the least good outcomes – a point that now seems obvious but clearly did not occur to many involved in the care system in the 1940s and 1950s. At least none of these children was ever eligible for shipping to Australia, given that country's 'whites only' policy; the children who were sent there from Britain often had the most terrible time and were used as child labour.[94]

As for adoption, what seems so extraordinary in reading about these various attempts to adopt mixed-race GI babies is that the adoption rate was so low. I am not able to compare directly the number of white children adopted as opposed to black and mixed-race, but the number of adoptions overall increased greatly after the war: from 1945 to 1949 there were an average of 17,000 adoptions per year in England and Wales, nearly three times the 1939 figure. And apparently babies and young children available for adoption were in short supply in the immediate post-war period.[95] From this one can surmise that white babies and young children given up for adoption did not on the whole remain in children's homes for long (although this would be different for those labelled disabled). Adoption agencies said that no one wanted to adopt 'half-castes', but from all accounts this was not true. Somerset County Council received well over a hundred applications from people in Britain wishing to adopt the children, and there were nearly 300 responses to the *Daily Mirror*/LCP article in July 1947. But few actual adoptions appear to have resulted from these requests. As for the United States, the Chicago Organizing Committee had over 500 potential adopters for Britain's 'brown babies'. The LCP received over 200 letters from the US asking to adopt, while Somerset received eighty-five. The latter had to be converted into 'aunts' and 'uncles' as opposed to potential adoptive parents because the British government had changed its mind yet again.

While the last chapter examined why there was so little adoption of the 'brown babies' in Britain, this chapter has demonstrated that the obstacles to the children's adoption in the US related to the fluctuating policy of the British government. Like the 'leading social worker' mentioned by the LCP, the government might also have thought the children 'unassimilable' as a result of equating Britishness with 'whiteness'. The government was clearly indecisive as to how to act, oscillating between attempts to simply remove the 'problem' (exclusion through American adoption) on the one hand, and voicing a lukewarm commitment to some kind of inclusion on the other. While in February 1946 the Home Office thought it undesirable to imply that 'there is no place for these coloured children in the United Kingdom',[96] by January 1948 Chuter Ede was in favour of the children being sent to the US – a position that Joseph-Mitchell characterised as looking 'as though coloured people were no longer wanted within the framework of British society'.[97] As Hazel Carby expresses it: 'These children were not imagined as present and future citizens but as "problems" that should be exported.'[98] In 1949 the Home Office changed its mind again, although it appeared to see these children as second-class citizens, never 'belonging' to the British nation by right of birth, although legally of course they did.

Did the adoption situation improve in the 1960s? A 1960 National Council for Civil Liberties' research project noted that there were only five British organisations – London County Council, agencies in Bristol and Edinburgh, the Church of England Children's Society and Dr Barnardo's – that even tried to find adopters for 'coloured' children.[99] But as far as Barnardo's was concerned, as its 1966 report *Racial Integration and Barnardo's* demonstrates, attempts were limited. While stating that 'colour should not be regarded in itself as a "difficulty"', it also noted that 'we do not admit many coloured children directly for adoption'. The reasons given were:

1. There do not appear to be sufficient applicants to adopt the large number of coloured (mainly half-caste) children for whom adoption seems to be desirable.
2. Very few coloured couples have so far applied to us to adopt children.

3. It is never easy to assess the motives underlying offers to adopt, and this is particularly true where white couples ask to adopt a coloured child.[100]

In relation to the second reason, there is no mention of efforts being made to recruit potential black or Asian adopters, something that only started being addressed in the 1990s.[101] In relation to the third reason, the social worker who condemned the two white women's desire to adopt Rosa as 'sickly sentimentality' again comes to mind. In 1965 the International Social Service of Great Britain and the Sociology Department of Bedford College, University of London, set up a four-year project to encourage the adoption of non-white children and to monitor the placements. Although committed to placing the children where possible with those of the same racial/ethnic background, the vast majority of the fifty-three children were adopted by white British couples.[102] This was the beginning of a fairly brief period when adoption agencies were happy to consider transracial adoption.

From the early 1980s this outlook shifted again, and the 'race matching' policy became dominant, initiated largely by black social workers. Testimonies from a number of black and mixed-race children who had been adopted by white families revealed that some of them suffered problems with identity, self-esteem and development.[103] The 1980s and 1990s saw greater awareness of the extent of racism and the view was taken that it was best for children to be with families who could reflect their cultural/ethnic backgrounds. Few local authorities would now countenance transracial adoption. However, research undertaken by Barbara Tizard and Ann Phoenix of fifty-eight mixed-race teenagers suggested that 'having a black identity or a positive identity, was not related to the colour of the parents the young people were growing up with'.[104] There was no necessary connection between identity issues and white adoptive parents; peers, neighbourhood and school were much more important, they argued.

In 2011 Martin Narey (head of Barnardo's from 2005 to 2011) was commissioned by the Department of Education to undertake an in-depth examination of adoption in England and Wales. He discovered that 'white children in care are three times more likely to be adopted than black children', due, he suggested, to local authorities having 'a rigid interpretation' of racial/ethnic requirements.[105] But there are other issues: why is there an over-representation of black children in the care system in the first place? And as Afua Hirsch suggests in her important book *Brit(ish)*, the delay in black children getting adopted was not the result of race matching but 'poor practice by social workers, who were pessimistic about black children's likelihood of being adopted, and were therefore failing to promote them as available for adoption'.[106] The similarity to attitudes in the 1940s and 1950s is worrying. The debate continues.

Notes

1   Interview with Tony M, 2 June 2014. Fashion designer Bruce Oldfield, the mixed-race, illegitimate son of a Jamaican boxer born in 1950, was also a 'Barnardo's boy' and also happily fostered, at least initially. He joined his foster mother, a dressmaker in County Durham, when he was eighteen months old, and stayed until he was thirteen, when he became too difficult for her to manage. Bruce Oldfield, *Rootless: An Autobiography* (London, 2004), p. 43. In contrast, mixed-race 'Barnardo's boy' John Williams, born 1948, had an unhappy childhood and took up criminal activities. After a long prison sentence he became an actor. John Williams, *Silver Threads: A Life Alone* (London, 1994).

2   Interview with Babs, 3 June 2014.

3   Akala, *Natives*, pp. 81–2.

4   Interview with Babs, 3 June 2014.

5   Telephone conversation with Babs, 13 June 2017.

6   Interview with Babs, 3 June 2014.

7   Telephone conversation with Babs, 13 June 2017.

8   Interview with Richard, 31 March 2017. Richard thinks the social services knew that he was made to work hard. It might have been expected that they would have been more careful, given the death of twelve-year-old Dennis O'Neill, who in 1945 was in foster care on a farm and died after numerous beatings. Keating, *A Child for Keeps*, p. 187.

9   Telephone and face-to-face interviews with Sandi H, 21 February 2015, 29 April 2016.

10 Interview with Dave B, 13 April 2017.

11 Case reports from Monmouthshire County Council, in Dave B's possession.

12 Email from Dave B, 10 June 2018.

13 The school-leaving age was raised from fourteen to fifteen under the 1944 Education Act.

14   Interview with Jim H, 16 August 2014.

15   Interview with Tony H, 19 October 2016.

16   Tony H's mother to Matron, Lady Stephenson House, Newcastle-upon-Tyne, 26 October 1951, in Tony H's possession.

17   FO Memo, CD Wiggins, 25 April 1947, FO 371/61017, TNA.

18   Quoted in letter from Preston Children's Department to Principal of National Children's Home and Orphanage, Highbury Park, N5, 14 November 1952, in Tony H's possession.

19   *Report of County Borough of Burnley Children's Department: Enquiries concerning Applicants*, 16 March 1959, in Tony H's possession.

20   Interview with Tony H, 19 October 2016.

21   Ronald Bedford, 'Colour-barred babies', *Daily Mirror*, 22 July 1947, p. 2. Bedford went on to become one of the paper's leading journalists in the area of science and medicine.

22   St Clair Drake, 'The League's Sociological Approach', Box 62/12.

23   John St Clair Drake, 'Possibility and Desirability of Adoption in Britain', Acc. no. 4910, LRO.

24   St Clair Drake, 'The League's Sociological Approach', Box 62/12. Emphasis in the original. The social worker is not identified in the source. St Clair Drake also noted, however, that 'colored leaders and ordinary citizens whom I talked to in Cardiff and Liverpool were, on the whole, sceptical of the wisdom of adoption by whites'. John St Clair Drake, 'Foster-home care and adoption', Acc. no. 4910, LRO.

25   Quoted in St Clair Drake, 'Possibility and Desirability of Adoption in Britain', LRO.

26   St Clair Drake, 'The League's Sociological Approach', Box 62/12.

27   Moynihan, 'Children against the colour bar'. On hostility towards interracial marriage, see Buettner, 'Would you let your daughter marry a Negro?'

28   Hazel V. Carby, 'Imperial Intimacies', unpublished manuscript in progress, 2017, p. 45. Many thanks to Hazel Carby for generously allowing me to read a section of her inspiring memoir.

29   'Let me give a home to twelve children, she asks', *Daily Mirror*, 30 March 1949, p. 3.

30   Harold King, clerk to the county council, to Tacchi-Morris, 30 March 1949; anonymous letter, undated, DD/TCM/15/14, Somerset Archives.

31   Cohen, *Family Secrets*, p. 139.

32   Interview with Ann, 28 November 2016.

33   Miss Bowerman to Janet J's adoptive parents, 13 January 1950, in Janet's possession.

34   Interview with Deborah, 17 October 2016.

35   Interview with Deborah, 17 October 2016.

36   Miss Bowerman to Janet J's adoptive parents, 11 December 1949, in Janet's possession.

37   Cohen, *Family Secrets*, p. 136.

38   Interview with Carole T, 9 September 2014.

39   On the fostering of African babies in Britain, see Jordanna Bailkin, *The Afterlife of Empire* (Berkeley, CA, 2012), pp. 164–201.

40   Interview with Janet J and her daughter, Karen, 9 June 2016. For Pauline Black's story, see Black, *Black by Design*.

41   W. M. G. 'Coloured Children of English Mothers and Negro Members of the United States Forces', 14 December 1945, FO 371/51617, AN3/3/45, TNA.

42   'Report of Conference on the position of the illegitimate child', MH 55/1656, TNA.

43   Quoted in Smith, *When Jim Crow Met John Bull*, p. 209.

44   Plummer, 'Brown babies', p. 77.

45   North American Department, Foreign Office to British Embassy, Washington, 19 February 1946, FO 371/51617, AN3/3/45, TNA.

46   Meeting of LaBadie at the Home Office, 6 February 1942, Acc. no. 4910, LRO.

47   Molly Huggins to Mrs Roosevelt, 26 May 1946, Records of NAACP, Box A642, Library of Congress, Washington DC.

48   St Clair Drake, 'The Brown Baby Problem', Box 60/15.

49   Andrea Levy, *Small Island* (London, 2004), p. 432.

50   Quoted in Smith, *When Jim Crow Met John Bull*, p. 21.

51   'Rankin opposes entry of brown babies', *Plain Dealer*, 21 May 1947.

52   James Hicks, 'State Dept. official calls colored British babies "apes"', *Plain Dealer*, 25 April 1947.

53   Theodore Acare, 9 May 1947, 'The "American Campaign" Debacle, 1946–47', St Clair Drake Archives, Box 61/2.

54   'Negroes will oppose coming of England's brown babies', *Plain Dealer*, 25 April 1947. I have been unable to establish whether Cain was Anglican or Catholic.

55   DuBois, 'Winds of change'.

56   'Harlem to aid British babies', *Chicago Defender*, 31 May 1947, p. 10.

57   See letters sent to NAACP in Records of NAACP, Box A642, Library of Congress.

58   See *Arkansas State Press*, 19 December 1947, p. 1.

59   'Britain's "brown Tiny Tims"', *Newsweek*, 29 December 1947, p. 24; 'The babies they left behind', *Life*, 23 August 1948, p. 41. There had

also been a short article, with photographs, in *Chicago Defender*, 9 August 1947: 'With the tan-Yank babies in England'.

60   The view expressed was that 'the child will have a far better chance if sent at an early age to the United States than if bought up in this country'. Maxwell, HO to Ministry of Health, 3 December 1946, MH 55/1656, TNA.

61   See Tara Zahra, *The Lost Children: Reconstructing Europe's Families after World War II* (Cambridge, MA, 2011).

62   Letter from Children's Branch, Home Office to Foreign Office, 21 November 1947, FO 371/AN3948/13/45, TNA. A week later the Children's Branch wrote again, this time mentioning (but providing no solution to) the possible 'embarrassment' that might result from 'the apparent inconsistency with earlier policy'; letter from Children's Branch, Home Office to Foreign Office, 29 November 1947. The International Social Service, founded in the interwar years to deal with refugees, had become a prominent coordinating agency for international adoptions, with offices in Europe, US, Africa and Japan. Fehrenbach, *Race after Hitler*, p. 152.

63   J. E. Jackson, Foreign Office, to B. Lyon, Home Office, 16 December 1947, FO 371/AN3949/13/45, TNA. Margaret Kornitzer, press officer for the Standing Conference of Societies Registered for Adoption, later referred to this new policy as an 'Anglo-American agreement'. Margaret Kornitzer, *Child Adoption in the Modern World* (London, 1952), p. 244.

64   J. E. Jackson, Foreign Office, to B. Lyon, Home Office, 16 December 1947, FO 371/AN3949/13/45, TNA.

65   Home Office to Foreign Office, 24 December 1947, FO 371/AN4342/13/45, TNA.

66   *Parliamentary Debates: Commons* (Hansard, 1948–49), col. 186, 29 January 1948. For the successful 'Brown Baby Plan', 1951–54, which enabled African Americans to adopt Afro-German GI babies and was orchestrated by black American Mabel Grammer and by the African-American press, see Yara-Colette Lemke Muniz de Faria, '"Germany's 'brown babies' must be helped! Will you?" US adoption plans for Afro-German children, 1950–1955', *Callaloo*, 26.2 (2003), pp. 354–7; Fehrenbach, *Race after Hitler*, pp. 147–8.

67   Somerset County Council, 'Maternity and Child Welfare', minute 2194, C/CC/M/2/19, 305, Somerset Archives.

68   Celia Bangham to Mrs Herbert, 13 February 1948; E. Roosevelt to White, 17 March, 1948; Herbert to White, 23 March 1948; White to J. Glenn, 30 March 1948; Records of NAACP, Box A642, Library of Congress.

69   *Newsletter of LCP*, vol. XVII, October–December 1948: DD/

TCM/15/14, Somerset Archives; St Clair Drake, 'Possibility and Desirability of Adoption in Britain', LRO.

70   *Brown Babies*, Touch Productions, Channel 4, 11 October 1999. See Bailkin, *The Afterlife of Empire*, p. 194, on how, similarly, putative West Indian fathers in Britain wanting to raise their children were overruled by mothers wanting their children to be adopted.

71   Anne Moore, 'GI babies', *Daily Express Magazine*, 2 October 1999; *Brown Babies*, Channel 4. Another example of a black US father trying to get his daughter out to the US is that of Susan Stacey's father, who wrote to Celia Bangham on 26 February 1946, wanting Susan to come to Atlanta, Georgia. Her mother had given up all rights. FO 371/51618, TNA. I do not know the outcome of his request.

72   Telephone interview with Carole M, 8 November 2016. A *Daily Mirror* article in 1957 about a seven-year-old mixed-race Barnardo's boy reports: 'When Peter has his nightly bath, he often asks the woman who cares for him: "If I wash myself VERY HARD will my skin become white like yours?"'; quoted in Caballero and Aspinall, *Mixed Race Britain*, pp. 354–5.

73   John S on *Woman's Hour*, Radio 4, 11 January 2018; see also Chris Mullard, *Black Britain* (London, 1973), p. 15.

74   'Our brown baby', *Pittsburgh Courier*, 19 February 1949. My thanks to Leon for sending me the *Pittsburgh Courier* cuttings.

75   'Courier finds first "brown baby"', *Pittsburgh Courier*, 12 February 1949.

76   'First adopted "brown baby" is here!', *Pittsburgh Courier*, 12 February 1949.

77   'Scores seek "brown babies"', *Pittsburgh Courier*, 26 February 1949.

78   'Here's how Lomax couple got baby', *Pittsburgh Courier*, 19 February 1949; 'First adopted "brown baby" is here!', *Pittsburgh Courier*, 12 February 1949. I have unfortunately been unable to discover anything more about Dr Wingate or find the article in which he features.

79   'First adopted "brown baby" is here!'; 'Here's how Lomax couple got baby'.

80   Telephone interview with Leon Lomax, 10 October 2014.

81   Kornitzer, *Child Adoption*, pp. 244–5. Despite the limited numbers, she saw the process as 'an excellent example of what can be done at the international level to ensure a good adoption'.

82   The deputation included five of the six Somerset MPs. Somerset County Council, minutes of the Children's Committee, CH1/1, p. 110, Somerset Heritage Centre.

83   'Ban adoption by US of brown war babies', *Chicago Defender*, 9

April 1949, p. 1; this is reproduced with slightly different wording in George Padmore, 'Decides brown babies must stay in England', *Chicago Defender*, 23 April 1949.

84   *Life* magazine, 23 August 1948.

85   *Memorandum on Coloured Children*, 5 April, 1949, CH1/1, Somerset Archives.

86   *LCP Newsletter*, vol. XVII, October–December 1948, Somerset Archives.

87   Padmore, 'Decides brown babies must stay in England'.

88   Celia Bangham to Mrs Herbert, 13 February 1948.

89   George Padmore claimed that Chuter Ede changed his mind because of pressure from black organisations; Padmore, 'Decides brown babies must stay in England'.

90   Fryer, *Staying Power*, p. 373; Paul, *Whitewashing Britain*, pp. 9–10, 14–17.

91   Paul, *Whitewashing Britain*, pp. 111–30.

92   Quoted in Mike and Trevor Phillips, *Windrush: The Irresistible Rise of Multi-Racial Britain* (London, 1998), p. 75.

93   Laura Tabili, 'Outsiders in the land of their birth: exogamy, citizenship, and identity in war and peace', *Journal of British Studies*, 44.4 (2005), p. 797. Had their British mothers married their American boyfriends, their mothers would have lost their British nationality, until the law changed with the 1948 Nationality Act (ibid., p. 812).

94   See Margaret Humphreys, *Empty Cradles* (London, 1994); David Hill, *The Forgotten Children: Fairbridge Farm School and its Betrayal of Britain's Child Migrants* (London, 2008).

95   Gill Rossini, *A History of Adoption in England and Wales, 1850–1961* (Barnsley, 2014), pp. 134–5.

96   North American Department, Foreign Office to British Embassy, Washington, 19 February 1946, TNA.

97   Joseph-Mitchell, 'The Colour Problem among Juveniles', p. 5, DD/TCM/15/14, Somerset Archives.

98   Hazel Carby, 'Becoming modern racialized subjects', *Cultural Studies*, 23.4 (2009), p. 650.

99   Ivor Gaber, 'Transracial placements: a history', in Gaber and Aldridge (eds), *In the Best Interests of the Child*, p. 15.

100 Barnardo's, *Racial Integration and Barnardo's*, p. 23.

101 See Julie Selwyn, Lesley Frazer and Angela Fitzgerald, *Finding Adoptive Families for Black, Asian and Black Mixed-parentage Children: Agency, Policy and Practice* (London, 2004). Thanks to Annie Hudson for this reference.

102 Lois Raynor, *Adoption of Non-White Children* (London, 1970).

103 See Gaber and Aldridge (eds), *In the Best Interests of the Child*.

104   Tizard and Phoenix, *Black, White or Mixed-Race?*, p. 176.
105   Martin Narey, *The Narey Report: A Blueprint for the Nation's Lost Children* (London, 2011).
106   Afua Hirsch, *Brit(ish): On Race, Identity and Belonging* (London, 2018), pp. 139–40.

5

Secrets and lies: searching for mothers and fathers

For nearly every British 'brown baby', the identity of their American father was a total mystery. This led many of them, once they were older, on a search for their father and for their unknown American relatives. Those who were placed in children's homes knew little or nothing about either parent, and the first parent they usually searched for was their mother. Before the rise of the internet in the 1990s and increasing access to many different kinds of records, this search for mothers was not necessarily easy. As Elaine (whose story appears in Chapter 6) expresses it, 'that intense longing to find and to know where one comes from and that sense of roots and belonging underpins many of those who have the courage to go and search'.[1]

Finding mothers

Aged twelve, Billy, who was in St Luke's children's home, was told that his parents were dead. In 1959, aged fourteen, he had to attend a nearby clinic for a TB jab and was handed his medical record card. While waiting in the surgery

> I looked at this card and saw a strange address in Devon ... I memorised the address as best I could ... A few months later, at Christmastime, I sent a card to the address. I didn't know who to address the card to so I put 'To Sir or Madam'. We were told at school that that was what you had to write when you did not know the name. So that's what I did, wishing whoever it was a Happy Christmas, and then sent the card off. Then after Christmas I received a letter. It was from my mother.

His mother wrote movingly and lovingly: 'I was so thrilled to receive your Xmas card … I have often thought about you.' She had not been in touch before because of her husband. 'I hope and pray that you will make your way in the world all right.' She signed off: 'with my sincerest best wishes from your friend, Eileen'. Billy did not reply but kept the letter (and still has it), thinking that one day he 'would do something about it'. In his twenties, Billy's friend Tom helped him contact his mother. Tom wrote to her at her address in Devon and they arranged a meeting in Plymouth, under Drake's statue on Plymouth Hoe.

> So Tom and I went to Plymouth by train and got on to the Hoe nice and early, and every time a single woman went by we would think, is that her? No, is it that one? No. And then Tom said, 'Here she comes.' He was right. He recognised her in me or vice versa. Then Tom left us and my mother and I had a meal in a hotel.

5.1 Billy and his mother

They spent the day together. 'We knew we were going to be great friends, and always have been. I call her Eileen – not mother.' He saw her once a year after that first meeting, then more often. She lived to the age of 96, dying in April 2018.[2]

Brian first started to search for his mother in 1965, when he was 21. Everyone, including children, was given an identity card during the war,

> and this came into my possession when I was around about fifteen and what I did was I noticed the changes of addresses from where I was born … When I left Fazakerley Cottage Homes, I got this identity card and aunt Grace [an 'aunt' who used to take him out] … said, 'Well let's pay a visit to this address.' … I was about 21, 22 … we went to the Roman Catholic parish priest and he knew the family … and so the following Sunday, when … my mother's aunts came to worship at the church, he collared them you see, and that was a big shock to them … Didn't want to know. Their excuse was 'In a few years' time you will have your own family, so you don't need Sheila [his mother].'[3]

Brian persevered: 'So I went to see one of the aunts in her home, taking with me Grace … The appearance of both of us on her doorstep, out of the blue, hammered home to her that we meant business, and would take no messing.'[4] His great-aunt agreed to contact his mother, who had moved to Florida and married a white American GI. In July 1966 she came to Britain for a six-week holiday. His great-aunt

> said to meet outside a public house in Liverpool. So I, for Dutch courage, took a friend with me and we waited outside this public house and then this lady comes out of the pub and they'd been in there drinking of course … we got talking and then the tears started flowing. But it was a very emotional occasion when I first met my mother and the six weeks I spent with her were tremendous.

Two years later his mother developed breast cancer. Brian visited her in Florida, taking his future wife with him. It did not go well: 'I wanted her to see the girl I was going to marry, and my family tell me now that it was the worst thing I could have done … because she'd have wanted me for herself you see … the way she treated my wife was horrendous really.'[5] Brian was her only child and she was possessive of him, despite having given him up. But she had been only sixteen at the time. Brian and his wife carried on going out to Florida to see her over the years, until she died a few years ago.

Richard's mother came once to visit him, with a social worker, while he was fostered on the farm. He could not speak to her because the foster carers were there, but she secretly slipped him her address. After he left the farm for good he thought he would find his father. So he went and visited his mother, who lived in Bristol, to ask for information.

> I said, 'Do you have anything?' … She said, 'I may have some old letters.' And she went upstairs and brought me a pile of letters, which he'd been writing to her … I read the letters. I dissected the information I needed. And I said, 'Do you want them back?' 'No.' Then, I said, 'Then I must destroy them, then.' Because they were love letters.

He did not see his mother again for a long time. But then

> it was brought to my attention that she was in [a nursing home], and she wanted to see me. So I went down to see her. [Becoming upset] And she put her arms around me. Held me tight. 'Sorry' … I said, 'I'm living, and I never starved.' And she died happy then.[6]

The story of Richard finding his father comes later in this chapter.

Colin found his mother when he was about twenty. He managed to get her address from the Church of England Children's Society and just turned up, without warning. His mother was a bit shocked, but her husband, whom she had married about five years after having Colin, invited him in. He never saw her again; Celia, Colin's ex-wife, is not sure why.[7]

Dave B had been brought up in children's homes. When he turned thirteen he asked about his mother. To their credit, the children's home's officials thought 'it would be in David's best interest if this information were given to him'. They could not immediately find her, but after seven months the home was in contact with the McCarthys, who said that 'David's mother was taken in by them off the streets when she was due to have her baby. She returned to them after

David was born and lived there for two years. David was taken to the Children's Home without their knowledge.' Through them Dave got to meet his mother, but later it was reported that he did not want to have anything more to do with her, since 'she was not bothered about him for the first twelve years of his life'.[8] However, Dave later changed his mind: 'When I got married I thought, "Oh, it'd be nice to have my mother here."' It was 1972 and he was aged 27. He got her address in Wales from the children's home and wrote to her.

> She turned up with this brown paper bag with this hat and it was like Carmen Miranda, you know. Putting the fruit on it. [Carmen Miranda was a Brazilian samba singer who wore hats covered in fruit.] ... I met her from the train ... It wasn't emotional. It wasn't anything ... it was all over – two days, she was gone. I mean, we did the wedding – [laughs] she was gone the next morning, you know. That was it. Fleeting in and out.[9]

Like Colin, he never saw his mother again.

Deborah, who had been adopted, was able to find her mother's two daughters, Deborah's older half-sisters, with the help of David Stanley, former deputy director of Somerset social services.

> Now, Betty, who's the eldest one – she was born in 1941 – was very, very suspicious – ... eventually, when she agreed to – for me to meet my mother, I had to pretend I was her friend. So I met my mother ... she was in her nineties – she died at 94, 95 – so, she was about 92 when I met her – and pretend I was my sister's friend from Australia. Which was logical, because my sister does have a friend in Australia [and Deborah lives in Australia]. ... That was the only condition she'd allow me to come into the house ... Excuse was that my mother's current husband of the day was a bit crazy. He was – he was very crazy, actually. And she was worried about how he'd react if he knew that my mother had had me, that kind of thing. Which is quite – probably is a reasonable explanation. But I regret I didn't have more courage to say: 'Well, blow that! This is probably the only chance I'm going to have to sort of connect.' But I think my mother knew who I was, because the first thing she said when I came in – she said: 'Oh – *you* look familiar!' I thought: 'You canny old cow! Of course I look familiar! [Laughs] *You* know who I am!' I

think she knew who I was! … One of Betty's … grandchildren – she said: 'Actually, you look more like Granny than the other two do.' … It's annoying to me … that I didn't say: 'Hi mum! Can you please tell me who my dad is?'[10]

Like Brian and Colin, she never saw her mother again.

Leon Y found his mother in November 1984 when he was 40 and she was 69. With the help of Somerset social services, he discovered that she lived only five miles away from his home in Frome, Somerset. When Leon was born his mother had been unmarried and already had two children; she was living with her mother, brother, unmarried sister and her three children – all in a four-roomed house. When he met his mother, Leon felt 'on cloud nine'.[11] 'But he over-indulged his new family financially and time-wise. He had no family experience or values concerning the "norm".' Things changed when Lesley, his wife-to-be, arrived on the scene the following year. Like Brian's mother, Leon's mother 'wasn't happy about sharing him'.[12]

The unsolicited arrival of mothers

When Babs was about fourteen, the Barnardo's matron

> was sitting there with a big grin on her face and she said, 'I've got excellent news for you … after all of this time your mother's coming to take you home', and I thought she meant my foster mother. So, I was really pleased … I waited and I waited and I waited and there was no sign of this person turning up at the time she said she was going to turn up and so I thought, 'Well, I better get ready for bed.' … It got to something like quarter-to-ten at night and they were very strict in Barnardo's, you were usually in bed for eight o' clock, never mind quarter-to-ten and so I started going up the stairs and just as I did, I heard the doorbell go and the next thing was I was called down into the matron's office and she just said to me, 'Meet your mother' and there was this total stranger and I just looked at this woman and I said, 'She's not my mother' and she said, 'Yes she is and she's going to take you home' and I was shocked and I think the thing that hit me hard was it wasn't my foster mother but then if this was my mother, why was there a difference between us

complexion-wise, I couldn't understand this … And so anyway, I had to travel that night with her and we had to travel up to London and her plan was she had a sister that lived in Pentonville Road which was a pretty rough area, it was just by the prison and we walked there from the station at Kings Cross … Then when we got to the road where her sister lived, her sister obviously didn't know what was happening and refused to answer the door.

It was about one in the morning.

So, then it meant a walk right back to the station again and then waiting for the mail train and eventually we boarded that and arrived in York which was where she lived, six o'clock in the morning or something like that … And in all of this time of meeting her in Colchester and arriving at the family home, not one word passed from her lips to me, not one word … When I was in the house she wouldn't have a conversation with me, she always spoke through another person, a third person.

There were three other children and her stepfather, who

seemed a very peaceful man but they fought, they really did, and I always became the scapegoat for the arguments in the family home. There were huge debt problems, she had quite a major nicotine addiction … she was a very violent woman as well, I never felt safe. She would throw knives as well and it was a very unsafe environment and I wasn't just the only victim, the other children were in danger as well … When it came to holidays, when it came to Christmas, when it came to birthdays they all got presents and they got taken on holiday but I was totally, totally excluded and they would go away to Scotland, they would go away to various places and I would be in the house on my own. I didn't mind, I was quite relieved to be honest, under the circumstances.

Although Babs is very intelligent she had to leave school at fifteen as her mother wanted her to earn. She got a job in a shop which she liked but she had to leave after three weeks as they were cutting back. Her mother's reaction was 'that she didn't get me out of Barnardo's to keep me, I was there to pay my way … I was thrown out on the street.'

Luckily Babs had a good friend at school who she was able to go and stay with. She did not go back to her mother.[13]

Tony H's daughter Tracey, who was born in 1967, remembers that when she was six or seven 'this lady and this man come out this car. So we was just playing opposite our house there, like right in front, and I remember she had like a turban, 'cause it was the early seventies.' She wondered,

> why is this white woman calling me dad by some name that I've never heard of [Raymond, his original name], saying that she's my grandma, 'cause then she starts saying, 'Well he's my son, I'm your grandma.' And I'm like: 'My grandma's black and she lives in Jamaica. Who are you?'

Tony remembers that 'she was lovely. Very, very small, very petite ... that would have been the first time actually I met my biological mother [since his being put in a home].' She had come with her new husband, George, not the one who had taken her sons away. Tracey reflects that her sudden appearance was almost unreal:

> then she went away and we never really heard from [her] again, it was just like back to normal, like, I've got my black grandma in Jamaica who sends us letters from time to time, and, and this other woman who's also my grandma but let's not discuss her.

However, Tony 'went to their [his mother and George's] twenty-fifth wedding anniversary and ... both brothers were there with their wives, and I've got a nice photograph where we're all together'. He has stayed friends with his half-brothers, with whom his mother had managed to reconnect.[14]

Rejected by mothers

In the late 1970s, after her beloved adoptive parents had died, Ann thought she would try and find her birth mother.

> I was told I had to go through social services ... Well, I knew a woman that was working for them ... she said, 'I'll help you while

I can, Ann.' And she contacted them. Well, poor old Phyllis nearly
had a heart attack … my biological mother. Phyllis, her name was.
Went straight to the solicitors and said, 'Look, I signed the adoption
certificate. When I signed it, there was no way that she could track
me down. So now, I want an injunction brought out on her.' And
the solicitor enlightened her: in 1975, everything was changed – we
were all, we all had a right to our legal birth certificate. 'Well, I want
an injunction.' 'I can't put an injunction on her, she hasn't done
anything.' … So what she said was: 'Please ask her not to get in
touch with me, because my husband is racist. And he would never
forgive me.'

He knew nothing about Ann: 'No – I was dead, wasn't I? 'Cause she'd
lost this baby that he'd married her for … I was told not to get in
contact with her because it would bring on a divorce. So I didn't get in
contact, I left it at that.' Then in the early 1980s a friend told her that
she had read in a newspaper that Ann's mother's husband had died.

> So I waited for a good while, and then I wrote to her. And she
> was quite fearful: 'Please don't contact me, I don't want nobody to
> find out, no-one knows anything about you.' … Three times I was
> supposed to have met her and on the day before, she'd – well, in the
> night she'd phone up to say she couldn't make it.[15]

Ann never met her birth mother and gave up trying. However, after
her mother died, Ann contacted the vicar who had performed her
funeral.

> I told him I was looking for my sister and gave her name, and he
> said he would go and see her … he just went there and said, 'A lady
> has phoned me who claims to be your sister.' He gave her my phone
> number and she phoned me and said it wasn't possible as she was
> the only child. So I explained the situation to her and she was quite
> surprised but within two weeks we met up … We talked and got on
> really well. She never queried that I was her mother's daughter …
> she said I resembled her … we still keep in contact.[16]

Sandi H was told by the children's home that her father had died
in the war and her mother did not want her or could not look after

her. However, when she was about eight, a social worker arranged for her to meet her mother in Bath: 'I was put in a room with my mum who never attempted to talk. She said: "It's best you forget all about me, you've your own life to live."' Then in the 1980s Sandi saw a TV programme about the GI war babies. It took ten years to find her mother, who still lived in Bristol but had moved.

> She was made up to see me. She was aware [who I was]. The first thing I asked her was: 'Who do I look like?' And I'm forty-three. And she said: 'You look like me.' And she was smiling when she done it. So that really encouraged me in a way of feeling good, 'cause I thought, 'Ooh a white woman seeing herself in a black woman.' I'd just turned up on her doorstep with two of my daughters. And then her husband just put the cap on it. I wanted her to *see* me, and who I was, how I felt. And I wanted to see *her*. And I got that – just about fifteen minutes on the doorstep was all I saw of her. I wrote to her for about fifteen years – birthday cards, even wedding anniversary cards to include her husband … even though he'd been really nasty to me. All that … she never got back. But it's quite possible, I think, she was under her husband's thumb, kind of thing. Just 'cause of the way he spoke to me, and how he was gonna call the police on me and say I had broke in and entered his home.

He had said this to her when she went to visit her mother another time, on Mother's Day.[17]

Looking for fathers

While the 1970s saw a growing interest in genealogy, the search by the 'brown babies' for their fathers cannot be seen as simply a reflection of family history's new popularity.[18] Not knowing about their fathers singled out these men and women as lacking what they felt was a basic right: knowledge of one's immediate origins. For whether or not they were in a children's home or living with their mother or grandmother, it appears that most of Britain's 'brown babies' were told little or nothing about their birth fathers, and the little they were told was often inaccurate or misleading. In the last chapter I mentioned how Denise's grandmother never replied to Denise's father when he asked about his daughter, thereby obstructing their contact. Even where a grandmother was the prime carer of her grandchild, she was sometimes the one who ensured that all contact between her daughter and her grandchild's father was terminated. She may have thought it was the best thing in the long run, but it would inevitably mean that it was much harder for the child to find his or her father later on. The stories here of those who searched for their fathers are very moving. They also demonstrate great initiative, amazing perseverance in the face of huge obstacles and impressive detective skills.

A few people, such as Richard, whose account of finding his father is given below, managed it all on their own. For many others, there was help in the form of two organisations set up in the 1980s: War Babes, founded by white GI baby Shirley McGlade, and TRACE, set up by Pamela Winfield, a GI bride who returned to Britain as a widow (Winfield and her organisation helped Sandi H find her mother).[19] TRACE is now online and renamed GI trace.[20] In trying to obtain information about her father in the 1980s, McGlade came up against enormous barriers, as did all the GI babies. This was before the arrival of email and of digital data accessible via the internet; there was no easy way of searching. But the greatest barrier was the stonewalling of the US military. It was true that many US military records had gone up in flames in 1973 at the National Personnel Records Center in St Louis. The fire destroyed approximately 80 per cent of the personnel records for army veterans discharged between 1912 and 1960, and there were no back-up records. But remnants from the fire had been retrieved and it did not affect all military veterans. However, the US army refused to divulge *any* information, such as addresses, invoking the Privacy Act. With great determination, McGlade, aided by several civil rights lawyers in the US, took on 'the Archivist of the National Archives and Records Administration, which controls the NPRC, and the Secretary of the Department of Defense at the Pentagon'. McGlade felt 'like the mouse who roared'.[21] War Babes finally managed to change the law in 1990 and the US military from then on was obliged to help under Freedom of Information legislation. With the recent and extensive use of DNA testing, finding US relatives is now proving a great deal easier, although it is rare that a father is still alive. AncestryDNA (a central part of Ancestry.com which was set up in 1999) has the largest US data set with over five million people registered.[22] Those searching for American relatives are also crucially assisted by the very helpful management analyst at the NPRC in St Louis, Dr Neils Zussblatt.

It was difficult enough for the 'brown babies' not knowing who their fathers were, but the difficulty was exacerbated by their learning that their fathers were American: America appeared huge and impossibly far away. The realisation that their 'different' skin colour and hair texture stemmed from these unknown fathers compounded the mystery. Even when a mother kept her child, she would often not fully answer questions about the child's father. While a mother may have loved the man, she usually believed that there was no future with him, and that she and her child had to make a life without him. Negating him or playing down his existence was one common strategy. As mentioned in Chapter 2, Monica's mother was very evasive when asked about Monica's father, saying that he had died in the war. However, she did eventually tell Monica his name: 'She said his name was Mack. I said, "That's a strange name." She said, "Well that's his name, that's all I know about him," and I asked where he was from. She said, "I don't know, he lived in America."' Monica has talked to other people in GI trace and found out that some mothers 'went to the grave and just absolutely refused to give the name of the man ... it seemed to be just the same for most of us'.[23]

Finding fathers

Seven of my interviewees have met their birth fathers, including Leon L, who was adopted by his father at the age of three and whose story was told in the last chapter. Unlike many mothers, Richard's helped him to find his father by giving him the letters he had sent her: 'in one letter he said he got married in England [after the war], to a British woman'.

I wrote to Somerset House for the marriage certificate ... And I never heard anything for nearly two years. And I thought, 'Oh, that's it.' And then all of a sudden, it came ... the mail had been stolen ... Now that gave me a lot of information. Where my father [Augustus] lived in America ... Then I wrote to Augustus's address in America. Worcester ... that took nearly twelve months, and that letter came back, 'no longer exists'.

Richard was now in the merchant navy and inquired

> 'Have you got any ships going to Massachusetts?' ... I was nineteen-and-a-half at the time. We get there, and I said to the captain, 'I'm just going to see my father, alright?' I said, 'Now what time does the ship leave?' And I get into Rhode Island, I go into the town. Greyhound bus ... and I get into Worcester ... about seven o'clock. It was dark. I went to the taxi rank, and I said, 'Would you take me to 31 Laurel Street?' '[It's] not there.' 'Take me to the nearest pub, bar, there, please.' He did. I went into this bar. It was pitch black! And all the people were pitch black ... I had this photograph with me [of his dad, given to him by his mother] ... There was a woman there, by herself at the bar. And I didn't look at her. I daren't look at her in case she thinks I was going to try to chat her up. It was pitch black. And the bar was nearly full ... And I went round every table. I said, 'Have you ever seen this ... ?' 'No, no. Are you the FBI?' I said, "No, I'm just a friend!' I must have been about ten minutes. That's a long time, going round. By the time I went back ... I turned to this woman and I said, 'Have you ever seen that? No?' And she said, 'Yes, come back to my place.' ... I went into this flat ... she got the phonebook out. Dialled the number. [Becoming emotional] I couldn't believe it. She said, 'Augustus, somebody wants to speak to you.' I took the phone, and I said, 'It's David' – my oldest half-brother ... he *knew* David ... he was fourteen at the time [when his father knew his mother] ... I said, 'Could you come?' He said, 'Yeah, I'll come.' He's about forty miles away ... And I heard him coming up the stairs [becoming emotional]. My heart-rate's going. He came in. So I – what I did, I went straight up to him and shook his hand. 'Hiya Gus. Alright? How you doing?' And he looked. He said, 'You're not David.' ... And he says, 'You're my son aren't you?' I said, 'Yeah.' ... We got in the car and he said, 'Are you gonna kill me?' ... And I looked at him. [Sobs] And I just cried ... And so did he. We just cried. It was ... wonderful. I just cried ... I'd never cried before in my life.

He was taken back to meet Mary, his father's wife. 'She was brilliant. She didn't say "Why?", she said, "Gus, why didn't you tell me? He could've been living here with us, in this home."' His father wanted him to stay and jump ship. 'I said, "I can't do that." ... We kept in contact for a long time. And I used to go over there, for months, when

5.2a Richard   **5.2b** Richard's father

I was on leave. Go and stay with him, stay with the family.' Richard had not known he had a black father until he saw the photograph when he was sixteen: 'I just looked at him and I thought, "Don't we look alike."'[24]

Dave G was unusual in that he was always told about his father by his mother. His mother 'used to show me his photographs: "This is your dad." [She] loved him, with a passion.' When Dave was about twelve,

> out of the blue, there arrived a Valentine's card – two Valentine's cards, one to my mum, one to me, and a photograph of him … So I wrote to him, and he wrote another letter back, told him about how I had been getting on at school, my athletic prowess [laughs] and how I was doing.

This went on for a while, then a letter was returned; he must have moved house. Years later, in 1999, Dave's friend Chris, a Mormon, offered to help. The Mormons – the Church of Jesus Christ of Latter-Day Saints – own the world's largest genealogical database, which is run by the non-profit company FamilySearch.[25] The Church's founder, the nineteenth-century American Joseph Smith, preached the need for Church members to offer baptism to all their ancestors – hence the need to trace lineages. Via access to this database,

> Chris had given me this list of possibles with the name Greene in different parts of the States, and I phoned this guy, and I had in my mind that my father's name was David Otis. Mum always thought his middle name was Otis. I get this list of names, and I think – well OK, I will go through them. I phoned a couple: no, no, this is a white person, 'My husband's dead.' … And I said: 'Do you mind me asking, is your husband African-American?' 'No, he's white and, you know, he's dead.' Then I spoke to this guy – said: 'I'm calling from England. I'm trying to locate David Otis Greene.' 'My name's David *Otto* Greene' [in angry voice] and he was really stroppy about it – came across really stroppy, quite a refined voice. I thought – crikey! I had a vision of a Germanic person on the other end of the phone getting quite stroppy. I said: 'OK, sorry to have troubled you.'

Dave got a bit more information about where his father was likely to be living and a few months later he rang this number again:

> The guy lives in Brooklyn, New York. Phone rings, he picks it up: 'The *news* is on! Don't you know the news is on?!' 'Yeah, yeah, but I'm phoning from England, and I'm looking for David Otis Greene.' He said: 'I'm David *Otto* Greene.' I said, 'Well, I'm phoning from Yeovil in Somerset. Were you there during the war?' He said, 'Well, yeah, I was.' 'Do you know Joan Bagwell?' 'Yeah, I do.' I said: 'That's my mum … You're my dad!'

Two-and-a-half hours later they were still chatting, and later Dave flew out to the US. Dave's stepfather 'was overjoyed for me when I finally met my father'.[26]

Pauline Nat had also always been told about her father, but not the whole truth. 'I was told that he was an American soldier and he had worked with doctors.' However, 'part of my family … I recall coming away thinking, oh he was killed in the war.' When she was about ten,

> I came across a stone wall memorial with all these names on, it said, 'World War Two' … and I thought, 'Oh I wonder if my soldier

5.3 Dave G and his father

dad is on there' and I remember looking for Natividad. The very next thing I recall doing ... I can vividly picture myself doing it, very determinedly walking around to the phone box and pulling open the big heavy door, getting the book out and I'm looking for Natividad in the Southampton phone book, not knowing it was Southampton and this heavy book, I must have thought the world was in it.

Pauline married and put the thought of her father on the back-burner. It was in the early 1980s, 'after I split up with my ex-husband that I started thinking far more about my father than I ever had and set out to try and find out what had happened'. But one problem was that although she had, unusually, been given his surname as her own, her mother and grandmother had got his first name wrong: they called him 'Paul'. In fact his name was Pilar (Paul was an Anglicisation).

I applied to the American Embassy, who couldn't help and referred me to the Military Records Office in St Louis and I tried the Salvation Army. Gave them a bit of information I knew of my mother and my father and some years later, I found that they couldn't help because my parents were not married – extremely judgemental because it wasn't my fault! ... We had a lot of doors almost slammed in our faces trying to do this search and back then it wasn't easy cost-wise to call the USA. So, we were doing longhand letters and all kinds of stuff ... I wanted to try and find out where my father was from in America ... Towards the end of the search I'd gone back to my birth certificate which does have my father's name on and it had a description of his profession being a copper sampler.

She discovered that there were copper deposits in Mexico and on the Mexican border.

I then found phone books in the reference library. Still no internet, we have to remember, and longhand I started writing to all the Natividads I could find along the Mexican border. So, there was no Paul but I thought maybe there was some family ... There was a Victor Natividad in El Paso, Texas.

Pauline had given the US Military Records Office her father's service number and they came back saying there was no Paul with that number but there was a Pilar. (For some reason they were clearly being more helpful that they were with many other people trying to find their fathers.) She then realised she had got the name wrong. A friend of Pauline rang Victor Natividad:

Victor answered the phone ... and was told the call was on behalf of a lady in England who had been searching for her GI father for some time, Pilar Natividad, and he was a US army medic in Winchester ... and he said, 'Oh boy, it sounds like it must be my sister!'

On Thanksgiving Day, 24 November 1988, Pauline talked to her father on the telephone:

I was given the most important phone number I would ever have from the point of going in the phone box when I was a little girl, ended up with a phone call and one of the grandchildren answered the phone and said, 'Just a moment I'll get grandpa.' ... He was just so happy I'd been searching for him for so long. He was just absolutely amazed and we decided within the conversation that I would write letters, exchange photographs and I hoped to visit the following summer ... Next morning I went into the office in the bus depot where I worked on a high and my story was blurted out and they wrote in the canteen on the blackboard: 'Pauline in the cash office found her father after forty-four years!!' And then the girls started to arrive and we were all laughing and crying again and my story was apparently going around like wildfire and by midday, the secretary called me to her office and said: 'Sit down', and I said, 'I know, I haven't been working, I will.' 'Pauline, sit down and listen ... while you've been floating around on your cloud all morning, we've been having a collection for you and we want you to go for Christmas.' ... this was 25 November and they collected over five hundred pounds for my air ticket![27]

On 20 December she flew into Texas:

There were little children in front of the barrier in the arrival lounge. There was a sign, 'Welcome Pauline, we love you!' and there was

5.4 Pauline Nat and her father

5.5 James A's father

a group of children and adults. We hadn't had time to exchange photographs of how we looked at that point but there was a tall grey-haired man at the back and I just knew it was my father. There was no-one else and I just went over and grabbed him. It was just wonderful and those two weeks I was just thrown into a totally new culture.

Pauline was lucky enough to have her father for the next twenty-eight years, as he lived well into his nineties.

When James A was back living with his mother, he wanted to know about his father,

but my mother always said I was not to ask questions in front of Reg [his stepfather] … because it wouldn't be fair. It was rude to do so. So I didn't ask any more questions … I had no alternative but to go looking and see what information I could find.

James found a photograph and his mother confirmed that it was of his father, and she told him his name. Unfortunately she then took the photograph off him, but he found it again later on and hid it. She asked him not to look for his birth father until Reg had died. Reg died

5.6 James A, his father and his stepmother

in 1985 and some time later James's daughter galvanised him into searching for his father. James got his original birth certificate and found that his father had registered him, so his army number was included. In about 2000, with the help of Rhonda England, a GI trace member, James found his father. He had been a truck driver for the US airforce near Derby in the Midlands. That first moment when James talked to his father on the telephone, 'it was a great relief … Up to that point, I never felt *whole*. You know? There was a part of me missing. And finding me dad was that part. And then I was, I felt whole. I felt better and settled.'

> Every member of his family, relations, what have you, *all* knew about me. He never kept it a secret. He produced a photograph … which he carried around with him, in his wallet, all that time, all those years. And he hoped that one day I would try and find him … There was a lot of things to say. It was difficult. Because we were both choked up. Me dad – me mum said that dad cried – that's my American mum – I call her mum. He cried a lot.

James went out and visited him every other year and his father came to England. He lived until the age of 95 and they had a wonderful relationship.[28]

Michael tried to find his father and eventually approached Shirley McGlade for help, giving her all the information he had: his father's

5.7   Michael with his father

name and where he came from – South Carolina. She found him. Like James's dad, Michael's father had always told people 'I've got a son overseas' and had wondered 'if I'll ever meet my son'. He had met Michael's married mother Elizabeth at an ice-skating rink in Camborne, Cornwall, as a single man of 26; she was eight or nine years older, with four children. As her granddaughter Janine expressed it, 'I think he made a huge impression on her that never really faded.' Michael was born in March 1945. In 1989 Michael went over to the US. 'When he came back he was like a different person.' His father, William, was very welcoming and there was a strong resemblance: 'Both William and Michael loved fishing and had a boat. William was a longshore man in the docks.' Michael was an engineer in the navy for twenty-two years.

Michael returned soon to the US with his daughter Janine, aged seventeen, and she met William and William's wife:

> The wife said she understood that it must have been difficult for Elizabeth. He feared for his life being with a white woman. William took out a photo album and there was a photo of Elizabeth and Michael, taken at a professional photographer's. Elizabeth was so pleased that he had kept the photo.

Janine's grandfather took them to church (black churches were and still are central to African-American culture).[29] Michael was introduced as '"brother Gibbs's son from England" … It felt very emotional.' Janine started to cry but tried to do so discreetly. Her dad handed her a handkerchief; she looked up and saw that he was crying too. Sadly, Michael died of cancer two years later, aged 47. He was loved by the local community in Cornwall: 'Police came to his funeral and cordoned off the street for a quarter of a mile. The local surgery shut for his funeral. It was the first time that I saw every seat in the church taken.' Janine was going to take Elizabeth out to the US to see William, but then William died of a massive heart attack.[30]

For Richard, Dave G, Pauline Nat, James A and Michael, finding their fathers was life-changing, but a sense of resolution was not the outcome for everyone, as in the case of Carol E. When she was about sixteen, Carol started getting letters from Flora, an American cousin, the daughter of her father's sister. Carol's father Rufus must have had Carol's address because he had sent her a bright pink dress when she was in the Wellington children's home. When she moved, the home, unusually, must have given him her new address. On Rufus's behalf, Flora's letters would always ask Carol to visit the States, but she was not interested in going. But when Carol married and had two children, she decided to visit Flora; she was in her early thirties.

> Flora got in touch with my father and said, 'Look, Carol's coming over. Why don't you come over to the house and meet her?' So this is what happened. So we were there, and there was me and my husband and the two children, Flora and her husband and their two or three sons ... They'd only got a small room. We were all in this room ... And a little while later one of her sisters, or her cousin, came to the house. So there's another one. Little while after that, two more cousins come over ... And we've got a houseful.

Her father arrived but 'it was really strange. It was awkward, and I didn't know how to behave. Because I felt all these people watching me, you know what I mean? So it was just a "Hello".' She never saw him again and he died not long after. 'I would like to have spoken to him on a one-to-one because in your mind you've got so many questions you'd like to ask.'[31]

Traces of fathers

Carole B never got to meet her father. When she was about 27, she asked her mother who her father was and was shown a picture. (All her photographs were later stolen in a burglary.) In the 1990s, 'I had a file and I had all this information in front of me but I couldn't correlate it to get to this point where I could find him because every time I wrote, they used to take a year to reply.' Part of the problem was that 'I'd been looking in the wrong place because ... I got told he came from South Carolina but he was in ... Connecticut.' She finally found out that he had died six years previously,

> and he'd left a daughter and two sisters ... and one was called Lila May Carlos ... Anyway, it was midnight ... and I rang her and I said, 'Excuse me', I said, 'but ... are you the sister of James Leman Johnson?' and she said, 'Yes'. I said, 'I think you better sit down', and she goes, 'Why?' and I said, 'My name is Carole B and James Leman Johnson is my father.' So, the next thing she goes to me, 'Well what colour are you?' So, I went, 'Wow, I would say I'm a bit coffee coloured.' ... Then she was asking all sorts of questions and she said to me, 'Can you sing?' So, I went, 'Well, yes I can, why do you say that?' She said, 'Well your father had a beautiful singing voice.' I said, 'Actually so did my mum and ... my two daughters have got beautiful singing voices', and that was it and we were chatting away and ... she was absolutely amazing.

It was Carole's sixtieth birthday in December 2004,

> and my husband said to me, 'What would you like for your sixtieth birthday?' and I said, 'I'd like to go to America and see my family.' ... Now, she'd never seen a picture of me and when I came out of the airport, her [Lily May's] daughter knew me straight away because she said to me, 'You look like your father.' ... I had the most amazing, amazing ten days of my life.

Like Michael, she went with her American family to a Baptist church, where her aunt was the deacon. (Women have been and are central to the black Church.)[32]

> She says, 'Have we got any *new* people in the church?' and I'm sitting there looking at her and she's gone like this, given me the nod ... she goes: 'Have we got any new people?' and I was going to her: 'No I'm not standing up.' So she goes: 'Carole, stand up, turn around and face these people and tell them who you are' and I

thought: 'I'm going to die.' So, I turned around and I said my name and I said, 'James Leman Johnson is my father' and they are all clapping, it was just totally amazing.

'It's quite sad really because we're sort of getting towards the end of our lives and I would have liked to have met him.' But finding her American family has made a huge difference: 'You look at these people [on the streets] and you think, these people have got a history, they know where they've come from, they know who they are and it's taken me *this long* to find out who I am.'[33]

Monica learned from her mother that her father's full name was Paris Mack and that he 'drove a truck between Liverpool docks and the many US bases around the North West of England'.[34]

> I used to spend hours daydreaming, I wonder where he is, I wonder if he's alive, I wonder what he looks like, I wonder what he does. Has he got married? Has he got a family? It was always on my mind. There was a permanent sadness ... all I knew he was Paris Mack and he lived in America.

In 1985 Monica, aged 40, had to have open heart surgery. Afterwards, she was

> plunged into a deep depression ... As I started to come to terms with it, I tried to find my way out of it, I decided I had to change things. I'd not been able to be honest in my life because all that had gone before. The race; the colour thing; the feeling imprisoned; the sadness at my dad. The loss of never knowing him and suspecting by this time he'd be dead. The depression crashed in and I figured to get out of it, I had to put things right ... I got divorced, went back to college ... and I got to fifty-eight ... thought about dad occasionally and things, but hadn't done anything.

That year, 2002, her son showed her how to use a computer.

> He said, 'Well, give me the name of something you want information on.' I said, 'My dad's name was Paris Mack.' ... He knew the GI story and all the background but he was nothing we talked about any more, it had been too long ... Well, he put it in, he said, 'Look mum,

found him.' I said, 'Oh yeah.' ... He said, 'No, come and have a look', and I walked over and looked at the computer screen and there was like a sort of official form ... It was a social security death index ... He died in 1994, eight years previously ... 'Don't touch it!' I had a moment then, I don't know, like the breath just left my body and he said, 'I won't touch it. It won't go away. I can get it back again.' ... There was a military number ... I wrote to Neils Zussblatt ... Just over a week I got a reply back ... He [her father] had two sisters that were older than him who was still alive in their eighties ... Alola and Edna. ... no wife's name on it and there was no children at his funeral ... So, I rang one night. I kept putting it off, putting the phone down, scared, fear, terror but finally I got round to it and I rang ... The girl in the library in Indiana had given me the number ... and an elderly lady answered and she had a deep southern accent ... oh, it was wonderful but it was a bit difficult because she was hard of hearing ... she couldn't understand a lot and then she got a bit confused and upset ... the phone went dead ... that happened a few times ... Anyhow, the phone didn't get answered for a week and I thought, 'Oh no I blew it' ... So, I started ringing the other sister ... but again she was very elderly and it was hard for her ... I said, 'Is there anyone else there I can speak to, please?' So I phoned back whenever it was, a few hours later, and this other lady said, 'I don't know what you're ringing here for but this must be a joke. Paris has died and he's not alive any more, please don't ring and upset my mum.' I said, 'Oh I'm not trying to upset her ... please, can I speak to you?' Anyhow, that phone got put down again, it didn't go very well ... so I was floundering a little bit but I rang back the first address; I decided I'd leave a message on the answer phone ... I said 'My name is Monica, this is my telephone number, I'm calling from the UK ... Paris was friendly with my family when he was over here ... if I could get in touch with anybody.' ... It took a few days but one day ... my phone at home rang, again this voice – southern but younger and she said, 'Hi, I'm Judy I'm Edna's daughter ... you've been calling, we thought it was a joke at first.' ... I decided to go for it at this point ... 'I believe Paris Mack was my father.' She said, 'Your father! What do you mean?' I said, 'Well, do you know he was a veteran in World War Two and he was in England? ... I was born in 1944.' ... All my life I'd been waiting for this moment and she said, 'Oh my God! Can this be real?' I said, 'It's a lot to tell you in a phone call, can I write to you?' ... I sat down and wrote this letter off to Judy telling her all about myself. I was searching for my dad ... I sent a bunch of pictures ... she phoned me back when she got those things. She said, 'Oh my gosh, you're my cousin, you're my biological cousin and you're English!' ... she believed it straight away ... If my health had been OK ... I would have tried to go just to see his grave, just to stand there where he's buried to see where – he was born in Mississippi – to go down to that place. I feel a deep connection to him ... She sent me photographs of him and the family and it was like all my birthdays and Christmas came at once when I looked at those photos.

Her daughter 'walked in and she looked and looked at it [a photo of Monica's dad] and she just burst into sobs ... I said "What, tell me?" "Oh my God, I've never seen ... it's you, it's you but in a male sort of face!"' Monica feels that it has transformed her life:

I am so joyful. I don't actually need anything else ... That's my dad. I know who I am and it just wipes out all the pain. All the emptiness and all the sadness. Full circle, just peace and joy ... But it's just a pity it took until I was so old before ... I found anything out about dad.[35]

5.8a Monica

5.8b Monica's father

Jennifer K was born in November 1944 in Essex to a single mother and a black GI. Her father was stationed in Debach near Woodbridge in Suffolk and was a barber in the US army. He used to write to her mother for years but he never came back to England. Jennifer never met her father, but she talked to him on the telephone when she was an adult. It was hard for her to travel to the US as she had become blind as a child, after developing an abscess in the brain. But 'talking to him was wonderful'.[36]

Jennifer B, who lived with her grandmother, found a bag of letters when she was about eleven:

and my grandma's seen me looking at these letters. And they disappeared. She must have burnt them. I suppose she wanted to close the past ... I'd started to question her. I said, 'It's got James Lennard Coleman here.' She says, 'Yes, that was his name.' I said, 'Where did he come from?' She says, 'Alabama.' She says, 'Don't keep asking about him, 'cause he's dead and gone. He were buried ... in the Pacific Ocean.' But that couldn't have been so ... There was quite a lot. It [an army bag] were more or less bulging with 'em. But they went, and that was it. She must have burnt them. I bet she thought, 'She's being bloody nosy with them, I'll burn them.'

But at least Jennifer B learned certain things about her father:

my dad ... he were very, very dark ... Grandma used to call him 'Midnight', and he didn't mind. She says he were lovely. Says he were a very nice person, very polite. In fact, the neighbour liked him. One or two of the neighbours, more so Mrs Walker ... And she says to me one day, she says, 'Ooh,' she says, 'you don't half get like your dad. You even walk like him.' I said, 'Did you know him, then, Mrs Walker?' She says, 'Yes! ... He were a lovely fella. Yeah, I used to talk to him!' And that's what she says: 'You look like him and you even walk like him.' You know, it filled me up a little bit ... He was in my life for twelve months. He used to borrow somebody's pushchair, or pram, whatever it was, and take me around the streets.[37]

Thus although neither of the two Jennifers met her father, they both felt a connection: Jennifer K managed to speak to her father on the telephone, Jennifer B was told that she looked very like him and that he had helped to look after her as a baby.

In his early twenties Lloyd had to get his birth certificate when he joined the army, and found that he was illegitimate. His mother came to visit him to explain:

> I said, 'Well why didn't you tell me before?' ... after all the boo-hooing and the tears and sadness, she *still* wouldn't tell me about him! ... And she didn't want to talk about it cos it would upset my stepfather. And when I asked my stepfather, he told me [laughing] he couldn't talk about it cos it would upset my mother! So between them, they didn't do anything. They wouldn't tell me.

But his mother did give Lloyd his father's name and an address in Braddock, Pennsylvania. Lloyd went to the US some time in the 1980s with a plan:

> I took some sheet music with me. So I went in old people's homes and, quid pro quo, I played ... in return for which they let me ask them questions. But then, they'd never heard of him, and most of them had never heard of Wood Way [the area he was from]. Because when I was there, it was a derelict town. It was like a ghost town, really. It had been a steelworks and very prosperous, but it wasn't when I got there ... And in the end, I wrote to the president. It was when Reagan was on the throne.

One of Reagan's aides replied and gave a telephone number, but they had found the wrong man. 'When I mentioned colour to the family, his daughter went hysterical. "No! No colour in our family!"' Then browsing the internet in 2012, he found details of the mayor of Braddock and emailed him. Within two days he got a reply: the mayor had found a cousin. 'My mother had given me a photograph of myself as a baby. And ... one of my relatives sent me a photograph that I thought: "This is identical." And sure enough, my brother and my sister-in-law had got the original photo.'

> They welcomed me straight away ... Went to the first reunion, which was 2014 ... I was thrilled to be there ... they're very religious. We got caught out every meal, I should think, forgetting to say grace

... Ooh, I love the church thing. Singing and shouting ... and the one we went to – one was just a tin hut there. And it was a female, a woman pastor. And she was so brilliant. And at one point, she lay on the floor [laughs]. It's right up my street! That's how it should be. And the pianist they had, at the same place – they're in this tin hut, and they've just got a piano. She's a real, mean, dirty-blues-playing piano woman ... The last reunion I went to, I'd got my sunglasses on, and a cap. And I was taking my sunglasses off, and she [a relative] shrieked. And she said it was such a shock. She said when I took the sunglasses off she thought she was looking at my father.[38]

As with Jennifer B, the physical likeness created a real bond to the father he had never met.

Sandra S lived with her grandmother until she was ten. 'Granny had a big box behind the sofa. There was a picture of a man in there with a Panama hat. I was told that it was Cha [short for Charles]: "He's probably dead now, he was an American soldier – looked like Errol Flynn – your GI father."' Like Jennifer B's grandmother, Sandra's grandmother suggested that he had died. In 2000, when Sandra's daughter, her only child, moved to South Africa, she decided she must find her American family. She knew her father's name from her uncle, who had been in the merchant navy and knew her father. Her uncle gave Sandra a letter from her father which claimed that he had been writing and sending presents for about seven years; it seemed that her grandmother had hidden or destroyed them. There was an address at the top, in south side Chicago, but her uncle said the area had been pulled down, so she did not write. However, four years later she returned to her search. She got help from GI trace and found a half-sister, Effie. 'Effie rang three times – at 3 a.m.!' Their father had always told her about Sandra, their sister in England. He had died in 1998. In 2006 Sandra had a huge and wonderful reunion with her US family: she has three half-sisters and two half-brothers; there were eighty people at the party in Chicago.[39]

Trevor was told that his father was American and 'probably now riding the plains on a horse in the US'. After he married aged 24 he was told his father's name, Jessie, and that he came from Chicago. When Trevor's son, Sam, found his US family a few years ago, Trevor discovered that his father had died in the 1980s and had had fifteen other children with at least three women. The US relatives never questioned that Trevor was their father's son, never asked for proof, such as DNA,

5.9 Sandra S's father

possibly because he had had all these children – '[he] was a bit of a lad!' Trevor wonders 'if I have a sibling in France too!' Trevor looks like his father, although he was thicker-set and darker, though he denies that he has inherited his father's 'promiscuous gene'! Trevor's family now have a DNA link to US cousins but Trevor does not like flying so he may not be going to the States.[40]

Brian's mother would not tell him his father's name. But one day

she came over from America to see me and she took me to see her friend, dancing friend of hers from years back and I went through the door ... this lady said to me, 'Oh you do look like your father, I'll never forget Ira Smith.' She had a photograph, this lady ... and she said, 'I've got Ira's photograph upstairs, I'll go and get it', and my mother ... didn't want me to have it but it was a photograph he gave out and in fact I've got the photograph now but it was signed and it was basically a portrait picture he had done for his mother but he used to give them out to his girlfriends.

5.10 Brian's father

Brian now had his father's name but he did not start to look for him for some years. 'I found my mother and I didn't really feel that it was necessary to find my father but I think it was because, although we weren't estranged, my mother and I, the relationship could have been better and I thought well, perhaps I ought to be looking for my father.'

> I narrowed it down to the black units and so I wrote to the army units in America in Kansas City I think it is and they wrote back to me and said they didn't have the personnel to search for Ira Smith. So I rang them, I kept trying to ring them and eventually my persistence paid off and they wrote to me out of the blue and gave me this document of the place, the ship that he was on and where he embarked in the army and where he disembarked but no addresses or contacts or anything. At least I knew the unit he was at and where he disembarked and that he died in a certain year.

He was advised by a helpful American to look at the obituaries:

> because in America obituaries are very big things. You know, they're not like the lines that we have, they're really big pages. So, I wrote to the *Kansas Star* and they sent this obituary back to me of my father,

I was surprised and it told me of all his family. He had a sister in a place called Muskogee Oklahoma. So I contacted her and she wasn't a bit surprised. He must have told her about me and she asked me for my photograph. So, I sent her a photograph and she had no doubts that I was his son ... I went first with a film crew, they took me first to Oklahoma in 1999. [This was for a programme called *Brown Babies*, made for Channel 4.][41]

Brian discovered that his father had had six children with his wife and three with his common-law wife, making ten children in all including Brian. His father was already married when he came to Britain, and he 'had a ten-month-old child when I was born'. After the war, Brian's father opened a barber shop in Muskogee. Brian met his father's wife, a 'very nice lady', and most of his siblings. He goes back for reunions.[42]

Sandi H found that her 'mother was really weepy when I'd ask her: "What about me dad? Who was he?" And I know I was born out of love, 'cause all his details are on my birth certificate, and me mother's, that's how I come to trace and find them.' He had been a quartermaster, stationed in Bristol. Like Pauline Nat, Sandi had also been given her father's surname.

When I traced and found me father, through the information Pamela Winfield gave me, two of my daughters happened to be living in Chicago at the time – where my father had lived. I got them to go and look at the addresses for reunions for army people. And they found my father's wife ... And me father had died ten months before I got there ... And when I got there ... Me dad's wife couldn't have any children. And they adopted a daughter. And me dad's wife was crying, saying: 'Your dad never stopped talking about you.' That was the first thing he told her when he met her. That he had a daughter in England. But all the neighbours come in, crying, saying exactly the same: 'Your dad never stopped talking about you.'

Finding her father's wife and hearing that her father always talked of her was a turning point:

I was like tumbleweed. You know – when you see them cowboy films and the tumbleweed's just blowing about where the wind takes it. I was like that. And I was aware of it, but I didn't know how to change it. And it's about roots. It's your roots that stabilise you ... Finding me father and meeting his wife and all the neighbours – it rebalanced the scales.[43]

When Billy met his mother in his twenties, she told him that his father was an American called William Flake Brown, that he had been stationed very close to Tavistock, and that he drove a truck, was a bugler and had known about Billy. Billy put this information to one side until his late forties when, prompted by the fortieth anniversary of the end of the war, he decided that he wanted to find his father. A friend knew a freelance researcher who discovered that the black US troops in Devon and Cornwall had come from Maryland and Virginia, so Billy wrote hundreds of letters to all the Browns in these states. He was getting nowhere until he received a letter from the Children's Society saying that someone was trying to trace him; it turned out to be David M. The Children's Society had given David his records, so Billy got his too and discovered his father's service number and that he had been a quartermaster from Oklahoma. He found a death certificate: his father, born in 1923, had died in 1990 of angina. It was now the mid-to-late 1990s. The death certificate gave next of kin, so Billy wrote to them. In February 1997 at 1.30 a.m. he received a telephone call from his half-sister, Joanne, in Salt Lake City. Billy went out and met them – a large, welcoming family of five half-siblings (and there had been two others who had died), an aunt and cousins. He got on very well with them. He was not a surprise to them: like the US relatives of James, Michael, Lloyd, Sandra, Brian and Sandi, 'they had all been told about having a half-brother in England. Junior said: "We thought you'd come over."'[44]

Heather P, whose stepfather had hinted in the 1970s that he was not her actual father, did not know for sure about her birth father until 2007 when she was in her sixties. Her mother first told, not Heather, but her husband Dave.

Dave said, 'You'd better go up and see your mother. She's got some-thing to tell you.' ... She said that ... after she'd married Tony, she met this bloke in the air force ... And they'd got on really well, and eventually she'd got pregnant with me ... She said: 'I asked Tony for a divorce, but he refused.'

They had met 'while my mother was stationed in Devon with the WAAF'.[45] Recently Heather has discovered that her father died in 1989, but with Sally Vincent's help she has found her two half-brothers, whom she is excitedly waiting to meet.

Terry's married mother had an affair with his father in 1943–44, but his father was moved from Leicestershire to South Wales while she was pregnant with Terry and his twin. He was never told much about his father, simply that he had died in the war:

> I was about eight or nine. And she didn't say where. She just said he was … killed in an aircraft accident. And all her siblings also had the same sort of story but slightly different in some respect. Some said in Germany, some said RAF Duxford, you know, and … I was confused … At a Christmas party, a few would be, 'Oh I know. Oh, your dad. Oh, I know what Mum has been doing,' you know. And I was about nine or ten. And I couldn't understand what they were talking about. But nevertheless, they wanted to express their opinions about Mum's relationship with my biological father. And there were times, when I was eleven, twelve, and I would sit down with my mother and my mother would turn round and say, 'Terry, I loved your father.' She would tell me that. 'I loved him.'

In 2009, when he was 65, Terry tried to find out what had happened to his father. Through a long process he discovered that his father had died in Cardiff in April 1944 (Terry had been born two months later).

> He was actually killed by an American shore patrol in Bute Street in Cardiff. And it was a situation whereby a white shore patrol had stopped this Land Rover [in fact it would have been a jeep] with six black GIs and told the vehicle to stop. It's alleged that it didn't stop, and so one of the white shore patrol shot at them. And it's alleged that it ricocheted and had gone through my father's heart.

At the subsequent court martial, despite the account from the black GIs that the white patrol would not let them take Terry's father to hospital for two hours and subjected them to racial abuse, saying 'If I had it my way, all you niggers would be dead', the white patrol were exonerated. Terry visited his father's grave in Madingley, the American cemetery near Cambridge where nearly 4,000 GIs are buried.

5.11 Terry at his father's grave

And when I saw his grave … what they do in the Cambridge … they have a gravestone, which is all white. Even the letters are white. And they had this special sand, which was flown back [from Omaha, Normandy] … And there was John! And it was a wonderful, wonderful experience! And I've … emotions coming up, I says, "Yeah! Dad! I've at least found you!"[46]

Elusive US relatives

Although Ann's mother refused to meet Ann, she did give her the name of her father, and told her that he was a lieutenant and that he came from Chicago. She got the first name wrong though, saying it was 'Eddie' when in fact it was James Edwin, though presumably he could have been known as Eddie. Ann 'got the directory and went through all the Stamps in Chicago'. She wrote masses of letters.

> And then this lady wrote back and said her son was Lieutenant Stamps and that he served in the Pacific ... so I wrote back and thanked her for all the information and hoped I didn't distress her in any way, but I'd been led to believe that James Edwin Stamps was my father. I had a letter returned within days. ... saying 'No, he can't be your father. Him and his wife have never had children ... And please don't write to me again.'

A few years later, Ann had a brain haemorrhage. When she recovered she wrote to her father's wife. Ann was encouraged to ring the wife, whose response was:

> 'How do you know it's your father?' 'Well', I said, 'I only know what my mother told me. I can't see as she'd have any reason to lie.' But – and you never know really, do you? And I said, 'I'm not going to bother you in any way, all I would like is a photograph of my father if that's possible.' 'I have some lovely pictures here, and I will ... get one copied for you and send it to you.' ... I wrote to her and thanked her very much and I'd also told her that I'd sent a photograph of myself and my children for her to see. And she told me that I should be satisfied, basically, with what I'd got.

Ann said to her,

> 'I'm going to Chicago in March.' I said, 'It would be ever so nice if I could meet you.' 'Yes, I look forward to that,' she said. 'Well, when I get there, I'll phone and let you know, yes?' Which I did, and she said to me then: 'And what makes you think that I want to meet my husband's indiscretion?'

She had been married to Ann's father at the time he was in Britain. She and her husband had been unable to have children and had adopted a little boy. 'I even wrote to his [adopted] son, and he didn't want to know either ... I think the worst thing of all is you're never accepted. And I wasn't accepted by either side.' Ann did meet her half-sister, her mother's other daughter, but they have never been close.

> On balance, I've found the only people who were truly pleased to see us – the only ones who made us feel welcome – were some of the nurses [from Holnicote House] and their families. They welcomed us into the homes and their lives, they were the people who made us feel important as children and continued this interest into our adult lives. To them, I say a sincere 'thank you'.[47]

Unusually, Babs learned her father's name from her mother. She discovered more from her cousin, Cynthia, who had been confided in by Babs's mother. Sally Vincent of GI trace helped her find her American relatives; they have so far not responded to her request for contact. Babs knows that her father died in 1989, and that she has a half-sibling and cousins.

Dave B as a child in a children's home had made the best of not having parents, telling other children that he had 'just sprouted'. However, on one occasion he did claim someone as his father: the county council told Dave that 'a child in your Sunday class whose sister was a missionary in Africa produced a photograph of an African and presented it to you. You took it home [Dave was being fostered at the time] and showed it as your father.'[48] So despite imaginatively suggesting that he had grown like a plant, Dave had a sense that he wanted (and lacked) a father. Recently, again with help from Sally Vincent, Dave has found American relatives and has asked for information about his father and for a photograph, but to date one has not been sent. He feels that having a photograph would make a huge difference to him, as it did for Monica. Janet J is also in the process of making contact. Others too, despite being in their seventies, are only now finding relatives.

Carole T's father was a steward in the US navy, based near Poole in Dorset:

> I seem to think that my father must have had access to stores because he used to bring food into the pub, mum used to say ... I know he

must have been here after D-Day because I wasn't conceived until July '44 … what I've been told is he used to go out on some boat in the day but he used to come back at night.

After Carole was born and her father had returned to the US,

> he used to send money for me but she [her mother] said one day she had this letter turn up from his wife, he was married … She'd obviously found out but she said it was not a nasty bitchy letter. It was a nice letter and she said that it said that she understood what had happened and that because with the war on and that, where everybody didn't know whether they were going to be here from one day to the next, so she said she understood all that but … she said please would Mum, now he's back, they wanted to get on with their life and would Mum please stop writing to him because half of him wants to be back here and it was tearing him apart … So, she begged Mum … Mum said if it had been a nasty letter, she would have probably carried on but because it was such a nice letter, she just felt it was the right thing to stop.[49]

Carole has been searching for her US family for many years. Now at last, through DNA matching, she has found and contacted some American relatives, but they have not yet responded. Receiving a message or telephone call from an unknown person out of the blue can understandably raise suspicions, as the initial response to Monica so clearly illustrates. Carole is hopeful that her relatives will eventually respond.

Joyce's search for her father led her to the wrong man for a time. She lived with her grandmother and 'my nan always said to me, "Don't forget you've got an American dad."' Later, her grandmother was insistent about his name: 'her exact words, "I don't care what anyone says, your dad is called Cornell Hill."' 'So I grew up thinking, oh, it was Cornell Hill … When I started looking, I wrote to Neils Zussblatt.' He found him.

> I wrote to this Cornell Hill for ten years before he answered … and then right out of the blue, right on Christmas he sent a Christmas card … 'to my loving daughter from your dad Mr Cornell Hill' and I thought, fine. So anyway then Neils Zussblatt got me his phone

number, so I actually phoned him and spoke to him … me and my friend went out and met him and I said, 'You know what Jane', I said, 'I don't think this is him.' … he was only a tiny little man. All my family had said about this great big man. So anyway, he met us and he was very nice and he apparently used to come … because my nan used to play the piano, so the Yanks used to buy the crates of beer and they used to come up and have a sing-song with the piano … they all used to sit on the lawn and laugh and joke and that and I said to him, 'You know exactly what happened?' and he said, 'Your mother turned up with you when you were a fortnight old and said "This is your daughter."'

However, later he contradicted himself and said he had not known that Joyce's mother was pregnant before he left England. He kept saying, 'I'm so proud I've got an English daughter', but Joyce remained unsure about him. Her friend suggested that she get her adoption papers (she had been formally adopted by her grandparents). She was required to talk to a counsellor:

He came in and I had a photograph up there which I'd taken with this Cornell Hill in America and he said, 'Who's that?' and I said, 'Well, presumably it's my dad.' So he said, 'What's his name?' I said, 'Cornell Hill.' He said, 'You better read this.' I said, 'You've got a piece of paper with another man's name on it haven't you?' … On there it stated that she'd had an affair with this black American by the name of William Page.

Joyce had been conned by a former GI who had presumably come to her mother's house during the war and was happy to go along with Joyce's misconception; for some reason he liked the idea of having 'an English daughter'. Joyce knows that her actual father, who was born in 1912, is no longer alive, but she has met her two half-sisters who are both lovely.[50]

Conclusion

Having a serious operation or illness acted as an impetus for a number of the 'brown babies' in their search or renewed search for their

American fathers. Monica and Ann both had serious illnesses that made them think that it was now or never. Recognition of the precariousness of their existence and of their mortality was the crucial spur. As Dave B expressed it:

> It'd be awful if you left this earth and not know. I've said I've had a great life, which I have – but it does affect you, you know. It does affect you. And I think when you get sort of older, and you think, 'Well, we're coming almost to the end of it all.' You just want a few things tidying up.[51]

Monica expressed a similar sentiment:

> We have many varied stories between us [those on GI trace] but there's one thing we have in common and that's the need to know who our fathers are or were. Nothing else seems as important and before we each 'shuffle off this mortal coil' then we should do all we can to find the answers.[52]

Arlene has not yet found her father or any relatives in the States. When she asked about her father years ago, her mother said: 'He said he was Louis Armstrong's son.' Arlene never got around to asking more:

> The last time I came up the road I thought: 'Right, next time I go back, I'm going to definitely ask.' And she died over that weekend … I can trace my mother's family back about six generations, and I've got all these pictures of all these different generations, but me – my other side, I stop at me. I don't even know his name, so I really just stop dead at me.

Arlene has the feeling 'that half of me is missing'.[53]

Notes

1   Email from Elaine, 23 October 2016.
2   Billy in Burningham, *When We Were Young*, pp. 265, 268; interview with Billy, 12 November 2016.
3   Interview with Brian, 24 March 2014.

4   Brian's website: www.muskogee007.com

5   Interview with Brian, 24 March 2014.

6   Interview with Richard, 31 March 2017.

7   Telephone interview with Celia, 23 March 2017.

8   Case reports from Monmouthshire County Council.

9   Interview with Dave B, 13 April 2017.

10 Interview with Deborah, 17 October 2016.

11 She appears in *No Father*.

12 Interview with Leon's wife, Lesley, 25 November 2016, and email 10 February 2018.

13 Interview with Babs, 3 June 2014.

14 Interview with Tony H and Tracey, 19 October 2016.

15 Interview with Ann, 28 November 2016.

16 Email from Ann, 17 June 2018.

17 Telephone and face-to-face interviews with Sandi H, 21 February 2015, 29 April 2016.

18 Cohen, *Family Secrets*, pp. 242–6; Alison Light, *Common People* (London, 2014), pp. xxi–xxii.

19 Winfield, *Bye Bye Baby*.

20 www.gitrace.org.

21 McGlade, *Daddy, Where Are You?*, p. 197.

22 AncestryDNA.co.uk.

23 Interview with Monica, 1 September 2014.

24 Interview with Richard, 31 March 2017.

25 See https://familysearch/org.

26 Interview with Dave G, 23 June 2016.

27 Interview with Pauline Nat, 17 April 2014.

28 Interview with James A, 19 April 2016.

29 Timothy Fulop and Albert Rabouteau (eds), *African-American Religion* (Durham, NC, 1990).

30 Telephone interview with Janine, Michael's daughter, 8 November 2016.

31 Interview with Carol E, 3 May 2017.

32 Evelyn Brooks Higginbotham, 'The Black Church: a gender perspective', in Fulop and Rabouteau (eds), *African-American Religion*, pp. 274–308.

33 Interview with Carole B, 1 September 2014.

34 'Monica's story', on GI trace.

35 Interview with Monica, 1 September 2014.

36 Telephone interview with Jennifer K, 29 August 2014.

37 Interview with Jennifer B, 14 December 2016.

38 Interview with Lloyd, 28 June 2017.

39 Interview with Sandra S, 28 October 2014.

40   Interview with Trevor, 15 July 2015.
41   *Brown Babies*, Touch Productions, Channel 4, 11 October 1999.
42   Interview with Brian, 24 March 2014.
43   Telephone and face-to-face interviews with Sandi H, 21 February 2015, 29 April 2016.
44   Interview with Billy, 12 November 2016.
45   Interview with Heather P, 7 September 2017.
46   Interview with Terry, 14 December 2016.
47   Email from Ann, 17 June 2018.
48   Gwent County Council to Dave B, 25 August 1995, in Dave B's possession. Interview with Dave B, 13 April 2017.
49   Interview with Carole T, 9 September 2014.
50   Interview with Joyce; telephone conversation, 17 July 2018.
51   Interview with Dave B, 13 April 2017.
52   Monica Roberts: email to GI trace, 25 September 2017.
53   Interview with Arlene, 7 November 2016.

6

After the war and beyond

In 1948 the *Empire Windrush* docked at Tilbury, Essex, bringing 802 people from the Caribbean. Until recently the figure had been given as 492, but records at the National Archives show a much higher figure.[1] Many had served in Britain during the war and were now return-ing. By 1958 over 125,000 West Indians had arrived since the war.[2] Throughout the 1950s into the early 1970s many more travelled to Britain from the West Indies and the Indian subcontinent; the racial make-up of Britain changed enormously. They had come primarily in response to Britain's labour shortage, although they were never embraced by the British government.[3] While most Britons had been welcoming to the black GIs and West Indians who had come earlier to aid the war effort, many now saw these new arrivals as a threat to their jobs, housing and the 'British way of life'. As Wendy Webster points out, they were now no longer uniformed 'allies' but 'immi-grants'.[4] Allan Wilmot, a Jamaican who had served in the RAF, had 'doors slammed in my face'.[5] Martin Noble, another Jamaican former airman, applied for jobs, but 'as soon as I presented myself and they saw I was black, the post would mysteriously have just been filled ... When it was a question of risking my life, fighting for this country, the colour of my skin was irrelevant, but now it was a different ballgame altogether.'[6] Notices were put up in windows warning 'No Irish, no blacks, no dogs'. In 1958 there were racist attacks in Nottingham and Notting Hill, in part a reaction to interracial relationships.[7]

Most West Indians arriving in Britain at this time were initially without children, with their children only being brought over later. However, mixed-race children were born in this period, mostly the product of relationships between Caribbean men and white British women – the women, like those in the war, were called names and labelled 'loose'. Antagonism towards miscegenation was as strong as ever.[8] A 1955 pamphlet produced by the British Council of Churches called *Your Neighbour from the West Indies* asked the reader to consider how a mixed-race child would be 'received by society'.[9] Immigration Acts restricting the entry of black and Asian people from the 'New Commonwealth' were introduced in 1962, 1968 and 1971.[10] What is now referred to as 'the Windrush generation' came before the doors into the 'mother country' slammed shut.[11]

1950s GI 'brown babies'

It was not just West Indians and Asians who were coming to Britain; there were still some black GIs arriving temporarily as part of the now desegregated American military, stationed in the UK during the Cold War. There were 46,000 GIs in Britain during the early 1950s, largely based in East Anglia and Burtonwood, Cheshire.[12] In response to my talking on the radio about this project on the children of African-American servicemen, six people approached me who had black GI fathers and had been born in the 1950s. I was interested to hear their stories to see if their experiences were significantly different from those of children born during the war. Did their parents marry, given that the wartime marriage restrictions were now presumably lifted with the 1948 desegregation of the US army? Was it easier for their parents to have a longer-term relationship than during the upheavals of war? Had the racism experienced by them lessened or worsened, given that the racial composition of Britain was changing?

Cynthia was born in October 1953 and is the only one of the mixed-race GI babies discussed in this book whose parents were married to each other. As mentioned in Chapter 1, her father, despite being from British Guiana, was studying in the US in 1941 and came to Britain as a GI.

> At the end of the war, he was given the choice of citizenship of the US or maintaining his citizenship of the British South American colony. He considered that his [future] children, being of mixed race, would have a better chance in the UK rather than the US where in many states the marriage would have been illegal.

Her father 'struggled to get work here. And he ended up doing very manual jobs. But he always used to read, he used to write … He was an academic [trained in agricultural science]. But he used to do the

6.1 Cynthia

most dreadful jobs to feed us.' There was also the problem of accommodation: 'Because it was all "No blacks. No Irish. No ... " whatever. So Mum would go and get somewhere, and then they'd turn up and then send them away.' Ultimately they settled in Birmingham, where Cynthia was 'the only black child in the school'. Cynthia was subjected to racism: 'I had my teeth knocked out when I was five. I was pinned against the wall.' Racism was still, of course, around when she went to Manchester University in the early 1970s:

> There weren't any other students that looked like me, and one of my colleagues ... was doing this long, complicated joke. And there was a big racial element to it. And I just stood there. And he looked at me. And he hadn't, just hadn't made the link. And he said, 'Oh ... I didn't mean you.' ... I remember just laughing it off and letting it go. The thing was, that racism then was more unconscious – people were brought up like that, so it was a part of their language, part of how they responded ... I remember this joke to this day. I don't remember what the joke was, but I remember standing there, and feeling I wanted the ground to swallow me up. Because of course, you're nineteen and you want to just fit in ... But then ... the other thing that happened, which was a benefit to me, was 'Young, Gifted and Black'. I remember walking down the street in Manchester, Oxford Road, singing, 'Young, Gifted and Black'.

The strong emotions of shame and embarrassment that Cynthia felt at the time remain with her, even while the specifics of the joke do not.[13] Comparing racism then to today, she reflects that 'to some extent, racism then was vocal. Now it's hidden.'[14]

The fathers of the other five 1950s babies arrived in Britain after the war. Elaine's mother Margaret met black GI Harold Grigsby when he was based at Lakenheath, Suffolk, in the early 1950s; he was sent back to the US before Elaine was born. When Margaret's father noticed her pregnancy he banished her from the house, and she went to London to a Magdalene laundry run by nuns. 'They were treated very badly … weren't properly fed and considered sinners, having to confess to the priest every week. Nearly all of them were having to give up their babies.' Margaret's aunt Flo told her brother – Elaine's grandfather – that 'unless he brought her [Margaret] back home, he would no longer be part of the family'. He was one of thirteen siblings, nearly all living locally. He brought his pregnant daughter home. Elaine was born in 1953 and brought up in Cambridge with her mother, aged twenty, her mother's two younger sisters and her grandparents. It was a white, working-class area. Her grandmother was not yet forty when Elaine was born and had lost a baby son four years earlier. Margaret was not very maternal, but fortunately Elaine's grandmother was. 'My grandparents were the stability in my life.'[15]

Elaine and her mother lived with the grandparents until she was seven, then they moved to Milton with her mother's new husband Colin. Elaine was adopted by Colin, whom she loved. When she was fourteen the couple divorced, which was very painful for Elaine: Margaret did not want another child but Colin wanted his own children. In fact Margaret had already had two other children by different fathers in the first four years of Elaine's life. Neither Colin not Elaine knew about these other children. Elaine only found out about her half-sisters when her grandfather died in 1989 and she discovered a letter. She went to Somerset House and learned that both girls had been adopted. The fact that her family had kept this secret contributed to her always feeling 'a bit separate from the family'. Elaine speculates that although as a child she did not consciously know about these children, at some level she was scared of asking about her father in case she too was given away. She suffered insecurity but also the stigma of illegitimacy. Like Lloyd, Elaine could 'pass' for white; she quotes Maya Angelou: 'Black people range from ebony to ivory with just a bit of plum.'[16] So although she was lucky not to be subjected to racism, she was the only child in the school who was illegitimate and 'was made fun of'. In frustration at the bullying 'I would come home and bang my head against the wall.'[17]

Margaret told Elaine about her having a black father when she was about fifteen. When she became a mother herself, Elaine asked for his name. She was also told where he had been based and that he was from Washington DC. After fourteen years of looking via all the official channels with no luck she met an American woman, Jane, who lived in Washington DC and helped Elaine to trace him. Jane found that there were twenty-one Harold Grigsbys, so in October 1996 Elaine wrote carefully worded letters to them all. She got a reply less than two weeks later – a lovely card which said 'I am the Harold Grigsby you are looking for.' On 29 December 1996 Elaine, with her husband and son, flew out for a three-week visit and were given a new year's 'welcome home' party by the whole family. Harold explained that although he had known about Elaine, he had done nothing because 'he had had a girlfriend back home and it would have been very difficult for them [him and Margaret] to live together in the US'. Elaine got on very well with her father from the start: 'We have so much in common which I didn't have with my maternal relatives. We both loved pottery, painting, creative things, same type of music and food.' He had three other children who had been told about Elaine when they were young. Elaine thus moved from thinking she was an only child to learning that she was the oldest of six: two sisters with the same mother and twin sisters and a brother with the same father. 'Sadly my dad died eight years after I found him but it was an amazing gift for me that I had those precious years getting to know him and more of who I am.'[18] 'In finding him I found the other half of me.'[19] As we have seen, this was a familiar story for many who at last found their fathers.

Carole M was born in 1956 in Dover to an eighteen-year-old mother and a black GI who was based at Mansfield, Kent. 'Mum always told me that I was a mistake.' Her grandmother brought her up, her mother leaving home for London:

> Granddad left home for two weeks when my nan brought me home but came back but never spoke to my mother. He said, 'It's me or her'; my nan said, 'It's her', meaning me. He felt shame because of me being mixed-race. He never talked to me in the seven years before he died.

Despite there being many more black people in Britain by the late 1950s, Dover was still a very white and racist town. Carole says she was the only black child in the area and was called a string of names: 'nignog, golliwog, blackjack, black bastard'. Despite her grandmother taking her on, she was hostile to Carole: 'Nan was a Romany gypsy and alcoholic. She said that I was "rotten to the core, the black in you is bad, the white in you is good".' When some of her grandmother's friends sexually abused her, 'I tried to tell Nan about the sexual abuse but Nan said it was the black in me lying and beat me with a hot poker from the fire.' At school she was singled out and a gang waited for her when school ended. She had two good friends, both white, and one in particular would fight her battles, but in return she was called 'nigger lover'. It was not just the other schoolchildren who gave her a hard time; she remembers an incident when the teacher told her that her feet were dirty and 'you cannot put them in my paddling pool'.

> I run out of school home to my nan in bare feet … My nan came back to the school with me, and made the teacher scrub my feet with carbolic soap and a scrubbing brush in front of the headmaster and some other teachers … The point she was making was my feet were sun-burnt and that's why the teacher thought they were dirty.

This was similar to when a teacher made Jennifer B scrub her hands until they bled. When she was eighteen, Carole moved to London where she 'met people who were brown and black. I then tried to be very black. Tried to talk in a different way. Never felt good enough. Not black enough.' This led to what she calls an identity crisis. It has taken a long time for her to be accepting of who she is.[20]

The other three 1950s mixed-race 'GI babies' were all born in Liverpool. Eugene was born in 1955 'in Everton, which was a white area. When I went out on the streets, from the age of three, and I can remember it, I was always just known as "Gene the Nigger" … just being the only black really, for miles.' He did have one mixed-race friend – Benny:

> For me to get to Benny's house, I'd have to go through this sort of gauntlet of gangs who all lived in these tenements. And there was two things going on. There was the race thing. They'd come after

me, like that: 'There he is! Let's get the nigger!' And they'd chase me. This was all when I was a little kid. I'd have to run. And it was all bombed ... And I'd have to hide behind bricks and get up and then I'd run to another place and then hide there. This was just to go to shops for me mother. And that's what I had *all* the time, living in Everton.

The second area of antagonism affecting Eugene was religion: Catholics versus Protestants. Everton had a large Irish population split by sectarianism. Eugene's mother was Protestant and he would sing: 'Ee-ay-ee-ay-ee-ay-oh, Paddy is a bastard, this I know. Ee-ay-ee-ay-ee-ay-oh, Billy is a hero, this I know.' He may not have known who 'Paddy' and 'Billy' were, but this was what the Everton Protestants sang.

Eugene was named after his father, who was stationed at RAF Sealand in north-east Wales from 1952.

My Pop was from Austin Texas, he was half African-American, half-Mohawk Native ... he was a colour sergeant. He was also a chaplain in the American Air Force ... He was around till I was three ... I know me mum and him fell out ... But he also had a wife in the States. I've got four sisters in the States. One was born '55, the same year as me. I was born in the July, Pam was born in the September.

Eugene did not meet his father again until 1999, when he went out to Texas.

I thought: 'Yeah! So that's where I've come from.' ... I've got loads of family there ... I just got a great welcome. It couldn't have gone better ... I do performance – spoken word. I did an open mic slot there. And me sisters were like: [American accent] 'You're just like Pop! You've got the same voice! It's not the same accent, but it's the same voice!' ... And me mother used to say that. She'd say: 'You're *just* like your dad.'

He drove around Texas with his father; in Eugene's wonderful autobiographical 'Drivin' with Pop' he recounts how his father reflected cynically on his time in the army:

6.2 Eugene's father

Thirty years in the Armed Services and then you're thrown on the scrap heap. That's the military for you, Son … When they're trying to recruit you for the Forces, they'll promise you everything – training, a career, pension, medical, but once you leave the service, it's like you never existed. No matter how much loyal service you give Massa, the ghetto always waiting at the end to devour you back up.[21]

Like many of those who visited the States once they had found fathers or American relatives, Eugene, who identifies as a Sufi, was struck by how religion was central to African-American culture:

I went to his church … everybody over there, they're all Southern Baptists. They don't drink, they don't smoke, they don't swear, but they've all got their own little churches that they go to. Churches are just like alehouses in England – there's one on every corner, and everybody's got their own. Go to me dad's … You're in church three hours … And the place is packed. The band's there, playing … It gets to the sermon now, and Pastor Reeves goes: 'Today's talk is about perseverance … We've got a young man that persevered, persevered for forty years.' … So I had to get up, and I'm like: 'I'm a Muslim, and there's a certain thing we say as Muslims – "alḥamdulillāh", which means "All praise be to God!"' And they were all like that: [American accent] 'Praise the Lord!' All women coming over, hugging me, kissing me. Guys coming and shaking me hand. I was just like the Prodigal Son! … And when I came back from there, I was just a different person. Because the half of me that was missing had been put back.[22]

Like Elaine and many others, in finding his father Eugene gained a sense of completion.

Karla was born in 1956, also in Liverpool. She lived with her older brother and her single mother: 'all the women I know were abandoned. So I lived in a completely single-mother matriarch.' It was a very cosmopolitan area:

I lived in the South End [Liverpool 8] right up till I was about six, because they moved everybody out. So – I'm living in the middle of Germans, Poles, Hungarians, black Americans, Africans, Jamaicans … Oh, and the Rileys over the road, right, 'cause they were a whole country on their own, them lot, right? Fabulous, they were. Fascinating! Just one big house, full of ninety-five hundred kids, dogs, cats and everything. And they were actually hanging out the windows. I used to want to go and live there with them.

She never knew her father but was surrounded by other black GIs:

I grew up with sort of afternoon parties going on – what they used to call shebeens … all you could see was grey legs, everywhere. I was in love with this GI called Pines. I was about three … he'd up and dance with me, like – yeh, instead of just sitting down … They'd bring all sorts of stuff home. We had jars of M&Ms before you knew what an M&M was … Rationing was still going on when my brother was born in '53.

But then

> we were moved up to Sidney Gardens, which was completely white.
> There was only me and our Paul there. They threw things at us the
> first day ... Me mother didn't help ... swearing in German at them
> ... they broke in, they destroyed the house – they did everything
> they possibly could ... And they scrawled 'black Nazi bastards' all
> over the walls.

Her mother was Irish but had married a German in 1933 and been in
Germany through the war:

> She was a fascist ... You can only have imagined this – me and my
> brother sitting in the tenements were the only two black kids up the
> Sidney Gardens. The telly's on – *World at War* comes on and my
> mother's standing there going 'Sieg, Heil!' at the telly ... I've grown
> up with my friends and other people saying to me: 'If your mother
> was a Nazi, Karla, how comes you're black?' And all I can see is
> there's a uniform fetish going on!

Even before they moved from the South End there were areas they
could not go because they would be attacked by Teddy boys who were
'going to do yer in. They don't care how old yer are.' But Karla was not
accepted by black people either. Similar to Carole M's experience, Karla
was told she was not black enough: at school she got sent to the back of
the class by a teacher and 'I sat next to Keith Higgins [a black boy] and
he told me I wasn't black enough to be at the back of the class.' Later
'I come up against a wall of black fascism: "Well, you're not a fucking
Jamaican! You're not African! You're not this!" "I'm a human being
– yeh!"' But when she was twelve she found a group of people that she
could relate to – hippies who lived over the road: 'I finally belong, and
what I belong to is a multitude of different people being themselves ...
you're not talking about rich hippies. We're talking about poor people
who were living in squats and one-rooms.' Then she got involved with
punks in what was a 'multiracial, anti-fascist movement'.[23]

Vanessa was born in April 1958 to a Liverpudlian mother and a
black GI based at Burtonwood air base; he did not know about the
birth. When her mother's family found out, her grandfather was very
disapproving. So Vanessa and her mother left Liverpool and went

to Norwich where her mother had good friends, all dating black GIs based at Lakenheath and Mildenhall:

> They had their own little community of mixed-race kids – like a large extended family. Some of the women ended up marrying black GIs and going to the US with them. One of my mum's friends and her husband were the first mixed-race couple approved to be married – 1956 at Burtonwood. Some went to Gretna Green to get married but the air force wouldn't pay for the wives to go over to the US. Some of the GIs went back to the US and were never heard of again.

Her mother then married a white English soldier who treated her badly. They lived on a little island off Wales, and Vanessa stuck out. 'He couldn't get past the fact of my mum having been with a black man. They were only together about a year and she never went with a white man again, only black Americans. She was very brave.' In 1966 her mother married a black GI who a year later adopted Vanessa. 'As a child, I adored my adoptive dad … He was adopted himself … He is light-skinned and everyone assumed I was his birth child.' At the air base she felt part of a protective family: 'At any air force base, there was always a contingent of British women. My extended "family" were British women with black GIs and their children … Bases have a lot of different races. The schools in the bases were a microcosm.' She went with her mother and adoptive father to the US when she was ten. Despite returning to England for a few years, she and her mother moved to the US permanently when she was sixteen, and she still lives there.

Vanessa never asked about her birth father until her mother and adoptive father separated. 'In the early years, I didn't feel bad about not having a dad as my friends in Norwich were in the same boat.' (This is a stark contrast to Elaine's experience of being the only child without a father.) In early 2016 she saw an advertisement on television about AncestryDNA. She did the test and found a half-brother. She discovered that her father had been born in 1921, had died in 1999 and had been 'a charming ladies' man – a Casanova. He never married.' He had joined the air force during the war and retired as a lieutenant-colonel, having fought in the Second World War, Korea and Vietnam. Like Vanessa, the half-brother had been brought up by

6.3 Vanessa and her mother

his white British mother and a black man who was not his father, but unlike Vanessa, he did not know his father was a different man.[24]

We can compare these six 1950s stories with those of the wartime 'brown babies'. Thinking first about racism, it is clear that it was as extensive and invidious in the 1950s and early 1960s as it had been in the 1940s, very probably more so. Interracial relationships were as frowned upon as ever, but there were more representations of such relationships in films, and the outcome not always presented as doomed.[25] Cynthia, Carole M, Eugene and Karla all experienced racism. Elaine was not subjected to racism because she does not seem to have been perceived as biracial. Vanessa was growing up in a protective community – near the air bases in the UK and the US – with other mixed-race children and only experienced minimal racism; she was also fully embraced and protected by her mother's family from the time she was born. Vanessa, Carole M and Karla all experienced rejection by black people as not being 'black enough'. Eugene also experienced this: 'I have been excluded by ignorant Black Nationalists who don't like mixed-race people. We get called "red", or "high yellow", or "brown" etc. I always remind them Bob Marley, Billie Holliday, Malcolm X, Langston Hughes, Cab Calloway, Pushkin, Ice T, and many more legendary "black" people are "red".'[26] With the black consciousness movement of the late 1960s to 1980s, some black people took an essentialist view of blackness, disapproving of interracial partnerships and people of mixed-race,[27] although contradictorily this attitude coexisted with the term 'Black' (capital B) being extended to include and unite politically those of mixed parentage and Asian heritage – all people who suffered racism.[28]

As for fathers, Cynthia is the only one of all those interviewed for this book who grew up with her biological father. Carole M searched for her father for years to no avail, Vanessa discovered that hers had died, while Karla has not looked for hers. Elaine and Eugene both found their fathers and their sentiments were similar to those born in the war: to quote James A: 'Up to that point, I never felt *whole* … There was a part of me missing.'[29] None of the six 1950s' 'brown babies' were put into care and they all knew their mothers, although like many of those born in the 1940s it was not always the mother who was the carer, as in the case of Carole M, who was looked after by her racist grandmother. The mothers of Cynthia, Eugene and Vanessa were all supportive and loving. Elaine's mother concealed the existence of two half-sisters, which caused something of a barrier; Karla felt no affinity towards her Nazi-loving mother. Although I cannot claim these six stories to be representative, they do illustrate continuities from the experiences of those born in the war around racism, the lack of fathers and the joy of finding them.

In what ways were the experiences of the 'brown babies' of the 1940s and 1950s different from those of West Indians who arrived after the war? While the vast majority of black or mixed-race people were subjected to racism in this period, where they lived made a difference to their sense of identity. Whereas most of the war babies had been born in very 'white' areas (those brought up Liverpool 8 being an exception), arrivals from the Caribbean generally lived in areas where there were other West Indians, such as slum housing in Brixton and Notting Hill in London, or Handsworth in Birmingham – often the only areas where, faced with the ubiquitous 'No blacks … ' signs, they could find somewhere to live.[30] Also, West Indians generally came to Britain as adults, with children coming later, either brought over from the Caribbean or born in Britain, although there were mixed-race children born too, who may also have experienced identity issues. Some of the GI 'brown babies' born in the 1950s, like those of the previous decade, felt very alone – the only person of colour in their family and neighbourhood.

South Pacific, Dutch, German and Austrian 'brown babies'

What about mixed-race children born to black GIs other than in Britain during and after the war? During the war two million US servicemen were based in the South Pacific. Most of the 4,000 war children born there to GIs and indigenous women did not have African-American fathers, but they were nevertheless mixed-race. As in Britain, marriages 'across the colour-line' were forbidden and men who wanted to stay with their South Pacific sweethearts were transferred elsewhere. Like other wartime 'brown babies', these children lacked knowledge of their biological fathers and experienced loss, silence and problems of identity. The children's stories and those of their mothers have been ignored until recently, but now interviews have been undertaken with many of these children and a few of their mothers. What is striking is that it was rare for these children to be adopted outside the family or put into care. The vast majority were absorbed into the wider family and community and grew up in a loving environment, as the title of an important book on this subject suggests: *Mothers' Darlings of the South Pacific*.[31] Research is also currently being undertaken on children born in Australia to Aboriginal woman and African-American servicemen.[32]

There were 'brown babies' born in the Netherlands, as a result of US troops passing through after D-Day. Mieke Kirkels has written a wonderful book telling the stories of twelve of the approximately seventy children born to black GIs in Limburg in the southern Netherlands; the US army liberated Limburg in September 1944.[33] After the war, in the period 1945–55, the US army occupied a large part of Germany and Austria. Of the 'occupation children' born in Germany, an estimated 4,000 were biracial.[34] A lot more has been written about these German 'brown babies' than their British equivalents.[35] In Germany

76 per cent of these children were kept by their birth mothers or other relatives and only 12 per cent were put into orphanages.[36] For the others, the black American journalist Mabel Grammer, aided by the African-American press, set up a successful 'brown baby plan' in the early 1950s which enabled African Americans to adopt hundreds of Afro-German GI babies.[37] Unlike Britain, German authorities did not appear to have qualms about their 'brown babies' being adopted by Americans. From the late 1950s to the 1970s, many such children were also adopted by Danes, often illegally.[38] There is now an international organisation that represents Afro-Germans – the Black German Heritage and Research Association.[39] Afro-Germans have a greater sense of a collective history than most of the British mixed-race war babies.

In the same post-war period 300–400 children were born to black GIs in Austria. Like the German babies, many were adopted by Americans. Unlike the Afro-Germans, they do not have a shared identity, although this changed somewhat with an impressive 2016 exhibition in Vienna created by historians and curators Niko Wahl, Philipp Rohrbach, and Tal Adler: *Black Austria: the children of African-American occupation soldiers.*[40] In November 2017 Philipp Rohrbach and Niko Wahl organised a two-day workshop in Vienna for nine people (myself included) who are researching children born to black GIs and European women. We found many parallels in the stories of unknown fathers, racism and stigma, and are producing a publication that compares these different experiences of mixed-race children born of war across Europe.[41] This will, I hope, complement the important comparative work of Sabine Lee and others on 'children born of war'.[42]

The working lives of the adult 'brown babies'

Returning to the British 'brown babies' interviewed for this book, although they primarily talked to me about their childhoods, a number also mentioned their working lives. They took on a range of occupations. Four of my interviewees became nurses. Arlene was originally into sport: 'They wanted me to be a sports teacher, because I was good at athletics … High jump and hurdles … I was in the top ten in Great Britain.' But to Arlene nursing seemed the only possibility:

I never knew why I wanted to do nursing. And it was only once I thought about it later that I was very aware that I only ever saw pictures of black people as nurses, so I thought ... that was the job that we had to do ... all the pictures in magazines and newspapers – the only black people I ever saw working were nurses.

She trained at Ancoats Hospital in Manchester:

I had such a shock when I went into nursing ... I'd walk into the sitting-room and there were two fireplaces, one at this end and one here, and it was all the black people, Africans, West Indians – I think there was one Asian – that were at this end, and all the white nurses were at that end, and I wasn't really accepted in either camp ... I didn't know which end to walk into.

It was not long, however, before she made friends from both 'camps'.[43]

In contrast, Deborah, who became a cadet nurse at sixteen at Southend Hospital, immediately felt she belonged: 'It was the first time I had anything to do with anybody else that was coloured [since Holnicote House nursery]. We had a couple of West Indian girls there, a Sri Lankan girl ... they were my natural buddies.' She moved to Australia in 1977 and won a scholarship to fund her PhD thesis: 'Cultural strengths and social needs of Aboriginal women with cancer'. She became chair of Palliative Care Queensland and from 2009 to 2014 was president of the Centaur Memorial Fund for Nurses. Deborah loved nursing, which she attributes 'to the wonderful Holnicote House nursery nurses who cared for me during my formative years'.[44]

Babs, however, was less keen. When she left her unpleasant mother, who had taken her out of Barnardo's once she could earn a wage, a friend's mother helped her into nursing as a form of escape. Later Babs taught nursing, but what she always wanted to do was play music. She now plays the flute to a high standard.[45] John F was trained as a psychiatric nurse and then looked after Mike Shaw, who had worked with the rock band The Who but had been rendered paraplegic after a car crash.[46] Gillian and Monica also worked in the medical profession. Gillian

started working as a medical secretary at a hospital in 1996 and I'm still working at the same hospital at the ripe old age of seventy-three years!! Whenever I leave, I get a phone call asking me to come back … I think the reason for this is because of being bullied by other children as a child; I wanted to prove myself in the working environment by being as good as anyone else or even better … [this is] how it was to work being 'different' in an all-white working environment.[47]

Monica 'started work at Pilkington's Glass company in St Helens as a clerk/typist', but later went back to college and studied psychology and social work. She 'became a volunteer in our local community working with women recovering from mental health problems. I really enjoyed it and got involved with similar volunteer projects until I retired.'[48]

At the age of 23 John S became the south-west's youngest and first black publican. Business trebled in his first year, although John suffered a lot of racism from white sailors in the town. Later he rigged electricity pylons all over the world, then took over his stepfather's chimney sweeping business.[49] Leon Y, who had been brought up in several children's homes in Somerset, worked for the railway for many years. In 1991 he saved a teenage girl who was clinging to the door of an accelerating train and being dragged under. At great risk to himself Leon managed to free her, and he was given an award for bravery by the Royal Humane Society. He tragically died in a car crash a few years later.[50] Lloyd picked cotton in the US, and then was a coal miner, a research engineer and an actor, playing Dickens in one-man shows in London to rave reviews.[51]

Dave G and Terry both joined the police force for a short time. Dave was the first black policeman in Somerset but was subjected to a lot of racism; Terry suffered more prejudice in the police than he had ever experienced in the Royal Marines. Both subsequently got involved in local politics. Dave became a town and county councillor and then chairman of South Somerset District Council. Terry became Leisure Services Officer in Leicester and in 1989 was in charge of the Special Olympics for people with disabilities, for which he was awarded an MBE. He has been chair of several charities including the African-Caribbean Citizens Forum.

While Terry has served in all three of the armed services – the air force, army and navy – Janet B, Jim H and Sandi H joined each respectively. Janet B joined the air force aged seventeen and trained as a dental hygienist. She later moved to Australia and undertook a

Masters in social work at the University of Melbourne. Her thesis, 'Lest We Forget: The Children they Left Behind: the life experience of adults born to black GIs and British women during the Second World War', tells the stories of eleven 'brown babies'; Rosa, Henry and one of the Joes, mentioned in my Chapters 2 and 3, are drawn from this excellent work. Jim H had been a golf caddy for the superintendent of Fazakerley Cottage Homes as a child. When he joined the army his interest in golf continued and a few years later he turned professional, in 1969 becoming the Professional Golfers Association's first black pro and Captain of the West Region PGA in 1991, and later its chairman. On his retirement he was sent a letter from Tiger Woods thanking him for opening the door to people of colour.[52] Golf has not been seen as a sport in which black people are 'naturally' proficient. One unfounded theory holds that 'black' sporting prowess lies in boxing and running, as a result of genes inherited from the surviving 'fittest' slaves, but as the writer Akala points out, Brazil, despite having had the greatest number of African slaves, has never excelled in either of these sports.[53] As with tennis and swimming, golf is only slowly become more racially diverse. That Jim succeeded in this 'white' sport is down to his huge ability and determination.

Sandi H joined the WRNS at seventeen. 'I met a sailor … and he was the first person that said he loved me … I used to read a little magazine called "True Romance", and it was always "happy ever after", and I suppose I was just aiming for that.' She had four children in five years; her husband was away in the navy two-thirds of the year, which suited her. But when he left the navy and came to live with her full-time, the marriage only lasted two more years. There was a lot of abuse, largely verbal, 'to the point that I felt like nothing'. He had always known she was a lesbian but had said, 'I like the challenge.' When she left him in 1970 and applied for custody of her children, she was deemed an 'unfit' mother. She thinks this was the first English lesbian-custody case. Sandi was now living in Liverpool, involved in both the black community (where she seemed to be the only lesbian) and the gay community (where she was the only person of colour).[54] She took a job in The Lisbon bar – one of Liverpool's most famous gay venues. 'Having had my own children taken away I felt a real need to nurture. People would come to me who needed help and I became like a mother to a lot of young teenage boys, boys who had been thrown out by their families because they were gay.'[55] Sandi is a DJ, photographer, independent film-maker and visual artist, managing her own production company, Shehugs. In 2012 she won a 'Lifetime Achievement' award from Liverpool Pride.

Eugene, a 1950s 'brown baby', is also a Liverpudlian. He is a poet, writer, percussionist, multi-instrumentalist and sound producer. Cynthia, another baby born in the 1950s, is a professor of dentistry at the London Institute of Dentistry and was the first woman to head a British school of dentistry. She received an CBE in 2006 and in 2013 was included in the Power List of the UK's most influential people of African and African-Caribbean descent.

Despite difficult beginnings – subjected to stigma, racism, adversity and knowing little about their parents – the majority of these 'brown babies' have done very well in their lives. There have been a number of 'firsts': John S was the south-west's first black publican, Dave G was Somerset's first black policeman, Jim H was the first black professional golfer, Cynthia the first woman to head a British school of dentistry. There have also been honours and awards: Deborah became president of the Centaur Memorial Fund for Nurses, Leon Y won an award for bravery, Dave G was chairman of South Somerset District Council, Terry received an MBE, Jim H became chair of West Region PGA as well as being honoured by Tiger Woods, Sandi H won a 'Lifetime Achievement' award, Cynthia was given an CBE and appeared on the 2013 Power List. Many have contributed to the health profession – Arlene, Deborah, Babs, John F, Gillian, Monica, Janet B and Cynthia – and to the arts – Babs, Lloyd, Eugene and Sandi H. And this is not counting all my other interviewees, who due to lack of space I have been unable to include. By any reckoning they are an impressive group, all the more remarkable when you take into account the odds stacked against them. Many developed resilience in the face of previous stress and childhood trauma.[56]

There have been meetings and reunions, including of those who were at Holnicote House. Ann remembers that when they met up, 'it was as if we'd always been in contact. There was never any walls between us. "Oh yes – Do you remember doing this or that?" "Well, I probably do, if you prompt my memory!"'[57] The men I interviewed from the African Churches Mission meet once a year at a gathering of former Fazakerley inmates. Every year there is also a get-together of contacts made through GI trace, which includes those with white GI fathers and well as black; there are often GI babies from Germany

6.4 1990s reunion: Deborah, Carol E, Ann and Leon Y in back row

too. Very close friendships have arisen from their shared experiences of rootlessness, of lacking and looking for their American fathers. GI trace provides huge support as well as practical help to those who are searching.

Identity, belonging and Britishness

In their childhood the vast majority of the British 'brown babies' suffered racism. Many developed strategies for addressing this: trying to ignore it (Jennifer B's response), tackling it by counter-insults or fighting (John S hitting out), taking pride in famous black people (as did Terry and Dave G), attempting to excel in a certain sphere (Jim H at golf, Gillian at her work).[58] They often felt caught between the white world in which they were raised and the world of black people in which they were outsiders. As this book has shown, some of the 'brown babies' went through a period of wanting to be white, even taking drastic action such as scrubbing their skin or eating chalk. Some mixed-race children of later generations have felt likewise, such as the writer Afua Hirsch, born in 1981 to a Ghanaian mother and a white father and brought up in white, middle-class Wimbledon, who reflects: 'I can't count the number of young black or mixed-race girls I've known to, like I once did, take to their skin with a Brillo pad, hoping to scrub the darkness away.'[59] The girls also felt frustrated that their hair did not meet white standards of beauty. As Janet B remembers: 'I was a teenager in the 60s, and if you didn't have dead straight, blond hair, you were absolutely just ignored, and if you had hair like mine you were pitied.' But even in later years, as Hirsch reflects, young black or mixed-race girls tried to 'rip their hair out of the scalp, hoping to make it thinner and floppier, which is – according to films, music videos, fashion shows, adverts and magazines – to make it objectively more beautiful'.[60]

What defines 'blackness'? The central character in Chimamanda Ngozi Adichie's novel *Americanah* is a Nigerian woman, Ifemelu, who goes to the US as a student and starts writing a blog. One item is entitled: 'Is Obama anything but Black?':

> lots of folk – mostly non-black – say Obama's not black, he's bira-cial, multiracial, black-and-white, anything but just black. Because his mother was white. But race is not biology; race is sociology. Race is not genotype [genetic constitution]; race is phenotype [vis-ible characteristics]. Race matters because of racism. And racism is absurd because it is about how you look. It about the shade of your skin and the shape of your nose and the kink of your hair.[61]

When Karen said of her mother Janet J that they (white people) 'might not have actually known that Mum was black … that's all to do with hair … [she] has wavy, wavy hair that is not afro',[62] she was referring to one central definer of 'blackness' – hair. The other, skin tone, can be 'read' sometimes as a suntan, as when Carole T notes that 'a lot of people say … to me now: "I didn't even think of you as directly black. We just think you've got a nice colour."' Or as Heather P was told, 'Oh, you've got a nice tan.'[63]

Although a few mixed-race people could 'pass' as white, or were assumed to have a suntan, others wanted to identify as black but were not seen as black enough. Eugene remembers

> when 'Black Awareness' came, we tried to kick that into touch, and we all became Black to some extent … I went through the Rasta thing. I had the locks, I was getting into 'Let's get back to Africa.' But I was getting a lot of rejection through being mixed-race.[64]

A younger generation are finding ways to address this. A mixed-race friend of the writer Reni Eddo-Lodge 'used to worry about not being black enough, but I am starting to feel that I am part of the diversity of blackness. There is more than one way of being black.'[65] Choudhry's study of 'interethnic' Asian/white young people revealed that some of her interviewees 'practised a situational/chameleon-like identity', presenting different selves to different people.[66] But this option may not be open of those of mixed-race who are 'seen' as black. For if many mixed-race people have not in the past been treated by black people in Britain as 'properly' black, this was not the case with white people who largely have seen and do see them *as black*. Identity is not only about how you feel about yourself and want to define yourself, but also and crucially about how others see you.[67] As Pauline Black (born 1953) understands it: 'Society defines me as black by virtue of my skin colour. It would be absurd for me to say "I'm half white."'[68] In the year of Pauline's birth the Trinidadian calypso singer Lord Kitchener recorded 'If You're Not White, You're Black' in which he warns: 'You cannot get away from the fact: if you're not white, you're considered black.' To Afua Hirsch, 'for all the modern talk of "fluidity" and race being a "social construct" ... in Britain, people see you, when you are mixed race, as "black".' Hirsch may be typical of many mixed-race people in Britain today when she writes: 'I am black; I am also mixed race.'[69] To Akala (born 1983), 'even though I am technically "mixed race" I am racialised as black ... perceived as a black man'.[70] The anthropologist Jayne Ifekwunigwe asks people in lectures 'my "zebra" question: "Is a 'zebra' black with white stripes, white with black stripes or ... ?"' She wants to know 'the extent to which individuals can envisage zebras as *both* black with white stripes and white with black stripes'.[71] But most mixed-race people of a black–white mix, if seen as like a zebra at all, will be labelled the 'black with white stripes' variety.

Britain's 'brown babies' were born in Britain and have British citizenship. The historian David Olusoga points to one of the claims made in Enoch Powell's scandalous 1968 'Rivers of Blood' speech: that British-born children of black immigrants could never become British, despite knowing no other homeland.[72] After writing an article for *The Times* the previous year, mixed-race Chris Mullard had received a racist letter which opened with: 'Get out of our country Black Rubbish! You can never, never be English.'[73] The question 'Where do you come from?' and the assumption that you cannot really be British/English is still widely thrown at those who are black or mixed-race. Hirsch writes of how: 'Being asked where you're from in your own country is a daily ritual of unsettling ... reserved for people who look differ-ent.'[74] A number of my interviewees offered stories of being asked this question or told to go back to their own country. Ann as a child was told, 'I should go back to where I belong.' Monica was aggres-sively asked, 'Where are you from? You're not from *our* country.' The Scottish mixed-race poet Jackie Kay writes in her evocative poem 'In My Country': 'a woman passed round me/ in a slow, watchful circle,/ as if I were a superstition;/ or the worst dregs of her imagination,/ ... *Where do you come from?/* "Here," I said, "Here. These parts."'[75] In 1995 the *Guardian* journalist Gary Younge wrote about how black Britons are still frequently asked 'Where are you from?':

> He answers, 'Hertfordshire.' They ask, 'But before then?' He replies, 'I was born there.' They persist, 'Well, where are your parents from?' 'Barbados.' 'Oh so you're from Barbados.' He responds, 'No I'm from Hertfordshire.'[76]

As recently as April 2016 James A told me: 'A couple of weeks ago, I did have one person come up and say: "Where are you from?" And I says: "Oh, Long Eaton." And he looked and walked away, and I thought: "Yes!"'[77] Hearing these stories has made me more aware of the privilege of being a white British person who is never subjected to these insulting and invasive questions.

In the 2011 census for England and Wales, 1.2 million people (2.2 per cent of the population) ticked one of the 'mixed' boxes – a significant increase from 672,000 in 2001.[78] First introduced in the 2001 census, the choices for 'mixed' are 'white and black Caribbean', 'white and black African', 'white and Asian' and 'any other mixed background'. There is no box for 'white and African-American'. I asked many of the interviewed 'brown babies' how they defined themselves and which box they ticked on the census form. The vast majority said they now called themselves 'mixed-race'. In the 1980s Sandi H identified as black, and 'now would say "mixed-race" on a form'. Arlene reflects: 'I was always an "other". There wasn't a category for me, and I always ticked myself as an "other", and then explained. Now "mixed-race". I think it was easier once Obama started to use it quite openly.' Many tick 'other' and then elaborate, James A for example: 'I often, with these boxes, put ... "Anglo-Black-African-American" ... I love put-ting that in the "other" ... just to throw one back!' Carol E ticks 'other' then puts 'Afro-American'. Adrian (who is not interested in looking for his father) calls himself 'English mixed-race'. Tony H, who was happily adopted by a Jamaican family, calls himself 'Afro-Caribbean'. In the past when the 'brown babies' met other black people, the vast majority were African-Caribbean, but the 'brown babies' did not generally identify with them and their culture. Tony H and his family are an exception. Tony's daughter Tracey, who has a white mother, states: 'Politically I'm Black … Liverpool, there's a lot of people like us – generally just go by "Black British".' Or she might put '"black Caribbean/white British", I don't say "Black-American", because my family, my black family, is Caribbean, not American'. Some generations disagree about self-definitions. Carole B calls herself 'mixed-race' and says to her daughter, 'I won't deny my mum, but she [her daughter] says I'm black, she's adamant I'm black.'

In Britain, the Second World War brought together for the first time in large numbers people with a common language but different race. The personal stories in this book demonstrate the lifelong impact that small and large acts of discrimination, racism and the stigma of illegitimacy had on the individual lives of the children born of those encounters. Britain was still very white in the immediate post-war period, although all that was to change in the following years. Of those I interviewed, nearly half were put into children's homes but scandalously few were adopted. Were there gender differences? Of those whose stories I have drawn on, nearly half were given up for adoption. Of those twenty-one, there were exactly double the number of boys to girls: fourteen to seven. Three girls were adopted (Ann, Deborah and Janet J) but only two boys (Tony H and Leon L) and one of those was adopted by his father. These findings concur with the common opinion at the time (the 1950s) that boys were more likely to be given up than girls and that girls were much easier to find adoptive parents for than boys. Most of these children were let down by the care system – their experiences a largely overlooked aspect of post-war welfarism. Another gender difference was that the girls were seemingly more mocked for, and thus more concerned about, not meeting white Western standards of beauty, especially in relation to their hair. Gender differences about attention to appearance and its policing affected and still affect girls much more than boys.[79]

These children's lives were often dominated by a sense of loss: lacking knowledge of their fathers and sometimes their mothers.

Something else I have learned from my interviewees is just how powerful the need for belonging is: not just feeling part of a country and a culture (and Britain has generally not been welcoming to black and mixed-race people), but having a sense of your heritage. As a white British woman who always knew who my parents and grandparents were, talking to my interviewees has given me a greater sense of what a lack of belonging might mean. Sandi H's idea of feeling like 'tumbleweed' until she discovered her father's family indicates the way in which a sense of belonging and having roots is not simply about where you grew up or live, but how you feel placed in the world, including your story of origin. Meeting their American fathers or relatives or simply seeing photographs gave the 'brown babies' a sense of completeness and often racial pride that many had lacked. Sandi felt 'I had no history of my own … I needed to know all this and understand it.' Having been weighed down by lack of knowledge of her beginnings, she now realises that she is 'not carrying any weight now – I feel light now'. And she also has a geographical belonging: 'I'm a Scouser now.'[80]

Conclusion

The historian David Olusoga refers to the '*Windrush* myth': 'the widespread misconception that black history began with the coming of that one ship'.[81] The children left behind by the African-American GIs during and after the war are part of this pre-*Windrush* black British history – a part that has very largely been overlooked. I thank all the 'brown babies' who were so generous in sharing their stories. In doing so, they have shone a light on an important part of recent history. This book is testimony to the difficulties and the resilience of the 'brown babies' and commits to print, for the first time, the memories of many of them. It is both a celebration of their lives and a reminder of the failings of official policy and society. The process of writing this book has been rich and rewarding, and I hope that Eugene's words echo a common sentiment among my contributors:

I have an official history, as a member of a collective, and as a person of indeterminate, hybrid ethnicity. It feels good, it also feels good to have an opportunity to contribute my small piece in the telling of that story … I feel like I belong here in the UK just that little bit more.[82]

Notes

1   Lucy Rodgers and Maryam Ahmed, '*Windrush*: who exactly was on board?', *BBC News*, 27 April 2018.

2   Fryer, *Staying Power*, p. 372.

3   Olusoga, *Black and British*, pp. 493–5.

4   Webster, *Mixing It*, p. 19.

5   Wilmot, *Now You Know*, p. 34.

6   Noble, *Jamaican Airman*, pp. 64–5. See also Beverley Bryan et al., *The Heart of the Race: Black Women's Lives in Britain* (London, 1985) for black women's experiences.

7   Paul, *Whitewashing Britain*, pp. 155–9; Olusoga, *Black and British*, pp. 509–11; Edward Pilkington, *Beyond the Mother Country: West Indians and the Notting Hill White Riots* (London, 1988). On the role of Teddy boys in the violence, see Paul Gilroy, *There Ain't no Black in the Union Jack* (London, 1987), p. 81.

8   See Webster, *Imagining Home*, pp. 47–52; Clair Wills, *Lovers and Strangers: An Immigrant History of Post-war Britain* (London, 2017), pp. 179–81; Buettner, 'Would you let your daughter marry a Negro?'

9   Quoted in *Windrush: Songs in a Strange Land*, exhibition, British Library, London 2018.

10 Paul, *Whitewashing Britain*, pp. 166–81; Sinclair, *British Immigration*, pp. 129–46.

11 Shockingly, in 2018, as the seventieth anniversary of the arrival of *Empire Windrush* was being celebrated, it was revealed that many of this generation were being denied access to the NHS and being deported for lack of 'proof' of their right to remain.

12 Reynolds, *Rich Relations*, p. 436.

13 On memory and emotion, see Abrams, 'Memory as both source and subject of study', pp. 102–6.

14 Interview with Cynthia, 12 September 2017.

15 Telephone interview with Elaine, 13 June 2018.

16 Email from Elaine, 23 October 2016.

17 Telephone interview with Elaine, 13 June 2018.

18 Email from Elaine, 23 October 2016.

19 Telephone interview with Elaine, 13 June 2018.

20 Telephone interview with Carole M, 8 November 2016.

21 E. S. Lange, 'Drivin' with Pop', in *Dread Poet in Austin* (Booksie.com, 2004).

22 Interview with Eugene, 29 April 2016.

23 Interview with Karla, 29 April 2016.

24   Telephone interview with Vanessa, 2 April 2018.

25   See Lola Young, *Fear of the Dark: 'Race', Gender and Sexuality in the Cinema* (London, 1996), pp. 84–114; Lynda Nead, *The Tiger in the Smoke: Art and Culture in Post-war Britain* (London, 2017), pp. 151–84; Caballero and Aspinall, *Mixed Race Britain*, pp. 366–76; Clive Webb, 'Special relationships: mixed-race couples in post-war Britain and the United States', *Women's History Review*, 26.1 (2017), pp. 110–29.

26   Email from Eugene, 25 October 2016. 'Beatrice', a GI child in a Barnardo's home, 'found she was shunned by the other children for being neither black nor white'; Winfield, *Bye Bye Baby*, p. 96. Bruce Oldfield, born in 1950, was 'shunned by black people for not being one of their own'; Oldfield, *Rootless*, p. 93.

27   Caballero and Aspinall, *Mixed Race Britain*, pp. 429–30.

28   See Avtar Brah, 'Difference, diversity and differentiation', in James Donald and Ali Rattansi (eds), *'Race', Culture and Difference* (London, 1992), pp. 126–45.

29   Interview with James A, 19 April 2016.

30   See Wills, *Lovers and Strangers*, pp. 247–60; Susan Benson, *Ambiguous Ethnicity: Interracial Families in London* (Cambridge, 1981), pp. 23–38.

31   Judith A. Bennett and Angela Wanhalla (eds), *Mothers' Darlings of the South Pacific: The Children of Indigenous Women and US Servicemen, World War II* (Honolulu, HI, 2016).

32   See Karen Hughes, 'Mobilising across colour lines: intimate encounters between Aboriginal women and African Americans and other allied servicemen on the World War II Australian home front', *Aboriginal History*, 41 (2017).

33   Mieke Kirkels, *Children of African American Liberators* (Nijmegen, 2017). The historian Magda Altena is currently extending this research.

34   Lee, *Children Born of War*, p. 76.

35   See Ika Hugel-Marshall, *Invisible Woman: Growing up Black in Germany* (New York, 2001); Lemke Muniz de Faria, 'Germany's "brown babies" must be helped!', pp. 342–62; Fehrenbach, *Race after Hitler*; Lee, 'A forgotten legacy'; Lee, *Children Born of War*; Ute Baur-Timmerbrink, *Wir Besatzungskinder* [*We Occupation Children*] (Berlin, 2015).

36   Lemke Muniz de Faria, 'Germany's "brown babies" must be helped!', p. 344.

37   Fehrenbach, *Race after Hitler*, p. 148.

38   Matilde Hormand-Pallesen, *Children Import: A Dark Chapter in International Adoption in Denmark* (2013).

39 The president of this organisation is herself a German 'brown baby', Rosemarie Peña.

40 See Niko Wahl, Phillip Rohrbach and Tal Adler, *Schwarz Osterreich [Black Austria]* (Vienna, 2016). The project continues as *Lost in Administration*, based at the University of Salzburg.

41 'Black Occupation Children in the Context of Post-War Societies', special issue of *Zeitgeschichte* (*Contemporary History*).

42 Lee, *Children Born of War*; Victoria Grieves, 'Children born of war: a neglected legacy of troops among civilians', *The Conversation*, 12 August 2014.

43 Interview with Arlene, 7 November 2016. See also a similar dilemma faced by Lola (born late 1970s), Nigerian but fostered by a white couple, when she went to university; Hirsch, *Brit(ish)*, p. 136.

44 Interview with Deborah, 17 October 2016.

45 Interview with Babs, 3 June 2014.

46 Telephone interview with Adam, John F's son, 22 August 2017.

47 Email from Gillian, 18 July 2018.

48 Email from Monica, 17 July 2018.

49 Interview with John S, 20 June 2016.

50 Interview with Leon's widow, Lesley, and daughter, Amy, 25 November 2016.

51 Interview with Lloyd, 28 June 2017.

52 Interview with Jim H, 16 August 2014.

53 Akala, *Natives*, pp. 100–1.

54 Interview with Sandi H, 29 April 2016.

55 *Liverpool Echo*, 29 June 2011.

56 See Baker, 'Lest We Forget', pp. 106–9.

57 Interview with Ann, 28 November 2016.

58 Young mixed-race people in the 1990s had similar strategies; Tizard and Phoenix, *Black, White or Mixed Race?*, p. 168.

59 Hirsch, *Brit(ish)*, p. 109.

60 Ibid.

61 Adichie, *Americanah*, p. 337. Or as Hirsch puts it: race 'is a social construct, designed in relatively recent human history to artificially distinguish between members of the same biological species. Does that make it meaningless? Not in my view, since humanity evolved to self-identify along cultural lines, and to discriminate based on visual differences'; Hirsch, *Brit(ish)*, p. 24. See Choudhry, *Multifaceted Identity*, pp. 186–91 on Barack Obama.

62 Interview with Janet J and her daughter, Karen, 9 June 2016.

63 Interviews with Carole T, 9 September 2014, and Heather P, 7 September 2017. See Sara Ahmed, '"It's a sun-tan, isn't it?": auto-

biography as an identificatory practice', in Heidi Safia Mirza (ed.), *Black British Feminism* (London, 1997), pp. 153–67.

64 Interview with Eugene, 29 April 2016.
65 Eddo-Lodge, *Why I Am No Longer*, p. 107.
66 Choudhry, *Multifaceted Identity*, p. 179.
67 On the complexity of the term and its multiple uses, see Paul Gilroy, *Between Camps: Nations, Culture and the Allure of Race* (London, 2000), pp. 97–133.
68 Black, *Black by Design*, p. 378.
69 Hirsch, *Brit(ish)*, pp. 159–60, 121.
70 Akala, *Natives*, p. 256.
71 Jayne O. Ifekuwunigwe, *Scattered Belongings: Cultural Paradoxes of 'Race', Nation and Gender* (London, 1999), p. 181.
72 Olusoga, *Black and British*, p. 313. On Powell, see Bill Schwarz, *The White Man's Burden* (Oxford, 2011).
73 Mullard, *Black Britain*, p. 17.
74 Hirsch, *Brit(ish)*, p. 33.
75 Jackie Kay, 'In My Country', in Jackie Kay, *Other Lovers* (Newcastle-upon-Tyne, 1993), p. 24.
76 *Guardian*, 4 July 1995, quoted in Paul, *Whitewashing Britain*, p. 189. See also Andrea Levy on being English, https://www.theguardian.com/books/2000/feb/19/society1 (accessed 14 December 2018).
77 Interview with James A, 19 April 2016.
78 Caballero and Aspinall, *Mixed Race Britain*, p. 478.
79 See Naomi Wolf, *The Beauty Myth* (London, 1990).
80 Telephone and face-to-face interviews with Sandi H, 21 February 2015, 29 April 2016.
81 Olusoga, *Black and British*, p. 523.
82 Email from Eugene, 7 August 2018.

Appendix:
the case study 'brown babies'

Name	DoB	Birthplace	Mother's marital status	Kept (K) or relinquished (R)	Father/ US relatives found	Taped interview in Black Cultural Archives
Adrian	Aug. 1945	Plymouth	M	R		Y
Ann	Feb. 1945	Somerset	M	R (adopted)	Y	Y
Arlene	Oct. 1943	Nr Manchester	M	K		Y
Babs	Oct. 1944	Ipswich	M	R	ongoing	Y
Billy	June 1945	Plymouth	M	R	Y	
Brian	May 1944	Liverpool	S	R	Y	Y
Carol E	Feb. 1945	Somerset	M	R	Y (father)	Y
Carole B	Dec. 1944	Birkenhead	S	K	Y	
Carole T	Feb. 1945	Poole	M	K	ongoing	Y
Colin	Dec. 1946	Gloucestershire	S	R		
Dave B	Mar. 1945	Pontypool	M	R	ongoing	Y
Dave G	Aug. 1945	Somerset	S	K	Y (father)	Y
David M	Sept. 1945	Bristol	S	R		Y
Deborah	Mar. 1945	Somerset	Widowed	R (adopted)		Y
Gillian	Feb. 1945	Stafford	S	K	Y	Y
Heather T	May 1945	Ipswich	S	K		Y
James A	Nov. 1944	Derbyshire	M	R (reclaimed aged 8)	Y (father)	Y
Janet B	Jan. 1946	Bournemouth	M	K	Y	
Janet J	Oct. 1945	Somerset	S	R (adopted)	ongoing	Y
Jean	Dec. 1944	Somerset	S	K		
Jennifer B	Dec. 1944	Leicester	S	K	ongoing	Y
Jennifer K	Nov. 1944	Essex	S	K	Y	
Jim H	Sept. 1943	Liverpool	S	R		Y
John F	Jan. 1945	Cornwall	Separated	K		
John S	May 1945	Weymouth	M	K	ongoing	Y
Joyce	Jan. 1945	Portsmouth	S	K	Y	Y
Leon L	Dec. 1945	Essex	S	R (adopted by father)	Y (father)	
Leon Y	Nov. 1944	Somerset	S	R		
Lloyd	June 1944	Derby	S	K	Y	Y

Appendix (cont.)

Name	DoB	Birthplace	Mother's marital status	Kept (K) or relinquished (R)	Father/ US relatives found	Taped interview in Black Cultural Archives
Michael	Mar. 1945	Cornwall	M	K	Y (father)	
Monica	Nov. 1944	Liverpool	S	K	Y	Y
Pauline Nat	Jan. 1945	Southampton	S	K	Y (father)	Y
Peter	Oct. 1946	Lancashire	S	K	ongoing	
Richard	May 1945	Devon	M	R	Y (father)	Y
Roger	1943	Cheshire	?	R		
Sandi H	Aug. 1943	Bristol	M	R	Y	Y
Sandra S	Aug. 1943	Bristol	S	K	Y	
Stephen	May 1944	Nottinghamshire	S	K		
Terry	June 1944	Leicestershire	M	K		Y
Tony B	June 1945	Merseyside	S	K		
Tony H	Jan. 1945	Liverpool	M	R (adopted)		Y
Tony M	May 1946	London	?	R (fostered)		Y
Trevor	Feb. 1946	Kidderminster	S	K	Y	

Memoirs

Pauline Nevins	1944	Northampton-shire	M	K		
Suzi Hamilton	April 1945	?	M	R		

Born to West Indian fathers in the 1940s

Bryn	June 1942	Staffordshire	S	R (reclaimed)		
Heather P	Mar. 1946	London	M	K	ongoing	

Born to black GI fathers in the 1950s

Carole M	1956	Kent	S	K		
Cynthia	Oct. 1953	Guyana	M	K	Lived with father	Y
Elaine	1953	Cambridge	S	K	Y	
Eugene	1955	Liverpool	S	K	Y (father)	Y
Karla	1956	Liverpool	S	K		Y
Vanessa	1958	Liverpool	S	K	Y	

Bibliography

Archives

Barnardo's
Night and Day: the Barnardo's Magazine

British Library
Hansard House of Commons Debates

Library of Congress, Washington DC
Records of NAACP, Box A642

Liverpool Record Office, Liverpool Central Library
Acc. no. 4910

Mass-Observation Archives, University of Sussex
Women in Pubs, December 1943, file report 1970

National Archives, Kew
Colonial Office: CO 875/19/14
Colonial Office: CO 876/14
Colonial Office: CO 876/24.
Foreign Office: FO 3H/61016
Foreign Office: FO 371/AN3948/13/45
Foreign Office: FO 371/AN3949/13/45
Foreign Office: FO 371/AN4342/13/45
Foreign Office: FO 371/34126
Foreign Office: FO 371/44601
Foreign Office: FO 371/51617, AN3/3/45
Foreign Office: FO 371/61017
Foreign Office: FO 371/97/AN668/13/45
Foreign Office: FO 954/298
Home Office: HO 45/25604
Ministry of Health: MH 10/150
Ministry of Health: MH 93216/7/16

Ministry of Health: MH 55/1656
Ministry of Information: INF 1/292.
Prime Minister's Office: PREM 4/26/9

Rhodes House Library, Oxford
MSS Brit Emp S19DH/7/14

St Clair Drake Archives, Schomburg Center for Research in Black Culture, New York
'The Brown Baby Problem', Box 60/15
'The "American Campaign" Debacle, 1946–47', Box 60/15
'The League's Sociological Approach', Box 62/12
'Black Babies – Research Notes', Box 63/5
'Correspondents and Documents', Box 64/3

Somerset Heritage Centre, Taunton, Somerset
C/CC/M/2/19, 305
CH1/1
DD/TCM/15/14

Newspapers

American newspapers
Afro-American
Chicago Defender
The Crisis
Ebony
Liberty
Life
Newsweek
Pittsburgh Courier
Plain Dealer
The Sun (New York)

UK newspapers and magazines
Daily Express
Daily Express Magazine
Daily Herald
Daily Mail
Daily Mirror
Guardian

Keys
The Listener
Liverpool Echo
New Stateman
Picture Post
Reynolds's News
Sunday Pictorial
Woman's Own

Books, articles, theses and published reports

Abra, Allison, *Dancing in the English Style: Consumption, Americanisation and National Identity in Britain, 1918–50* (Manchester, 2017)

Abra, Allison, 'Doing the Lambeth Walk: novelty dances and the British nation', *Twentieth Century British History*, 20.3 (2009), pp. 346–69

Abrams, Lynn, 'Memory as both source and subject of study: the transformations of oral history', in Stefan Berger and Bill Niven (eds), *Writing the History of Memory* (London, 2014), pp. 89–109

Abrams, Lynn, *Oral History Theory* (London, 2010)

Addison, Paul, and Jeremy A. Crang (eds), *Listening to Britain* (London, 2010)

Adichie, Chimamanda Ngozi, *Americanah* (London, 2013)

Adie, Kate, *Nobody's Child* (London, 2005)

Ahmed, Sara, '"It's a sun-tan, isn't it?": autobiography as an identificatory practice', in Heidi Safia Mirza (ed.), *Black British Feminism* (London, 1997), pp. 153–67

Akala, *Natives: Race and Class in the Ruins of Empire* (London, 2018)

Ali, Hakim, and Marika Sherwood, *The 1945 Manchester Pan-African Congress Revisited* (London, 1995)

Anionwu, Elizabeth, *Mixed Blessings from a Cambridge Union* (self-published, 2016)

Back, Les, 'Syncopated synergy: dance, embodiment and the call of the Jitterbug', in Vron Ware and Les Back, *Out of Whiteness* (Chicago, 2002), pp. 169–95

Bailkin, Jordanna, *The Afterlife of Empire* (Berkeley, CA, 2012)

Baker, Janet, '"Lest We Forget": The Children We Left Behind: The Life Experience of Adults Born to Black GIs and British Women during the Second World War', unpublished Masters thesis, University of Melbourne, 2000

Barnardo's, *Racial Integration and Barnardo's: Report of a Working Party* (Hertford, 1966)

Barrett, Duncan, and Nuala Calvi, *GI Brides* (London, 2013)

Baur-Timmerbrink, Ute, *Wir Besatzungskinder* (Berlin, 2015)

Belchem, John, *Before the Windrush: Race Relations in Twentieth-century Liverpool* (Liverpool, 2014)

Bennett, Judith A., and Angela Wanhalla (eds), *Mothers' Darlings of the South Pacific: The Children of Indigenous Women and US Servicemen, World War II* (Honolulu, HI, 2016).

Bethencourt, Francisco, *Racisms: From the Crusades to the Twentieth Century* (Princeton, NJ, 2013)

Black, Pauline, *Black by Design: A 2-tone Memoir* (London, 2011)

Bland, Lucy, 'British eugenics and "race crossing:": a study of an interwar investigation', *New Formations*, 60 (2007), special issue on 'Eugenics Old and New', pp. 66–78

Bland, Lucy, *Modern Women on Trial: Sexual Transgression in the Age of the Flapper* (Manchester, 2013)

Bland, Lucy, and Frank Mort, '"Look out for the goodtime girl": dangerous sexualities as a threat to national health', in *Formations of Nation and People* (London, 1984), pp. 131–51

Bourne, Stephen, *Mother Country: Britain's Black Community on the Home Front, 1939–45* (Stroud, 2010)

Bowlby, John, *Maternal Care and Mental Health* (London, 1951)

Brah, Avtar, 'Difference, diversity and differentiation', in James Donald and Ali Rattansi (eds), *'Race', Culture and Difference* (London, 1992), pp. 126–45

Braybon, Gail, and Penny Summerfield, *Out of the Cage: Women's Experiences in Two World Wars* (London, 1987)

Bressey, Caroline, 'Forgotten histories: three stories of black girls from Barnardo's Victorian archive', *Women's History Review*, 11.3 (2002), pp. 351–74

Bressey, Caroline, 'Geographies of belonging: white women and black history', *Women's History Review*, 22.4 (2013), pp. 541–58

Brown, Jacqueline Nassy, *Dropping Anchor, Setting Sail: Geographies of Race in Black Liverpool* (Princeton, NJ, 2005)

Bryan, Beverley, et al., *The Heart of the Race: Black Women's Lives in Britain* (London, 1985)

Buettner, Elizabeth, '"Would you let your daughter marry a Negro?": race and sex in 1950s Britain', in Philippa Levine and Susan R. Grayzel (eds), *Gender, Labour, War and Empire* (London, 2009), pp. 219–37

Burningham, John, *When We Were Young: A Compendium of Childhood* (London, 2004)

Caballero, Chamion, and Peter Aspinall, *Mixed Race Britain in the Twentieth Century* (London, 2018)

Carby, Hazel, 'Becoming modern racialized subjects', *Cultural Studies*, 23.4 (2009), pp. 624–57

Carby, Hazel, 'Imperial Intimacies', unpublished manuscript in progress, 2017

Chesser, Eustace, *Unwanted Child* (London, 1947)

Choudhry, Sultana, *Multifaceted Identity of Interethnic Young People* (London, 2010)

Cohen, Deborah, *Family Secrets: Living with Shame from the Victorians to the Present Day* (London, 2013)

Constantine, Learie, *Colour Bar* (London, 1954)

Cunard, Nancy, and George Padmore, 'The White Man's Duty: an analysis of the colonial question in light of the Atlantic', in Maureen Moynagh (ed.), *Essays on Race and Empire: Nancy Cunard* (Peterborough, Ont., 2002), pp. 127–77

Davenport, Ormus, 'U.S. prejudice dooms 1,000 British babies', *Reynolds's News*, 9 February 1947, p. 2

Dover, Cedric, *Half-Caste* (London, 1937)

DuBois, W. E. B., *The Souls of Black Folk* (Chicago, 1903)

DuBois, W. E. B., 'The winds of change', *Chicago Defender*, 15 June 1946

Dyer, Richard, *White* (London, 1997)

Eddo-Lodge, Reni, *Why I Am No Longer Talking to White People about Race* (London, 2018)

Ellison, Ralph, 'In a strange country', in Dorothy Sterling (ed.), *I Have Seen War: The Story of World War II* (New York, 1960), pp. 103–10

Farmer, Richard, *Cinemas and Cinemagoing in Wartime Britain, 1939–45* (Manchester, 2016)

Fehrenbach, Heide, *Race after Hitler: Black Occupation Children in Post-war Germany and America* (Princeton, NJ, 2005)

Ferguson, Sheila, and Hilde Fitzgerald, *History of the Second World War: Studies in the Social Services* (London, 1954)

Frampton, Phil, *The Golly in the Cupboard* (Manchester, 2004)

Freud, Anna, and Sophie Dann, 'An experiment in group upbringing', *Psychoanalytic Study of the Child*, 6 (1951), pp. 127–68

Fryer, Peter, *Staying Power: The History of Black People in Britain* (London, 1984)

Fulop, Timothy, and Albert Rabouteau (eds), *African-American Religion* (Durham, NC, 1990)

Gaber, Ivor, and Jane Aldridge (eds), *In the Best Interests of the Child* (London, 1994)

Gaines, Kevin, 'Scholar-activist St Clair Drake and the transatlantic world of black radicalism', in Robin D. G. Kelly and Stephen Tuck (eds), *The*

Other Special Relationship: Race, Rights and Riots in Britain and the United States (London, 2015), pp. 75–93

Gardiner, Juliet, *Over Here! The GIs in Wartime Britain* (London, 1992)

Gilroy, Paul, *Between Camps: Nations, Culture and the Allure of Race* (London, 2000)

Gilroy, Paul, *There Ain't no Black in the Union Jack* (London, 1987)

Goodman, Phil, '"Patriotic femininity": women's morals and men's morale during the Second World War', *Gender & History*, 10.2 (1998), pp. 278–93

Gowing, Laura, *Common Bodies: Women, Touch, and Power in Seventeenth-Century England* (New Haven, CT, 2003)

Grant, Colin, *Negro with a Hat: The Rise and Fall of Marcus Garvey and His Dream of Mother Africa* (London, 2008)

Grieves, Victoria, 'Children born of war: a neglected legacy of troops among civilians', *The Conversation*, 12 August 2014

Hall, Catherine, *Civilising Subjects: Metropole and Colony in the English Imagination, 1830–1867* (Cambridge, 2002)

Hall, Stuart, 'New ethnicities', in James Donald and Ali Rattansi (eds), *'Race', Culture and Difference* (London, 1992), pp. 252–9

Hall, Stuart, with Bill Schwarz, *Familiar Stranger* (London, 2017)

Hamilton, Suzi, *Notice Me! A Barnardo's Child Scrapbook of Memories: 1946 to 1961* (Ely, 2012)

Hendrick, Harry, *Child Warfare* (Bristol, 2003)

Hervieux, Linda, *Forgotten: The Untold Story of D-Day's Black Heroes, at Home and at War* (New York, 2015)

Higginbotham, Evelyn Brooks, 'The Black Church: a gender perspective', in Timothy Fulop and Albert Rabouteau (eds), *African-American Religion* (Durham, NC, 1990), pp. 274–308

Higginbotham, Peter, *Children's Homes: A History of Institutional Care for Britain's Young* (Barnsley, 2017)

Hill, David, *The Forgotten Children: Fairbridge Farm School and its Betrayal of Britain's Child Migrants* (London, 2008)

Hirsch, Afua, *Brit(ish): On Race, Identity and Belonging* (London, 2018)

Hormand-Pallesen, Matilde, *Children Import: A Dark Chapter in International Adoption in Denmark* (2013)

Hubble, Nick, *Mass Observation and Everyday Life: Culture, History, Theory* (London, 2006)

Hugel-Marshall, Ika, *Invisible Woman: Growing up Black in Germany* (New York, 2001)

Hughes, Karen, 'Mobilising across colour lines: intimate encounters between Aboriginal women and African Americans and other allied servicemen on the World War II Australian home front', *Aboriginal History*, 41 (2017), pp. 47–70

Humphreys, Margaret, *Empty Cradles* (London, 1994)

Ifekuwunigwe, Jayne O., *'Mixed Race' Studies: A Reader* (London, 2004)

Ifekuwunigwe, Jayne O., *Scattered Belongings: Cultural Paradoxes of 'Race', Nation and Gender* (London, 1999)

James, Leslie, *George Padmore and Decolonization from Below* (London, 2015)

Jones, Amanda, 'The Wartime Child in Women's Fiction and Psychoanalysis 1930–1960', unpublished PhD thesis, Anglia Ruskin University, 2015

Kay, Jackie, *Other Lovers* (Newcastle-upon-Tyne, 1993)

Keating, Jenny, *A Child for Keeps: The History of Adoption in England, 1918–45* (London, 2009)

Killingray, David, '"To do something for the race": Harold Moody and the League of Coloured Peoples', in Bill Schwarz (ed.), *West Indian Intellectuals in Britain* (Manchester, 2003), pp. 51–70

King, Constance, and Harold King, *Two Nations: The Life and Work of the Liverpool University Settlement* (Liverpool, 1938)

Kirkels, Mieke, *Children of African American Liberators* (Nijmegen, 2017)

Kirton, Derek, *'Race', Ethnicity and Adoption* (Buckingham, 2000)

Kornitzer, Margaret, *Adoption & Family Life* (London, 1968)

Kornitzer, Margaret, *Child Adoption in the Modern World* (London, 1952)

Lake, Marilyn, 'The desire for a Yank: sexual relations between Australian women and American servicemen during World War II', *Journal of the History of Sexuality*, 2.4 (1991), pp. 621–33

Lange, E. S., 'Drivin' with Pop', in *Dread Poet in Austin* (Booksie.com, 2004)

Langhamer, Claire, *The English in Love* (Oxford, 2013)

Langhamer, Claire, 'Love and courtship in mid-twentieth century England', *The Historical Journal*, 20.1 (2007), pp. 173–96

Lee, Sabine, *Children Born of War in the Twentieth Century* (Manchester, 2017)

Lee, Sabine, 'A forgotten legacy of the Second World War: GI children in post-war Britain and Germany', *Contemporary European History*, 20.2 (2011), pp. 157–81

Lemke Muniz de Faria, Yara-Colette, '"Germany's 'brown babies' must be helped! Will you?" US adoption plans for Afro-German children, 1950–1955', *Callaloo*, 26.2 (2003), pp. 342–62

Levy, Andrea, *Small Island* (London, 2004)

Light, Alison, *Common People* (London, 2014)

Little, Kenneth, *Negroes in Britain* (1947) (Oxford, 2010)

Longmate, Norman, *The GIs: The Americans in Britain, 1942–1945* (London, 1975)

MacKeith, Lucy, *Local Black History: A Beginning in Devon* (Archives and Museum of Black History, 2003)

Malcolmson, Patricia, and Robert Malcolmson (eds), *Nella Last in the 1950s* (London, 2010)

McCarthy, Liam, 'Racism, Violence and Sex: An Alternative History of American Troops in Leicester during the Second World War', unpublished MRes thesis, University of Leicester, 2016

McClintock, Anne, *Imperial Leather: Race, Gender and Sexuality in the Colonial Context* (New York, 1995)

McCormick, Leanne, '"One Yank and they're off": interaction between US troops and Northern Irish women, 1942–1945', *Journal of the History of Sexuality*, 15.2 (2006), pp. 228–57

McCormick, Leanne, *Regulating Sexuality: Women in Twentieth-century Northern Ireland* (Manchester, 2009)

McGlade, Shirley, *Daddy, Where are You?* (London, 1992)

McKenzie-Mavinga, Isha, and Thelma Perkins, *In Search of Mr McKenzie: Two Sisters' Quest for an Unknown Father* (London, 1991)

McNeill, Sylvia, *Illegitimate Children Born in Britain of English Mothers and Coloured Americans: Report of a Survey* (London, 1946)

Mead, Margaret, *The American Troops and the British Community* (London, 1944)

Mercer, Kobena, *Welcome to the Jungle: New Positions in Black Cultural Studies* (New York, 1994)

Ministry of Information, *British Public Feeling about America: A Report by Home Intelligence Division* (London, 1943)

Moody, Harold, 'Anglo-American coloured children', appendix 6 in Sylvia McNeill, *Illegitimate Children Born in Britain of English Mothers and Coloured Americans: Report of a Survey* (London, 1946), pp. 15–17

Moody, Harold, *The Colour Bar* (London, 1944)

Moye, J. Todd, *Freedom Flyers: The Tuskegee Airmen of World War II* (Oxford, 2010)

Moynagh, Maureen (ed.), *Essays on Race and Empire: Nancy Cunard* (Peterborough, Ont., 2002)

Moynihan, Lisa, 'Children against the colour bar', *London Magazine*, 29 October 1949

Mullard, Chris, *Black Britain* (London, 1973)

Murdoch, Lydia, *Imagined Orphans* (New Brunswick, NJ, 2006)

Murphy-Shigematsu, Stephen, *Multicultural Encounters* (New York, 2002)

Murphy-Shigematsu, Stephen, *When Half is Whole* (Stanford, CA, 2012)

Narey, Martin, *The Narey Report: A Blueprint for the Nation's Lost Children* (London, 2011)

Nava, Mica, *Visceral Cosmopolitanism* (London, 2007)

Nead, Lynda, *The Tiger in the Smoke: Art and Culture in Post-war Britain* (London, 2017)

Nevins, Pauline, *'Fudge': The Downs and Ups of a Biracial, Half-Irish British War Baby: A Memoir* (self-published, 2015)

Newley, Patrick, *You Lucky People! The Tommy Trinder Story* (London, 2008)

Noble, E. Martin, *Jamaican Airman: A Black Airman in Britain 1943 and After* (London, 1984)

Nott, James, *Going to the Palais: A Social and Cultural History of Dance and Dance Halls in Britain 1918–1960* (Oxford, 2015)

Oldfield, Bruce, *Rootless: An Autobiography* (London, 2004)

Olusoga, David, *Black and British: A Forgotten History* (London, 2016)

Padmore, George, 'Decides brown babies must stay in England', *Chicago Defender*, 23 April 1949

Parker, Louisa Adjoa, *1944 We Were Here: African American GIs in Dorset* (Dorset, n.d.)

Parker, Louisa Adjoa, *Dorset's Hidden Histories* (Dorset, 2007)

Partridge, Frances, *Everything to Lose: Diaries, May 1945–Dec. 1960* (London, 1985)

Paul, Kathleen, *Whitewashing Britain: Race and Citizenship in the Postwar Era* (New York, 1997)

Perks, Robert, and Alistair Thomson (eds), *The Oral History Reader* (London, 3rd edn, 2016)

Phillips, Caryl, *Crossing the River* (London, 1993)

Phillips, Mike, and Trevor Phillips, *Windrush: The Irresistible Rise of Multi-Racial Britain* (London, 1998)

Pilkington, Edward, *Beyond the Mother Country: West Indians and the Notting Hill White Riots* (London, 1988)

Plummer, Brenda Gayle, 'Brown babies: race, gender and policy after World War II', in Brenda Gayle Plummer (ed.), *Window on Freedom: Race, Civil Rights, and Foreign Affairs, 1945–1988* (Chapel Hill, NC, 2003), pp. 67–91

Portelli, Allessandro, 'The peculiarities of oral history', *History Workshop*, 12 (1981), pp. 96–107

Ramamurthy, Anandi, *Imperial Persuaders: Images of Africa and Asia in British Advertising* (Manchester, 2003)

Raynor, Lois, *Adoption of Non-White Children* (London, 1970).

Reynolds, David, *Rich Relations: The American Occupation of Britain, 1942–1945* (London, 1996)

Rich, Paul B., *Race and Empire in British Politics* (Cambridge, 1986)

Richards, Jeffrey, *The Age of the Dream Palace: Cinema and Society in 1930s Britain* (London, 2010)

Richmond, Anthony, *Colour Prejudice in Britain: A Study of West Indian Workers in Liverpool, 1941–1951* (London, 1954)

Riley, Denise, *War in the Nursery: Theories of the Child and Mother* (London, 1983)

Robinson, Jane, *In the Family Way: Illegitimacy between the Great War and the Swinging Sixties* (London, 2015)

Rose, June, *For the Sake of the Children: Inside Dr Barnardo's* (London, 1987)

Rose, Sonya, 'Girls and GIs: race, sex, and diplomacy in Second World War Britain', *International History Review*, 19.1 (1997), pp. 146–60

Rose, Sonya, *Which People's War? National Identity and Citizenship in Britain 1939–1945* (Oxford, 2003)

Rossini, Gill, *A History of Adoption in England and Wales, 1850–1961* (Barnsley, 2014)

Sage, Lorna, *Bad Blood: A Memoir* (London, 2000)

Sato, Kiyotaka, *Life Story of Mr Terry Harrison, MBE: His Identity as a Person of Mixed Heritage* (Tokyo, 2013)

Schwarz, Bill, *The White Man's Burden* (Oxford, 2011)

Selwyn, Julie, Lesley Frazer and Angela Fitzgerald, *Finding Adoptive Families for Black, Asian and Black Mixed-Parentage Children* (London, 2004)

Sherwood, Marika, *Many Struggles: West Indian Workers and Service Personnel in Britain (1939–45)* (London, 1985)

Sherwood, Marika, *Pastor Daniels Ekarte and the African Churches Mission* (London, 1994)

Shute, Nevil, *The Chequer Board* (1947) (London, 2000)

Smith, Graham, *When Jim Crow Met John Bull* (London, 1987)

Soares, Claudia, 'Neither Waif nor Stray: Home, Family and Belonging in the Victorian Children's Institution, 1881–1914', unpublished PhD thesis, University of Manchester, 2014

Spencer, Ian R., *British Immigration Policy since 1939: The Making of Multiracial Britain* (London, 1997)

St Clair Drake, John, 'Values Systems, Social Structure and Race Relations in the British Isles', unpublished PhD thesis, University of Chicago, 1954

Stevenson, Raymond, *Interim Report on Child Abuse: Shirley Oaks Children's Home 'Looking for a Place Called Home'* (London, 2016)

Summerfield, Penny, *Histories of the Self* (London, 2018)

Summerfield, Penny, *Reconstructing Women's Wartime Lives: Discourse and Subjectivity in Oral Histories of the Second World War* (Manchester, 1998)

Summerfield, Penny, *Women Workers in the Second World War* (London, 1989)

Summerfield, Penny, and Nicola Crockett, '"You weren't taught that with the welding": lessons in sexuality in the Second World War', *Women's History Review*, 1.3 (1992), pp. 435–54

Swain, Shurlee, and Margo Hillel, *Child, Nation, Race and Empire* (Manchester, 2010)

Tabili, Laura, 'Outsiders in the land of their birth: exogamy, citizenship, and identity in war and peace', *Journal of British Studies*, 44.4 (2005), pp. 796–815

Thane, Pat, and Tanya Evans, *Sinners? Scroungers? Saints? Unmarried Motherhood in Twentieth-century England* (Oxford, 2012)

Thorne, Christopher, 'British and the black GI: racial issues and Anglo-American relations in 1942', *New Community*, 111.3 (1974), pp. 262–71

Timmins, Nicholas, *The Five Giants: A Biography of the Welfare State* (London, 2001)

Tizard, Barbara, and Ann Phoenix, *Black, White or Mixed Race? Race and Racism in the Lives of Young People of Mixed Parentage* (London, 1993)

Virden, Jenel, *Good-bye, Piccadilly: British War Brides in America* (Urbana, IL, 1996)

Wahl, Nico, Phillip Rohrbach and Tal Adler, *Schwarz Osterreich* (Vienna, 2016)

Webb, Clive, 'Special relationships: mixed-race couples in post-war Britain and the United States', *Women's History Review*, 26.1 (2017), pp. 110–29

Webster, Wendy, *Englishness and Empire, 1939–1965* (Oxford, 2005)

Webster, Wendy, '"Fit to fight, fit to mix": sexual patriotism in Second World War Britain', *Women's History Review*, 22.4 (2013), pp. 607–24

Webster, Wendy, *Imagining Home: Gender, 'Race' and National Identity, 1945–64* (London, 1998)

Webster, Wendy, *Mixing It: Diversity in World War Two Britain* (Oxford, 2018)

Wells, Ida B., *Southern Horrors: Lynch Law in All its Phases* (New York, 1892)

White, Walter, *A Man called White* (New York, 1948)

White, Walter, *A Rising Wind* (New York, 1945)

Williams, John, *Silver Threads: A Life Alone* (London, 1994)

Williams, Susan, *Colour Bar: The Triumph of Seretse Khama and his Nation* (London, 2006)

Wills, Claire, *Lovers and Strangers: An Immigrant History of Post-war Britain* (London, 2017)

Wilmot, Allan, *Now You Know: The Memories of Allan Charles Wilmot, WWII Serviceman and Post-war Entertainer* (London, 2015)

Wilson, Carlton E., 'Racism and private assistance: the support of the West Indian and African missions in Liverpool, England, during the inter-war years', *African Studies Review*, 35.2 (1992), pp. 55–73

Winfield, Pamela, *Bye Bye Baby: The Story of the Children the GIs Left Behind* (London, 1992)

Wolf, Naomi, *The Beauty Myth* (London, 1990)

Wynn, Neil A., *The African American Experience during World War II* (Plymouth, 2010)

Young, Lola, *Fear of the Dark: 'Race', Gender and Sexuality in the Cinema* (London, 1996)

Zahra, Tara, *The Lost Children: Reconstructing Europe's Families after World War II* (Cambridge, MA, 2011)

Films

Brown Babies (Touch Productions, Channel 4, October 1999)

Housewife 49 (dir. Gavin Millar, 2006)

Mixed Britannia, episode 2, 1940–65 (dir. Kate Misrahi, BBC2, 2011)

No Mother, No Father, No Uncle Sam (dir. Sebastian Robinson, West HTV, 1988)

Tiger Brides: Memories of Love and War from the GI Brides of Tiger Bay (dir. Simon and Anthony Campbell, with Valerie Hill-Jackson, 2013)

VE Day: First Days of Peace: Race Relations (dir. Alistair McKee, BBC, 2015)

Welcome to Britain (dir. Anthony Asquith, 1943)

Index